CW00863135

Jim,

Thanks so much for your
vision about mm & gender. You
heart is in the right place.

All the Best,
Rod Kopp

Jan 17, 2013

THE NATURALLY
GOOD MAN

And the Ten Thousand Blades of Life

ROD E. KEAYS

Order this book online at www.trafford.com
or email orders@trafford.com

Most Trafford titles are also available at major online book retailers.

Also available in E-Book from: Trafford.com or booksellers online.

Bibliography and Index included.

Printed in the United States of America.

ISBN: 978-1-4669-1924-2 (sc)
ISBN: 978-1-4669-1923-5 (hc)

Library of Congress Control Number: 2012904244

Trafford rev. 10/18/2012

 www.trafford.com

North America & International
toll-free: 1 888 232 4444 (USA & Canada)
phone: 250 383 6864 ♦ fax: 812 355 4082

TABLE OF CONTENTS

ACKNOWLEDGEMENTS

Without the support of these men I could not have found the insight or the belief in myself to make the exploration necessary to write this book:

My father, John Elgin Keays first and foremost the greatest positive influence on my life, and without him I would not have survived.

James Richardson who introduced me to the men's movement and taught me about leadership.

Dr. Warren Farrell who encouraged me to keep writing after reading some of my early drafts.

David H. Gold, a friend who stood by me and supported my goals for the retreat site and his continued support for this book.

Dave Nordstrom who taught me about the male heart.

Harvey Maser who by his determination still maintains the talking stick men's group for so many years.

Keith Harris, President of The Victoria Men's Center who reminded me that I had something of value to contribute to the lives of men.

Earnie Ogilvie who through years of conversations, chance meetings and a standup comedy routine supported my goal of producing this book.

And finally, Robert Barlow who over many years of encounters including Island Men Journal, the retreat site and social gatherings taught me about "walking the walk."

For editing and support, I want to credit Marco for her patience while this book was being created. Also my additional thanks to Ineke Veefkind for kind but firm editing, and helpful proof reading of the manuscript by Dave Nordstrom, Jim Richardson, Robert Barlow and David Gold.

To the First Nations people of the southwest coast of British Columbia, I thank you for your wise culture and our shared love of the land.

Thanks to all.

PREFACE

As a young man I knew something was very strange about men. During my elementary schooling in the early 1960's my grade three class was herded into the gymnasium for a dance during the lunch hour. I recall as a rule we came into the gym in long lines, the boys in one and the girls in another. Nobody talked for fear of a detention. As we entered the gym the Principal stood on the stage behind a podium with his microphone. He told the boys to line up on one wall and the girls to line up all the way across the gym on the other. Then he told the boys to go ask a girl to dance! Well, I thought, you mean we have to go all the way over there to ask some girl we don't even know to dance? Are you nuts?

Why was it up to the boys and why did we fall for it? I was thinking, why don't we just meet in the middle or draw straws or something? But no we had to go ask some girl her permission to dance, yuck! How humiliating. This event changed my life. From then on I knew something was very odd in the lives of men, yet at the same time I felt good about being male. Why was that?

Like many boys, I went through many childhood traumas, including schoolyard beatings, beatings by teachers, competition for girls, the last boy chosen for the team and other humiliations, yet during all this I made a decision: I would shed light on what was happening. I knew first off that I was a bit different from other boys and I knew that I would have to make a massive effort if I was ever to understand what was going on. This book then is my personal journey in the discovery of masculinity over the years. I had no choice-I had to do it or I probably would not have survived. Much that has been written is common to many men in many cultures so naturally I hope you will find something of value for your own growth and discovery. To encourage this growth I will include my blog address at the end of the book for a more personal conversation.

So here we go, and I am glad to say that I undertook the mission to learn what I did not know. I was about eleven or twelve when I actually started to undertake this. Somehow I knew if I was going to get to the bottom of it I was going to have to concentrate all my energies on the topic. So one afternoon after another beating at school I lay on my bed for about an hour and focused all the determination I could bring to thinking through all the weird things that had happened in my life up to that point. Suddenly as if a light went on in my brain I had an answer: it was not my fault! I some how had taken on the feeling that being different was wrong, and that being myself was wrong too. Knowing this I realized as well that my bullies were probably feeling victimized somehow as well, no doubt suffering as deeply or deeper than myself. However, they had not yet got to the point of questioning their conditioning, and hopefully one day they would realize it was not their fault too. So on that day I learned compassion for men and new hope for myself. Of course this was just the first layer of many in my understanding of my life.

All the other strange experiences could also be explained, but my awareness of them came much later in life. Some how I knew I had to make the attempt to understand, and as a result I came to relate almost empathically with a lot of other men and their lives.

My own father, John Elgin Keays had considerable influence on this new awareness. We often had long talks about philosophy, religion and government. I spent the summers sailing with him and learned peace of mind while watching changes on the water for wind and the value of quiet conversation. As well I learned critical thinking, and a passion to confront unjust social situations as well as the courage to own my feelings. Paradoxically, my greatest wounding came from him in the way he responded to insights I had. He would laugh at my "silly" ideas often humiliating me. From this experience though I learned to think critically as he had taught me, I had to in order to free myself from his ridicule. Eventually I realized to my horror he lacked the imagination to understand my perceptions. Again I learned compassion. It seemed in those years I was always learning compassion!

Honestly though, I went along with most things in my family when I was young, not thinking too much, it was in my nature to be compliant. That does not mean to say that I could be led into wrongdoing, but in those days I enjoyed being a part of the gang so much so that I was willing to go along. At the same time I enjoyed classical music, acid rock, blues and Sea Cadets. I rarely stepped out of line until I grew older. At 16 I grew long hair as was expected in the '60's, played bass in a rock group, which initiated a serious search for meaning, and began to challenge everything. I was a bit late, but my Dad was quite a decent guy so I never felt the need to turn against him. I just stiffened a bit when he laughed at my insights and tried to explain them so he would understand. What was hard for me to come to terms with was the fact that although I liked myself, I did not know who I was. Everyone else seemed so confident and sure of who they appeared to be, I was neither. My confidence began to grow when I realized that the confidence I thought I saw in others was often based on their fear of not looking in or questioning their lives in any deep way. Their confidence seemed superficial and they lacked any real depth to their character. It was a put-on. As I grew older I began to feel that these people had missed out on something quite important. I began to feel I had something to give to people and with that awareness I came to see value in my life, again.

Later, having finished high school and working out of a hiring hall I witnessed many unsafe work environments. I watched other men steal, saw men engage in prostitution, my own involvement with drugs and on and on and on; it seemed life couldn't get any stupider or more confusing. At the same time I was hard and stupid on my younger sisters and my lessors. What would drive us men do this? It was not as if we are born this way or are we? We learn this stuff some how, fit it into a way of living and that is that. We begin to realize something is wrong during our experience of hurt and the hurting of others if we are open to observing ourselves, that is. It has been called Patriarchy, and in a historical sense it began to dawn on me that it was possibly the result of survival in a difficult world. So what to do?

The only people who said they had answers of any kind were so conservative and fear oriented that I could not stand listening to them. They could not appreciate that I needed to question life. They felt the act of questioning was somehow the problem that needed fixing. I came to see that it was stopping my questioning of their reality that was the problem they felt needed fixing in me. They could not stand it. Earlier in my life it was my own guilt or fear of challenging the norms that existed before I was born that kept me ignorant. How dare I challenge my elders! This time it was my elder's fear of a challenge that attempted to stop me. It didn't work.

So I was looking for goodness in men and not finding it. If it existed at all, where was it? Was it all bad?

So I joined the hippies, hoping to find people whose word meant something and that the high morals I had heard about were real. I suppose you might say that I was a believer in the good of human nature. But as I watched, many other hippies fell into the competition trap of who could appear the most enlightened. I knew then this was another dying movement, and I withdrew from the counter-culture and got really depressed. Of course there are good people everywhere but at the time the understanding was not consciously available to me, or I couldn't see it. I came very close to suicide on a number of occasions. Fortunately I wanted to live for another blue sky, so I dragged myself into therapy and slowly worked out some of my bigger problems. My biggest ones involved not having a meaningful job and poverty.

Eventually I found work. By then I was beginning to think about men again and wanted to start a men's group. This was 1976 and at that time just to mention such a thing you might be immediately spurned or looked down upon with disbelief, or that long tense silence some people indulge in when they think you're weird or gay. Well, are you just trying to get me in a room by myself, they might think? Will you intimidate me or humiliate me?

At that time gayness was definitely not out in the open and it would be years until that was a legal and justified right. Yet my character could be interpreted as gay-like because of the desire to start a men's group and being a bit different, I suppose I appeared to have an ulterior motive. Eventually though it became obvious that many men's lives had similar twists and turns as mine. One thing lacking from the whole mess was the stark fact that men did not talk about their pain, or their joy for that matter. They might talk about what they bought or joke about losing money at the track but emotional highs or lows, forget it. It was only referred to as an afterthought, something that happened in the past and not something going on now, and definitely not important. From my circumspection years earlier and my willingness to talk openly and frankly with anyone I happened to meet, I again felt very isolated and wrong.

I realized that I wanted to live differently, I don't know why but during that early exploratory phase of my life emotions were important and if I felt something, another man might as well, if he could admit it that is. If I felt walked on by someone it was probably more his or her problem than mine. Although I had to ask myself what was being walked on and to make sure I had not previously walked on them. If I had, I urged myself to clear it up immediately so as to not poison the relationship.

Apologizing is never easy, as there are risks that the other person will get angrier or even violent. It is the exception though and not the rule. I liked to think I could be sympathetic to abusers but found this to be exceptionally difficult since one could be seen as enabling their behavior if one was too sympathetic. What I mean here is to be able to relate to abusive people with awareness and not become their victim. I failed quite badly, but I keep trying.

One personal issue that became very irritating occurs with some people that take my apology as a signal that they can learn nothing from our shared experience and decide that it was my error all along. In other words they are not involved. Usually a disagreement involves two people and both need to apologize. However I am more assertive now than a few years ago. I now attempt to pass on knowledge as well as learn. Life really is about being able to hear, to acknowledge other people's words, to feel, and acknowledge our own feelings, to stand our ground or give way, to find a win/win solution or suffer the consequences, and to honor the process as a part of living successfully. At least that is what I tell myself, as experience suggests that at times it is easier to just walk away.

When I was twenty-one I had this hair-brained idea that if I went in chase of a particular woman who had left town in order to get away from me, I could somehow get her back. Well she threw me out on my insulted butt. On the way out the door (in mid-air actually) she gave me a book on Buddhist meditation; it actually changed my life. I never saw her again, but I have a lot to thank her for if that meeting ever occurs. I began to meditate. As I went deeper many troubling questions from my childhood surfaced again and again: they washed over me in waves of defeat and agony. I needed to know what drove me on. Why do I bother looking inside so much? What was different about me that allowed or encouraged or permitted this exploration? Was I sick or normal? What was different? Through meditation I realized that it was the fear of the discovery that you are more aware in the now than you thought that keeps people from exploring their inner natures. People fear their inner wisdom because it often goes against the accepted or outer standards. I did not always listen to mine either because I too was afraid. I played the enlightenment game too. I did learn to honor my path in time and I do value my willingness to look inward. I am sometimes irritated by the unwillingness of others to do the same, but have come to the conclusion that this may well be my contribution to others, a small contribution to peace.

So how to keep track of my emotions? Well, after understanding the basis for my motivations, such as how fear rules me, or how when I am angry with you, it might just be that I am really angry at myself and the past, or I actually did some thing that hurt you.

These convoluted mind warps in logic had to be understood before I could be sure of anything. Emotions are true for the moment but can change or grow the instant a different perspective is added in. One must be prepared to be always searching for the clearest and most honest expression, even though it might be made irrelevant a second later. Letting go of being right is a valuable skill, and I am no expert.

It has only been in the last twenty-five years or so that I began an academic study of men and masculinity. Prior to this time my experience of men was largely observational and remote. As I hinted at earlier, I did not like men and found them arrogant and self-important. I had no idea why, even though they often reminded me of the bullies from my childhood. Learning to stand up for myself was a difficult process, and telling someone to f—off, and seeing that this magic phrase would gain me a kind of respect was the weirdest thing of all. It seemed incredulous at the time that it would work. From my early childhood experiences of learning to be compassionate regarding other people's behavior it seemed inconsiderate to speak in such a way. They may have seen me as wishy-washy or patronizing but of course no one came up to me and said, "Rod, what we really need from you right now is a show of strength so we can trust you." It was more brutal than that-another mystery to unravel-something to do with a survival mechanism. It only became clear in men's groups, and a lot of therapy. Then, I understood what men were seeking from me. They wanted to see my boundaries and what I would do to defend myself, and by extension, if I would be there to defend them as well. These men seem to see life like a sport and that being on the right team was the basis of all social relationships. With that understanding they could relax.

Another factor that had huge implications for my sense of self was the misfortune or the opportunity to be born to a woman who took her own life when I was sixteen. During her illness of about eight years my father single handedly held the family together. He is probably unaware of the fact my sisters and I have so much gratitude for this act of strength, yet we would have been blown away like dust if not for him. Probably his sense of humor is what saved him, and by way of the example below you will see how he could be.

One day Dad and I were out walking as we often did on my visits with him. We entered the train station so I could return home, but Dad seeing a security guard sitting in a kiosk could not resist striking up a conversation with him. So he went up to the counter and said "So do you feel secure in there?" Most of the time people laugh and strike up a genial yak with him that go on and on forever, but this time the guard just grunted and that was that. Dad gave me the "Oh well" look and we walked away.

The devastation of my mother's death left a huge hole in me that has affected me my whole life, but again I was fortunate to encounter another woman who taught me to be my own mother. So I did and it worked. At least pretty good any way. Relating to women was very easy for me since it seemed we were on the same wavelength. However I was secretly asking the question, do you like me, as a man? Yet from well meaning women I found only definitions that applied to women about masculinity and how they viewed men. In those days at about twenty-eight years of age, masculinity was a largely unknown factor, so it seemed appropriate at the time to ask women. They seemed to know who they were and men would not talk. Eventually I had to face up to the fact that women had few meaningful answers for me. Many women were as confused about men as I was. Romantic relationships with women were another matter entirely, for without knowing it and for many years into my adult life I idolized many feminine characteristics. Compassion, gentleness, sweetness and the graceful beauty of women drew me in and left me overwhelmed and lost. They were good qualities that I admired and wanted as part of my own character. This was fine but as for admirable male characteristics I had no idea. Other men did not seem to appreciate these qualities in me as I did and I still did not like a lot of the male behavior around me.

My idealization of women reached a crescendo with a young college beauty. She was as Carl Jung defines such women as shining with the light of the sun,[1] and yes she blinded me in the astonishment of her beauty. Wow! They are anima[2] figures, as two of the greatest interpreters of the human soul, Carl Jung and Schopenhauer suggest: Jung sees my projection as "the archetype of life itself." And Schopenhauer[3] going further suggests "one's secret intention for oneself", and that was certainly true of me in those years.

This attraction was at the time unknown reflections of my own disconnect with masculinity. I wanted to be a brilliant light source for myself, but failing that to the extent I had, I fell for her. She was my greatest unknown danger like the moth to a light bulb that circles it frantically and irresistibly attracted, then with a sudden touch the moth spirals downward exhausted, unable to co-exist with such brilliance.

So do you think I was in love[4] or what?

As you can probably imagine it was a bomb that left me curled up in a fetal position for what seemed like months.

At the time it was largely impossible to talk about it with other men or guys my age in order to get some kind of idea of what to do. Talking to men about a problem was tantamount to asking for either humiliating criticism or never ending lectures on manliness. Women seemed far more compassionate; yet I still wanted contact with older more mature men. It would be many years later, until I experienced this male mentoring from older men. This was a kind of blessing all men need, and it cannot come from women. Women do it for other women; men do it for other men.

In addition to these issues my spiritual life was going nowhere, with too many answers that did not satisfy me, in a world where good answers[5] are not really available, they were becoming a bad habit, leading nowhere. Like all bad habits, it was leading to a cycle of dependency where I felt totally useless and hopeless. It does seem that things eventually come to an end, even finding a spiritual direction or purpose. I recall during the years of searching for belief that I would spend hours in bookstores trying to learn about my chosen direction often feeling more frustrated than enlightened by the effort. Eventually I gave up, started a program of visits to a psychiatrist to sort out some of my phobias and an anxiety disorder. What I discovered changed my life. After a few weeks the therapist began to paraphrase what I had said to him, his clarity shook me. What he stated was first of all, I had a personality disorder of which I knew quite clearly was true, but how it had been created was the interesting bit. I saw the world as outside of myself, with its demands, roles, and obligations. I did not feel qualified to live in that world, hence the anxiety. He then described my inner world, full of my values, beliefs, desires and creative energies, this was the person I knew myself to be. He simply said that I have been attempting to fit my world into the outer one and that was impossible. What I had to do was fit the outer world into my world. In other words live my life out of my own values, beliefs, desires and creative energies and give the outer one much less importance. I had to decide which world I was going to live in and truthfully, it was quite simple. Shortly thereafter, my anxiety went away. I stopped fretting about not finding work and began to plan my life on what I wanted. I left college, moved to a rural seashore village and did nothing for a year and a half. I stopped buying books and started practicing peace of mind. Many internal barriers had to be overcome in order to do this; but progress was happening.

With the new change in my perspective, my experience of a given issue became meaningful in a new way. For example, my spiritual direction has almost always remained the same, but my interpretation of it has changed immensely. From my first experience of it I am less idealistic and more realistic about outcomes. Passion is not belief. It is the truth of it that maintains the belief. We all have to find our own answers to life's questions and mine is now living my life every second.

Dealing with men and masculinity issues was still my largest challenge since most of the images of men I saw at the time I did not like very much. The killer, the controller, or the taker, were all enigmas to me. These were big issues for me and I had to resolve them. I could see them all in me, in my revenge fantasies, my sexual lust for women, my desire to overwhelm women with my "awareness" such as it was. Eventually I came to understand my violent fantasies towards my peers. I knew at the time I was not big enough inside in order to make a surgically thought out defense for myself. I held back from fighting because my bruised emotions would have come out in a raging torrent, without focus or direction. I had to master myself first and it took a long time. I started having fun, but in the end I kept running up against my unmastered life; I hurt a lot of women and got hurt by just as many too. At that point I began to learn about love and choices, but more on that later.

This urge to join a support group for men kept raising its fearsome head and when I eventually faced my fear with a solid yes, another world opened to me again. This was one of the better decisions of my life. It was a group run by a psychologist and it helped to fill the deep unmet need I had sensed was there. It was a re-birth as a man by the mature presence of other men. Having sought it for years without really knowing where it was, by asking women to tell me what masculinity was, by hating the evil in other men, by hurting and being hurt and knowing again and again an answer was there, but where, and was now found.

No longer idealizing women, yet still appreciating their beauty and everything else that is wonderful and feminine I came to a renewed sense of the natural goodness in being a man. No longer alone, my eyes had started to creak open. Through deep conversation, trust building exercises and weekend group campouts a core feeling of "connectedness" began to develop and my life felt "right" for the first time. I learned about ritual and ceremony to make events special. Women became more of an acceptable mystery now than a problem or an intense need. This need had always baffled me; now an understanding of what was missing was there to use.

This led group eventually faded for me until eventually I decided to leave it and start my own group built from men of a spiritual community I had recently joined. I decided on a leap of faith to invite new members from all the men in this community and from outside of it that I respected or admired in some way. It was a very difficult yet tremendously empowering experience for me. I learned so much about myself and other men, especially about ritual and standing my ground with all these new guys in my life. These men could be brutally honest and yet still be willing to listen to my story. So many wonderful healing experiences!

Then after almost twelve years in men's groups I decided to do something different, to give back to the larger civic community. My plan at almost forty-five years old was to create the kind of men's community that I had needed for myself while being a young and uninitiated man, with the intention that other men would not have to go through what I had endured. Good fortune through a friend led me to a magazine called Island Men Journal. We wrote on the most bizarre aspects of manhood, from violence to pornography. We published about 15 issues, of which many spare copies are still in my basement. During this time, Island Men was also an event producing organization. We ran Men's Gatherings held on Equinox and Solstice weekends four times a year for about four years. We used theater games, ritual, comedy, self-exploration and drumming to break down the barriers to emotion and the intimidating presence of so many men. One event brought together almost one hundred men.

During this time there was talk in many men's groups about the need for a men's center. We could use it for meetings, father and son events and parenting courses for parents with boys. The potential was limitless and the need was so great. So from these musings the Victoria Men's Center did eventually open at the corner of Oak Bay Avenue and Foul Bay Road here in Victoria. We spent most of our time fundraising by doing car washes and garage sales. We were well received by the foot traffic but government funding was an impossible dream. Without it we had to shut down after only eight months in operation. Worth doing, but it was a bitter disappointment. Men were not seen as a disadvantaged group so government funding was not available. We were told we would get money and lots of it if we were willing to do workshops on men's violence against women. But shooting ourselves in the foot over and over was not the reason we had opened, so we closed the doors. In order to change this relationship between society and men, men were going to have to demand it just like all other minorities. Getting enough men to do this has always been the issue. It was a big deal for men to step out of the ordinary and defend men's needs for support and a compassionate response from society. After all men had always been competitors: for females, jobs, status or physical prowess. Regardless, we knew many men were fed up with this scripted competition and saw a larger picture of a more generous and inclusive male society. The benefits to all of society were obvious and especially to boys. We had a strong vision yet the resistance was large as well, and remains so although cracks are forming.

Every recent civil upheaval has had a target or a bad guy they could point to, so they could name their oppressor. In the new men's movement, was the target other men, the legal system, corporations, or the military? Or was it us, our fathers, or even our mothers? Is there someone to point to that is responsible for men's enculturalization? If not, then how can we move forward, do we really need an enemy to move forward?

With the primordial memories of other times so far away, way back along the dusty tracks of history we have forgotten our egalitarian ways (assuming they did exist, once) on the mad and desperate race for survival. Yet many men are truly weary of the struggle and desire new alliances with women and other men. The new paradigm has been occurring quietly (since at least the 60's) and for me grew out of the songs written by The Beatles, The Moody Blues and others who created an idealistic world that became the counter-culture. It wasn't perfect but women gained much new territory, and men found a new voice, including myself, even with the drawbacks.

For many years during the 60's and 70's, the deepest and most meaningful conversations were with other male friends. We would talk about everything and anything often long into the night. We wrote poetry, put some of it to music and sang them at dances we put on. We had a ball during these very heady and idealistic times. Of course it did not last. It was often the ones who got greedy or quietly appeared cool on the outside but really had swallowed the hierarchical system hook, line and sinker that spoiled it for everyone else. The beautiful people who always looked great, wore clothes from Pakistan, or India, but would never stoop to tell you how they really felt about themselves. Heaven forbid admitting a weakness. In those days enlightenment was the goal and many people learned how to fake it, while on the side they were filling their pockets and believing not a word of the Zen teachings they threw at you if they caught you committing some trivial mistake. Funny thing, I really believed the New Age stuff (like I said earlier) was the salvation for the world, oh well. On the bright side, many people did in fact begin a major shift away from traditional values and reconnected with nature or began careers in biology or environmental sciences, ecology or farming. In a few circles the New Age philosophy is still practiced and continues the love of nature and of earth stewardship. Drumming and prayers for the earth are still enjoyed by many and their children are learning the ways of living in ecological balance with their surroundings. It seems there is a resurgence.

In the current men's movement there were the opportunistic kind as well: the therapists, the hip lecturers or civil servants who all look great, have one or two homes, lots of bucks and talk a good line about men's issues. Yet in my hometown the Men's Center closed due to a lack of funds—not a lack of programs or enough volunteers or even a bad location. It closed because a profit was not in the making by the very men who did the big talk. Real change takes both: the big talk and the big walk! Many well heeled men would come to our Men's Health Day events, pay five dollars at the door, get cutting edge information on current health research as well as opportunities to join men's groups or other on-going programs but walk away when asked to support a Men's Center.

I stayed on the Board of the Men's Center as a director but the writing was on the wall. It was time for me to move on with a rural retreat center for men on my horizon. This would be a place where men of all ages could rest, yes, just rest. It was embedded in my mind from an earlier experience of living alone on a mountain for eight months. It was on top of a ridge overlooking Fulford Harbor on one of the Gulf Islands, Saltspring Island, near Victoria. My little cabin had everything needed for survival and the peace of mind I had been searching for. I wanted other men to experience this for themselves and possibly gain some of the insight of my experience. After my retreat I canvassed all the local social service organizations that help the kind of men who might get value out of a wilderness retreat. I got absolutely nowhere and totally frustrated. Everyone was very nice to me and very encouraging but not at all on side. Their generally perceived view of men at the time was that men were the problem in society. These groups recognized men had problems but they felt they were of their own making. They felt that when men made real changes the service agencies would be there to help. Well, ten years later and many accomplishments here in Victoria that should raise the flag of change, still little real support from the community is available, although to be honest, homelessness is now a big-ticket item in local politics. With most street people being male some real support in the form of housing is occurring, although not exactly what I had in mind. Some things have changed but not enough to really make a splash. I was discouraged. (Maybe it is time to go back and do the ask again.)

Then, almost right away a friend passed me the phone number of a fellow that was in a small group of men who wanted to start a men's retreat center. That was in 1996 and two groups sprang up from those meetings. The original Board, The Well Foundation[6] provides men's health education in the form of conferences and public events, whereas The Well Site Retreat Society provides a venue for events, campers and personal retreats. The Foundation presented in March 2007 The First Canadian Conference on Men's Health. I was somewhat involved by sitting on the content committee and bringing in some funds and presenting a poster in the registration area on the contents of this book.

Regarding the retreat center: cabins, outhouses, trails and an all weather shelter have been built and maintained. The majority of the building work had been completed by fathers and sons united by the common goal of working together for greater understanding and friendship. Many men's support groups have also helped out. We have yet to open to the public but the bare bones of it are there and ready to go. In addition, as of this date a log cabin is in the initial stages of construction with the site selected and the logs felled and stacked to dry for spring. I am hoping the site can be used for men with my original vision to heal and regenerate from their crises, illnesses and difficult decisions. Hopefully we can provide services for these kinds of problems in society by making the cabins available to men on a short or long term basis. As I witnessed personally significant healing can occur by being in nature. Yet here it is August 17, 2011 and the site is empty, the men have gone, and I believe I have lost the energy to keep it going. Maybe it was all a dream that meant something to me alone, yet I do believe in the rebirth of ideas. Maybe this vision too will get reborn.

Another common dream many men have is to see men's studies courses in all schools and campus's. Yet this has not had a lot of success anywhere. Only one college that I know of has a Men's studies program, at Wagner College[7] in New York. Whether it is based on pro-feminist or male-positive works I am not certain. The difference here is important. Male positive men's studies attempt to show the good males have created and the suffering involved in creating that good, whereas pro-feminist men's studies see only the damage done by males especially towards women and the environment. Both have value by being used as educational tools with the intention of spurring personal growth.

Looking through a gender lens analysis now, I have been aware of concerns that men's events or retreats are an issue for some women due to the fear of reestablishing patriarchy. As feminist writer Laura S. Brown[8] says about retreats, Robert Bly and others: […] are we trying to find this men's movement funny so that we are less frightened by the sight of groups of men together, impassioned and stripping themselves of polite conventions? In another context, they look and sound too much like the gangs of boys that have intimidated and raped us all through recorded time. [9]

I hear her fear in that quote and I understand her point of view. My point of view is that men have rarely broken out of the mould of providing and protecting and need to meet together to find healthier solutions for their own daily lives. Ms. Brown wrote about Adolph Hitler,[10] [he] too relied upon ritual, upon the special bonds between men, to build his movement.

On this, I get her point yet I feel impatient with her huge jumps in logic. I could say from a reactive place that she is suggesting that men should not meet in groups of more than two on street corners for more than one minute or face arrest for conspiring to rape every woman on the block, and that they should have validated passes to be out on their own. Absurd of course, but her words could be interpreted that way by a society gone mad protecting women and children all the while ignoring the contributions of millions of caring men. Many modern women are making very clear that they no longer wish to be protected or provided for as they were in the past. Of course there are always circumstances where men must be called upon to help a woman in an emergency. However many men I know are very reluctant to step in during a domestic dispute for fear that both might turn on him.

From my personal experience of leading and participating in many men's gatherings, our goals were anything but establishing a new hierarchy. I suppose it could be said that the men leading the rituals were the new elite, yet all the men present including myself would be perfectly willing to allow any man to step forward to speak his peace or lead a ceremony. For men who were unable to speak, every opportunity was made to encourage expression. In some ways this process is fundamental to the retreat environment. Often the shy men were the men who needed a sense of safety at the retreat before they would open up. In the city they would not talk to anyone. There was something about being around a fire, telling stories and camping in the mountains that would free up all the pain and hurt these men had experienced and kept hidden. When the tears started flowing the men in the circle would hang their heads in silence. It is a powerful experience and an honor to be so trusted by men we hardly knew.

Being realistic though there are men in this environment who could be Ms. Brown's worst nightmare, so I do not deny their existence. These men can be very charismatic and secretive. Anyone who looks for a guru may find a devil instead. We all have to look out for that one! They can be very dangerous to men too.

The average guy on the street seems to think this is the way it is; that hierarchy is part of us and against all evidence, our lives are generally isolationist, hierarchical, life shortening and not too inspired. However for myself I prefer a different kind of relationship with men. I do not enjoy competitive sports, sparing with people about who is right, the whole concept of winning, of insecurity driven pride, of deceptions and on and on. It is probably why I joined the active part of the Men's Movement so I could socialize with similar minded people. However, men seem to want the hierarchical model to solve the world's problems rather than doing things unanimously. They cannot imagine how to do it otherwise. People seem afraid to trust themselves, to know how to do this. One wonders at the fear!

People seem to like their slot because it gives a sense of reassurance to their lives. They like and fear power because they believe the stories they have been told about themselves by their culture, their families and friends. I think once a person sees that nothing is forever and that security does not exist no matter what you do—you still die, you still hurt, you still are fearful, lost and finite—this realization changes you. All this, and yet life is still a wonderful experience and the learning about it is God's/Ultimate entity/The Universe or whatever's way of telling us that evolution is ours for the asking. All we've got to do is deal with our problems as they come up and we will receive endless bounty. I believe it, I try to live it, and I see it more and more in others. It is hard and it takes a long time, just like unanimous decision-making, but the result of this way of thinking leads to a non-hierarchical social structure, and any competition that exists is understood to be with me only—me being the true measure.

However, it seems that (especially in support groups) hierarchy turns some men against women's movements or other male movements (like the gay community). Yet these men were probably looking for an excuse anyway. Hierarchy gave it to them. Instead of facing their fear of homosexuality or acknowledging their admiration of women, they fear it. Hierarchy encourages and promotes this behavior. Hierarchy exists because of this fear. Without the fear hierarchy disappears. Women's groups and gay groups also use hierarchy to benefit their agendas and are not innocent either. Hierarchy creates hierarchy. The result is that competition reigns supreme, and nobody wins. Until we give up our need to be right this will continue forever.

In an attempt to clarify these and other conflicting views this book will have a focus on the male positive view, although as you may have noticed in the beginning and through the introduction I have been quite angry with men. Hopefully there will be evidence of some growth in my maturity as you read through the work, and you will observe how difficult my process was and still is at times. Writing this book helped to ease this self-exploration.

In my continuing effort to show the difficulty for men to find resources in order to change, male-oriented education is still a long way off as shown in the following example. About ten years ago I approached the Chancellor of the University of Victoria at a public forum and asked him if he would back the idea of a Men's Studies Department at his school. He turned to the head of the Women's Studies Department and asked her if men's psychology was covered under her auspices to which she agreed. I could not believe that he accepted her word on that. It is like asking a male professor to design the Women's Studies program. It will not do the job. Similarly, while I was attempting to drum up support for a male-based curriculum I spoke to several male professors at the same school about assisting me with the job. They were very enthusiastic to lend support from the shadows but they clearly feared the loss of their tenure on campus if they put their name on anything. That shows how powerful the Women's Studies Department had become, where genuine and important research is being denied due to political interference. So I continued to work away at the retreat site (until recently) and the health conferences. My dream for these courses to be available on campus is still alive even if in reality it is only a smoldering wish.

I have not mentioned much of my family life up to now partly out of thinking it was not relevant to the book. However raising two sons is certainly relevant to men's work. It has been a long time watching them grow into young manhood, one is well on his way and another is 19. It is nice to see them turn out so well. With my worries aside, they will do fine in life hopefully better than me. No doubt they would say in unison, "Well Duh, Dad!"

To conclude this preface, the major impetus to begin the research for this book came from my need to know why the feminist movement was so angry with us men, as well as to make an attempt to understand my own anger and shame with other men. In other words, what was this all about? I needed to know. The talk in the street was you know: men are assholes, men cause all the problems and so on. I had to admit that generally, and if only for a while, I agreed. When I asked an angry woman why she was so angry nothing concrete was mentioned that could be seen as traits all men shared. As I grew through my own anger these bad men seemed to me to be only a few of us. So why was I getting the flak too? A secondary push was why some men were so angry about the feminist response instead of sympathetic since there was some truth to women's criticism. A third was to understand who were the men who totally agreed with the feminist view. To me all of it had semi-truths and semi-distortions, the need to explore what was available historically to help resolve these issues appeared the only way to go. So for myself and the other men who lived in this shadow world called masculinity I began to dig . . .

At this point I would like to add a note for men who may have challenges with academic reading. My goal is for as many men as possible to be able to understand what I had to learn in order to write this book. To that end I have tried to write it in a common script. As well I include a comment based on a friend's valuable input. Since he struggles with factual books, he finds the preface easier to read than what follows. He suggested that the challenged reader focus on the title of the chapter being read and frequently reassess the words or that very paragraph with the chapter title. Hopefully that will assist you. R.K.

AN INTRODUCTION TO
WHAT I DISCOVERED ABOUT
MY OWN LIFE

From the earliest times imaginable masculinity has been about defining energies peculiar to males, be this father to son, friend-to-friend, or athlete-to-athlete. This defining process has changed little throughout the centuries, as well as through the men as they have lived it. No individual possessed the knowledge as to where masculinity came from. They all seemed to inherit something. It was a process of exploration as well as the occasional exploitation by powerful ruling elite's or subtle shamanistic rituals. Rather than a clear and rigid definition, our roles were defined by the need for survival. Necessity too dictated the creation of many of our cultural institutions. These institutions maintained and reflected the definitions of masculine behavior of the times as well as restricting new or alternate codes of conduct. Along the way, much disappointment, as well as thanksgiving, recorded the passing of this something from father to son. Many cultures ritualized this disappointment and thanksgiving into initiation ceremonies of the young male into manhood. In the West, early European cultures relied on war and bravery in the face of challenges to bestow a fiercely sought after manly mantle and in the fascination the possibility of the crown of immortality through sacrifice. Although the immature male found the world a confusing and frightening place, unconsciously he knew that without a guide or a rite of passage he would be lost to himself and be of little use to his family or his tribe. To this end initiation ceremonies fulfilled this deep unmet need. This need is still there in modern males; young men sense a need but the initiatory heritage is lost to them. Instead some seek it out in the streets or the gaming rooms online or in drugs and violence. Others look to their fathers for a sign of manliness, sometimes finding it, sometimes not. It is hard to find clear meaning in the day-to-day struggles for survival. The broad vision of the experience of humanity is the ongoing story of history and requires years of study to even grasp minor details. Yet it is still worth doing.

In our confusing present times attempts at initiation do exist. The mythopoetic men's movement is one that embraced initiation more than most, with its primary spokesperson, the poet Robert Bly. In his pioneering book, "Iron John" he tells the story of a boy who stole a magical key[11] from under his mother's pillow. He asks us to describe the significance of the key. Over time I have come to see that the father has a key as well, hidden somewhere for the son to find and steal.

What does Bly mean by this key? Why do we have to violate our parents like this? No good son wants to be a part of this. If this defiance does not occur the son will never mature to think on his own feet. He will remain a child under parental influence his entire life. Yet it is natural for the mother to be unwilling to give up her influence so the son must "steal" it from her. It is similar for the son's relationship with his father. The son must understand the limits of his father's realm. If he does not experience it he will live forever in his father's shadow, and again be useless to himself and his community. This initiation process may have worked well in a pre-industrial society. However in European cultures during the Industrial Revolution something else happened that short-circuited this process by taking the initiatory experience away from the young male and forcing a "work ethic template"[12] onto his soul instead. In other words the real need is still there and has not been addressed adequately in modern societies. This is a critical understanding; the modern male has only been partly initiated and we must be prepared for the consequences.

An uninitiated male can be like a bull in a china shop. He has no idea what he is doing and can actually be a danger to himself and his community. The reality of this is shown by the prevalence of young urban but often-ghettoized males forming into gangs that are an ongoing reality in modern cities. Along this line of thought I am reminded of a conversation I had with a friend who recently returned from Ireland. He was there just after the conflict between the Catholics and the Protestants had cooled down. He noticed considerable numbers of angry young men roaming the streets with nothing to do and nowhere to go. Nobody could figure out how to deal with them. They were still angry and causing trouble wherever they went. I suppose in their minds the memories and the anger will never fade. Their desire for revenge must be overwhelming. But break the cycle of hatred they must. If only they could reach some kind of catharsis with their emotions. From men's studies I have learned that the best way to get the attention of any man is to thank them for what he considers is his most important contribution to society at the time. If it is laying his life on the line in civil conflict or helping his children learn to read, it can only be a meaningful honor if it means something to him. The angry young man seeking revenge or a release of frustration is all too common in mainly poor underdeveloped countries or ghettos of the wealthier nations. What is his driving purpose that takes him into the streets? If you had seen your sister raped, your father killed and your home burned to the ground, a possible driving purpose would be a search for fairness. Seeking fairness in an unfair and violent society that demands its young men to fight for the cause of religion or whatever and then to stifle those feelings is an unreasonable and nearly impossible expectation to lay on them. Without thanks for their contribution or some kind of acknowledgment they may very well stay angry the rest of their lives, however long it may be with that kind of powder keg inside them. Young men are truly wonderful and their willingness to help is outstanding. You just have to talk to them like they are important to you and they will respond to you in the same way. By your wisdom you initiate them into adulthood.

Our impatience with the elderly is another key indicator to this loss of the initiatory experience. Indeed, if the elders in our communities are no longer respected as examples for the young to emulate, or they do not feel it is their duty to initiate the young, we not only lose their wisdom but we do not know who we are, what our place is or where we are going. In essence, we are lost. The elders originally performed the initiation ceremonies, so if there is no historical connection, proper respect cannot exist.

However, to get a man in his eighties to stand up and speak his wisdom of the years of his life seems a hard thing to do these days. It's as if the old guy feels he won't be listened to even if he does speak up. After all, who cares!

Historically, elders of a tribe were responsible for passing on the legends, history and values of that tribe to younger less experienced individuals. What happened to our Western culture? Why don't the young go to the elders anymore? By the way, where are all the elders of our culture?

Well, a lot of the men probably worked themselves to death, or died of alcoholism, or suicide. The rest are mostly in nursing homes with only their memories to give them meaning. Of course there are always exceptions. Many elderly men managed to save a whole whack of money for their retirement. Many more did not however.

When I talk to an elder[13] male, he is a lot more than his memories or what he did for a living. Mainly he is a storyteller. He may talk about the past, but in a way that shows he was there. Something I can never do, that is, until it's my turn. I mean, just the fact that the guy has silver hair says something about success! He survived that long. There's got to be some value in his life somewhere. Yet who is listening?

One of the great pleasures of being a member of the Island Men Network was the occasional men's gathering that occurred at Goldstream Park. This is a place of tall ancient cedars, a rushing river, eagles and salmon. Whenever an elder man came to the event, I made sure he was acknowledged by the gathering and asked to speak about his life. Often the look on their faces as they stepped into the circle was one of great surprise as well as great pleasure. You could see clearly the feelings coming from a few moments basking in the light of the younger men. Then, a few words of his life . . . Those moments were special for me, just to see them honored. (I'm reminded of an honoring my father received there one winter night) It was clear to me as well as to the other younger men that the effect on our male elders was an essential and ancient part of being human. To be present in order to hear how the old ones lived is one of the great opportunities in life and is not available to most of us. So many men regret the lost closeness they had with their fathers and never mended those bridges. It is never too late though.

The great German poet Rainer Maria Rilke[14] warns us of this lack of actual available wisdom from an elder that may be closer to home than we realize:

> Sometimes a man stands up during supper and walks outdoors, and keeps on walking, because of a church that stands somewhere in the East.

> And his children say blessings on him as if he were dead.

> And another man, who remains inside his own house, dies there, inside the dishes and in the glasses, so that his children have to go far out into the world toward that same church, which he forgot.

Translated by Robert Bly

The image of "dies there inside the dishes and the glasses so that his children have to go far out into the world" is the key idea in the poem. Young men having to go far out into the world to find themselves suggests there is no father or initiatory experience from elders to be had near the home. Without the wisdom of these elders, the young men will look to other young uninitiated or poorly initiated males far out in the world for ideas or experiences of how to survive. Hence a basis for gangs and lost youth is created. The consequences down the road is that some of these young males end up heading large corporations that do unprecedented ecological damage or displace tribal peoples on a grand scale. More commonly we see lost individuals spending a lifetime in prison or be trapped in a drug-induced haze. These things have been witnessed or experienced by many of us. Yet few take responsibility for our own lack of vision. They cannot because they do not know what they are missing, and probably never will. If they can be exposed to the understanding of their elders and traditions they might begin to understand their own isolation and immaturity. This understanding of elders and other initiated males has been so belittled and ignored in contemporary society that it is no wonder male silence exists to such a level in modern culture. They are not leading themselves in any initiated way and as a result are led instead by genetics, bio-cultural survival urges and in the wealthy industrial nations, the economic dynamo of market manipulation.

In the corporate model, some initiations are not so kind or egalitarian. Family dynasties or the inner circle that own and run many major corporations have considerable expectations, one might call initiatory rites, that is, the hoops the young are expected to jump through. Through initiation, young men and now young women in corporations can expect to learn how to destroy competition, instead of learning from it, and manipulatively sell products to people where a real need does not exist. All this instead of fulfilling real needs, and keeping business matters secret from everyone except the inner circle. An initiation of distrust is what is being created here, instead of an environment of growth and generosity. As the Japanese say, "business is war."[15] Other types of initiation include lessons from conversations around the dinner table, family humor and knee jerk reactions in daily life. For example a sexist joke might be tolerable between two friends but around young children may be in very bad taste and inappropriate. Military, medical or legal training have their respective philosophies of what is appropriate or taboo. Everything is initiation to the young or the susceptible; both often go hand in hand. We have to choose carefully if we seek to be initiated and if we do not choose then we take on unconscious and non-communicated societal norms, which can include cynicism, bitterness, isolation, and the ultimate lonely place, the endless struggle for power and prestige. I want to go into just one example of this by describing a recent visit to my family dentist.

I had mentioned to him about writing this book and how happy I was with its development when he immediately began a testimony of his own perspective on the goodness of men. I include this not only because he is a great dentist, but because he is also a good man who has been generous in his community and to me personally. His comments I believe are important since they reflect a common view among professionals and men who have worked hard to establish a livelihood in our contemporary society.

During our conversation he kept repeating the phrase "History is by design and not by accident." Since my mouth was full of technology and I could only mumble, I had no choice but to listen. So I let him go on about the evils of the world and his view that much of our behavior occurs from a selfish first person basis rather than from any kind of egalitarian purpose. This would suggest he considers there to be a remote or at best a minor natural goodness in men. I believe he meant by his often repeated quote that powerful people conspire to direct how the big questions were addressed and that the rest of us are helpless victims who buy into the "evil plan" largely because we lack vision or we are preoccupied scratching out a living under their silent but coercive authority. While he did not exactly say it was a conspiracy he implied it well enough. I responded with a quote of my own that I thought encapsulated everything he had just said: "It is a lonely world for a good man." He did not blink an eye but responded immediately with a nod of approval. In a later e-mail he mentioned "It is not a lonely world for a good man, but at times a lonely world for many good men." I took his initial response to have been an insight to his personal reality and evidence of a common sense of isolation that many well-intentioned professionals experience on a regular basis. His second comment suggests men must remember to collaborate to avoid isolation. I would add that while this might be a common experience for all good men, professional and business leaders also maintain their isolation because for them to challenge themselves it would require an uncomfortable shift in perspective and economics. In other words, a distance from everyone else is built into their practice and is a direct result of their practice. However any change at all would deliver a big payoff, but with tremendous risk.

My dentist's enlightened cynicism suggests this evil is in all of us and there is nothing any of us can do to change it, and is therefore a "reality." His subsequent e-mail made it clearer: "When one does not care about others, evil sets in." Yet many will use this as a justification to avoid facing uncomfortable feelings, or having to live with the overwhelming despair of being human. This failure to care may be the basis of many spiritual dilemmas for we might feel that without the guidance of a multitude of enlightened beings, heroes or a God(s) we are completely lost. Such men believe we live in a hopeless world with no meaning what so ever. Just consider for a moment all the fears we maintain because we have convinced ourselves those fears are wise precautions: fear of criminals when rates of crime are known to be decreasing, fear of homosexuals because we believe they are after us, or even an unwillingness to uncover the root cause for a phobia. It is the way we are, we say.

A fear of life is not a vision or a way to move forward. It is stagnation. The religious response is similar in nature. Both are defeats of the human spirit. According to both beliefs, there is no hope or no hope without help from outside. I hope one day we will realize if transcendence does not come from us, it will not come at all. If we do not truly want it, God's help will not deliver it. If and when we do create it on our own we will realize we have far more control over our destiny than we had previously credited ourselves with. This frees us to do even more. Yet some will say it did not come from us regardless of the evidence.

So if it has to come from us, what is it? I will show throughout this book what that something is. In a phrase it is the natural goodness in all of us, but it is more than that. You will see how everything we value has come from individual effort and sacrifice over thousands of years. In the end you will have been initiated into that goodness, not by me but by recognizing it in yourself. Call it God's will if you want, but we are the ones who have to act regardless. You will find there is a way forward that defeats cynicism and frees you from imposed psychological dictatorships. I hope you will find how to create the paradise we all need and deserve to live in without claiming to have the right way of doing it. It will take work, we just have to wake up to it. It is there; you have to be willing to do one thing though—dump those fears.

Could we agree then that the study of human culture is in many ways a history of initiation? If so then the answer to the question of what kind of initiation is acceptable seems to be whatever is appropriate to the times. Many young people today have initiated themselves into renewable and sustainable technologies and new ways of thinking brought about by the Internet. So, if this is the case, this initiation is supposed to happen and everything we do has some level of responsibility and opportunity embedded in it. If every action is an initiatory experience we can account for the beliefs and fears of the human race. However let us not forget the hurts in ourselves and the hurts in others as the initiations occur with or without our awareness. As well, we have to be sure our initiation is giving us what we need to function, rather than doing what is expected. What about independent thought outside the box of our initiations? In other words how do we know initiations will create what we wish in the end? It seems we make up our own mind about what is true and our initiation confirms it. A commonly used quote suggests: "We create our own reality." We then create initiations to confirm it.

But is this what we want, and how would we know?

This book asks if we got what we needed from the past so that we can create a healthy and vibrant civil society in the present. If we did not get what we needed, where we will find it? As my dentist suggests we are moved in many different directions by influences often not in the global good, and often without our conscious knowledge or consent. We need to discover where we came from and what were the very first initiatory experiences we developed in our desperate need for survival. Somehow we got to where we are today, but how? The great democracies of the West did not develop on their own, people made decisions or designs (again my dentist) in order to create a state of reasonable fairness.

Yet surely we are not done?

We will cover many of the historical root causes that led to the development of democracy and how our masculine identity played a leading role in its formation. While it is fair to criticize masculinity and hold it responsible for so much oppression throughout history, and it is true that in many ways males can create mayhem, it is still important to note the positive contributions. For example, many men have negative memories of their fathers. However if pressed, as in a supportive men's circle, they will recount moments of pleasure even affection. These memories are inseparable from the negative and must be acknowledged. Not all action is purely evil or purely good. A full account must be taken, not just the politically correct or emotionally laden one. For example, it seems that current writers of masculine studies appear to have decided to step out of their bodies and ignore their own reality in order to write their books. They must distrust themselves to such a degree they can see no good in themselves or in any other man. I want to focus on this negative vision of masculinity for only a short time.

One of the leading writers focusing on masculinity is R. W. Connell[16] who wrote in "Masculinities", "If we recognize that very large-scale institutions such as the state and corporations are gendered[17], and that international relations, international trade and global markets are inherently an arena of gender politics, then we can recognize the existence of a world gender order."[18] He is suggesting that a conspiracy exists by men to rule the lives of the more "human" and "good" women and children. In a second example he states: "Politics as usual is men's politics. Women's attempts to gain a share of power have revealed a defense in depth operated by the men behind the barricades [...]." If men have this intent why is it that in 1920 Canadian women were given the right to vote[19] by these very same men? My belief is that women got the vote because they demanded it and that is the only and best way society changes. But there is more to this story. Consider this: "[...] people (men and women) receiving public charitable support or care in municipal poorhouses (who had not been enumerated in the past because they lacked a "home" address) could not vote until 1929. (Please see cited work #19 above). This historical fact, that men without property could not vote either, needs to be stated along with this debate. In fact there were times before 1920 where women could vote but lost it.

I hope men will experience a different understanding, one based upon as many sides of history as possible. Only this will provide a sense of hope for the future. Yet there is an immense struggle ahead. An important question to be addressed is how did these male property owners end up with so much power. How was it that democracy occurred at all? Why wasn't it stamped out in its initial years and who fought for it during the hundreds of centuries of human history?

I will present a quote from "The Masculine Mystique", a book by Andrew Kimbrell. He writes about contemporary men's roles in society that: "The view that men are biologically or intrinsically competitive, self-centered, autonomous, promiscuous, work-obsessed, and power-driven is simply not borne out[20] by reports on the behavior of men in other cultures and in other times." This is important because males in highly industrialized cultures such as Japan and now China seem to incorporate these problematic attributes more readily. One must ask why? Is it true? One possibility is that these industrialized males have a culturally distorted biological impulse that propels them to create great gobs of wealth in order to raise a family and protect them from harm. Yet Connell concludes that modern researchers have largely dismissed the biological[21] foundation behind male behavior. Given this conclusion, can we then argue that males will do whatever needs to be done within a given environment to survive? Whether it is in industrializing China or being a member of a hunter gathering tribe it seems so. Survival is the key and the requirements for survival change all the time. Thus we have to be careful about what we say is true for truth changes all the time as well.

As we know, assumptions are everywhere and to illustrate the danger of maintaining assumptions about people or Western men in particular, a very popular anthropologist, Jared Diamond, gave us an example of the danger of bias in the study of Aboriginal people that led to a misconception of violence in remote cultures. He pointed out that upon the first early contacts with Aboriginal societies, anthropologists idealized tribal societies as gentle and nonviolent because they observed no murder in a band of 25 people in the course of a three-year study. Later much more extensive long-term information about band and tribal societies revealed that murder[22] was in fact, a leading cause of death.

We will have to keep an open mind and admit we might not be so bad after all, let go of the guilt, and find out what seems so different in Western societies. Where did these negative views of men come from? Maybe so much of this is just as Diamond suggests in "Guns, Germs and Steel" that we had the raw materials[23] in the right combinations and locations to develop the technologies and skills to run amok on a planet wide shopping spree. While appearing to be different, in reality Europeans[24] are no different than any other people. Is it a recently acquired collective guilt that runs us? Without a doubt, some areas have been left untouched and need to be addressed. These areas take the form of critical differences in culture such as the needs of the culture and its beliefs or ethics, as well as where it is going, its apparent goals or a stated purpose. Some cultures just wish to feed and clothe their people and others are expansionist or materialistic. Is there a common thread in all the distinctiveness we see around the earth? If we base that answer on the acceptance that we are similar wherever we are there must be a common thread. But what is it?

So we have two questions to resolve: one is where did the negative views towards Western men come from? Secondly, if there is a common thread between men worldwide, what is it? These are not easy answers to address and will take the majority of this book to explore.

Yet a simple starting point could put it all down to the initiation experience, but to what purpose? Why bother initiating your people; it is a lot of work and takes so much time away from more interesting things such as having babies or building a house. The average person's reply is why bother with it, just do what you have to do instead.

We seem to do all these things for different reasons and it is the reasons that are important. They drive culture, the development of ideas, and maintenance of history, philosophy and religion. Without reasons or questions we could not adapt successfully to our environments. Reasons turn into initiations based upon cultural needs. Culture is the combined accumulation of the initiations of a given society. As we know there are many different cultures. For example, cultural differences between northern European males and African males would appear to have originated from very different initiatory rituals in order to survive. European males were "initiated" by the Church in the hope to be highly productive for God and human society, and by the Industrial Revolution to create wealth[25]. Whereas pre-contact African males were raised and initiated into warrior and hunting societies by chieftains always alert to attack by other tribes or striving to avoid food shortages. The needs of the two societies were very different. As the developing world begins to embrace its own versions of capitalism, the two cultures are merging. African males are clearly placing themselves in position of wealth generation and the development of a civil society. The example of the African Union, Africa's United Nations, is a major step in democratic thinking for all the nations of Africa.

European peoples were initiated in other ways with other important considerations. The Christian religion's influence and its story of the expulsion of Adam and Eve from Eden,[26] has a staggering effect on the Western mind, primarily on our relationship to the environment. Our consciousness believes itself to be permanently banished from the goodness of the Earth or Eden. We believe we have lost something and are inherently evil, and that we must be "saved" in order to do any good whatsoever. Eden will only be regained upon our death, but only if we are good. That is some initiation!

The Aboriginal mind was only influenced in this way a few hundred years ago and still values the old beliefs of the inseparability of man and nature. To the Aboriginal mind[27] there was no evil deed and no casting out from nature although there are many tales of bad behavior and legends meant to teach the young as a help to maturity. Any wonder other economies that have copied Western economic development, such as China, are polluting the environment and cutting down rain forests or destroying ecosystems? We have not built in any reason or initiation in our culture for a historical relationship with the earth and its sustainability. We were banished from it.

Can we really blame Adam and Eve completely for this? No, of course not! If instead God had welcomed them to Eden without condemnation over a minor transgression, would the world be the same today? Not very likely. We could have hoped for a very different relationship during the colonial years and between the genders. The slaughter of people in the Americas might have been different. Hard to say for sure—European diseases did after all play a major role in depopulating most of the world's Aboriginal peoples,[28] and to be fair there are many examples (the deforestation of Easter Island is a good example[29]) of cultures that devastated their environments prior to European contact yet hardly on the same scale as the European way. However, it still comes down to reasons and initiations to show us what to do and why we do what we do.

From anthropology we have learned that humans abandoned a hunter-gatherer life on the land for a more settled existence when farmers were able to create a surplus.[30] Many cultures though did not develop the Euro-centric model of nature in conflict with humanity or being "other." The land is neither the enemy nor a lost paradise. Much could be said of the way the Western mind has treated the environment, as if it were the enemy, something to be used and discarded. Many, especially in the "back to the land" movement, have attempted reconciliation with the land. This social revolution can be seen as a conscious expression of despair and a growing cry for a new relationship with nature as a part of modern thought. It shows the ambitious environmental changes demanded by a growing global appreciation for renewable energy, reusable products, not just recyclable ones. An attempt is being made to heal the psychic damage done to the Western mind over the centuries. But we should not take this bias too far; other cultures are not so innocent either. For the time being, let us look at these Western behaviors and how they came into being.

The story of Adam and Eve is a very small symptom of the thinking that drove Western society. Prior to the Industrial Revolution, males were initiated into a process that was greatly needed at that time. Young males usually followed their fathers into the same trade or guild and would stay there for their entire life, even with the obvious potential for disappointment. Then along came the Industrial Revolution with demands for new initiations by capitalists and the Church for the sole achievement of great wealth. This took its toll in stress and time away from home and children. In this new reality only the rich had any rights to speak of, everyone else had almost nothing. Over time improvements came to all. One group had been left out however. Actually men left themselves out but either way it must be obvious yet it is not. By way of example, in Canada healthy white males are the only culturally based group to not have a disadvantaged recognition attached to the consequences of their position in society. This is important because when these males fall apart due to divorce, bankruptcy or illness. What support is there for them? It is usually assumed that they will just pay for it themselves. However, not all of them have the resources to do that. Canada's medical system will cover only so many expenses, whereas every other group has other resources to call upon when in dire need.

Historically there has been a tremendous expectation placed on Western males to create huge amounts of wealth in the form of cash. Research into stress from overwork and other related illnesses has been done but not specifically referring to white males. Much more is being done with Japanese males[31] who are known for working themselves to death or engaging in "Karoshi-Death."[32] One report says that in the last twenty years in Japan, sudden deaths among top executives have increased by 1400 %. "Juristat" an on-line website of Statistics Canada[33] shows male deaths by suicide, incarceration rates and murders[34]. While not perfectly related to studies on stress effects, an argument can be made that stress contributes to suicide and criminality.[35]

Is it possible we are too ashamed of our past colonial atrocities, too overwhelmed by the responsibility of creating wealth, or so afraid to admit any vulnerability that we will not claim any disability? Are we afraid of admitting or even acknowledging our own past Aboriginal roots in pre-Christian Europe? Do we really believe the familiar feminist theory that "we are the problem?" All other gender, racial and ethnic groups have this recognition enabling them to claim damages from discrimination and receive federal charitable funding for improving their lives. The Victoria Men's Center[36] here in my hometown could get nothing. Yet the needs of boys failing in our education system are becoming more and more evident.[37]

As of today, in 2012 there is no Federal Ministry for the Male. No surprise? Is this the proof of our disposability, as a manipulation to keep us "in the saddle" as our role demands? There have been many improvements for men yet the stigma of the wealth creation specialist till exists. Throughout the culture in general, white males feel big consequences when they admit weakness or failure to achieve what is demanded of them. After all, they are supposed to be on top of the genetic pile. As a result they are not considered victims of oppression although they are victims in a different, more internalized and hidden way. It could be referred to as "achievement anxiety" where much acting out and behavioral problems can be seen in adolescent males. They did not invent these pressures and place them on their backs. They inherited them from their fathers and mentors who also inherited them from their fathers. These attitudes need to be challenged in today's culture. I have heard the slogan, "Don't be a man!" as a kind of revolutionary statement for men to rebel against their inherited oppression.

Men can still complete their bio-cultural programming without killing themselves in the process. Raising a family does not have to be "one man against the world."

In a previous section, recall how I came close to suicide while struggling with my own demons. My struggle was mostly financial. I needed to achieve something. The inner demands were so urgent, I nearly ended my life. The financial imperative is a deep and critical demand in all men and is not addressed in today's boardrooms or in the hiring halls. Every Western man knows this but it cannot be referred to as oppression. Instead it is an accepted obligation or mantle of manhood, something we grow into and absorb. We become initiated by it. The individual male has to do it himself and alone. Failure to get through this financial struggle is seen as unmanly. Along with this goal a whole plethora of assumptions, prejudices, even outright lying can accompany each man striving to achieve this goal. Often along with the lying is unconstrained bragging about accomplishments, occasionally resulting in physical confrontations between competitors in order to determine the strongest liar. More often the males recognize the "victor" and accept their reduced place without a physical confrontation.[38] Some women and other wiser men sit back and think: "How stupid can you get?" This confrontation is really just a symptom of male oppression. We talk about "men's issues" as if all history is a men's issue, it is not. A men's issue is rather the oppression of being male in a competitive and wealth driven culture with no apparent escape. This situation arose from the demands for survival. The consequences are real and devastating. Many males will never understand this in a radical way; that is, that they will not demand an end to their conscripted and exhausting role as provider and protector. In addition, if men's issues were to be explored, much of the current family violence we see would be addressed, partly by dealing with the frustrations men feel.

If we were not blinded by our oppression, we might see these roles as a temporary situation, one that ends when the children mature safely and move into their own "field of dreams." More likely, the children will live out their lives believing the initiation they received from their culture to be the truth and never knowing their hurt inside actually shows. (the not good enough, unless...) They will carry it around for life, like a zombie never questioning why he feels dead. It would almost seem as if we are "allowed" by some higher power to know only so much knowledge and after that we are told to stay put and shut up! It is then left to priests or accountants to save us from our "lowly nature." Who has not heard that story? Who has not been lectured by "those who know?" Is there no freedom from oppression?

Men wear this hurt as armor, a psychic shield that protects them from feeling emotion. Building on an earlier argument they attempt to deceive others about the truth inside. These men can never stop competing because if they do, they will feel the hurt and experience the fear of being labeled by other competitors as failures. The only escape for these men is the development of the "Hero" culture where violence and great, often dangerous, effort can be explained by a search for immortality through sacrifice.[39] Males know this almost instinctively. To be the hero and to remain one is the only reward for a lifetime of sacrifices, even if few males ever maintain the status of hero for long. Few understand their deep and often unmet need for recognition. The movie and entertainment industry exploits this need by relentlessly bringing out one hero movie after another where the "Great Wooden Brain" never dies and always wins the love of some dumb hero—worshiping bimbo. Hollywood is built upon the belief that some people are innately different from and better than the rest of us. This belief pervades all pagan mythology and classical legend; it surfaces as well in folk tales and fairy stories. Plato writing in "The Republic" called this a "noble lie,"[40] a fable in which he suggests that all men are made from earth, but in a few, the earth has been mixed with gold, rendering them inherently superior to their fellow men and fit to wield power. The example coincides with prince and princess encounters in romantic tales of love and of the great inheritances-yet it is mostly about the money and the power it brings. The "love" is there if the money and power are there too, somehow. We know we are not these people, we will never be, but we want to be, and yearn to receive this unearned privilege of birth, to believe we are so much better than the others. That we are so deserving. The inheritance of an indecipherable locket our Grandmother gave us entitles us to a Lordship, or similarly the gift of a fairytale castle are both fantasies built into our culture. This exposure to the "rewards" of being better by doing nothing is at the center of our hero culture and we males eat it up, and women cannot wait to meet one of these men. On the other hand men who endure a life time of never-ending sacrifice without recognition is also unacceptable. They might get a note in the obituaries but that is that. This is the on-going struggle to reclaim the King's land. A reality based on fairness and honesty. This is the basis for the development of Democracy, with new learning and more appropriate initiations instead of ones based on phantasy. One wonders who or what controls the initiations handed out.

My personal experience within the "men's movement" showed the desire was there to help soften the blow for men during difficult times. We shared our disappointment or loss. There was nothing to be ashamed of. We controled the initiations and as long as we knew this, we were in control of our existence. Otherwise we risked becoming the victims of other people and their initiations. The "men's movement" though did not address the oppression of males. It got males talking. However, the images of hero, magician, warrior and lover[41] as described by Robert Moore and Douglas Gillette reinforced our traditional oppression by referring to greatness as our salvation. Even though they did not mean to oppress us further, this reference to greatness as salvation does by creating an urge to heroic striving.

There is nothing wrong with striving to be good at something. However let me be the devil's advocate for a moment by sharing a wicked thought and hopefully provide a clearer example: two heroes of the ancient battles between Sparta and Athens, Alcibiades[42] and Achilles[43] were of this heroic mix.

Historically Alcibiades was seen as a great protector and hero of Athens during the wars with Sparta. He saw himself this way as well. My wicked thought is that men or women of great ambition or powerful ego who interrupt, dominate, or otherwise ignore all the accomplishments of others may in fact have a great unknown gift to share. They may have no idea what that gift is and remain intolerable by not achieving their vision, and their degree of arrogance reflects their potential capacity-but they and their worshipers do not see it as such.

We often see this in the young or in the criminal. They do not know how to put their gift to acceptable use; they are feared and eventually cast out or re-absorbed in some other way by mainstream society. Their gift might be destroyed or twisted into an unrecognizable form. It becomes lost and humanity is worse off for it. This is true of everyone; we all have gifts locked away. But what are they? The gift of Alcibiades might be a lesson to resist worshiping him and a warning to any individual who may seek a cult of followers.

The dark side of the gift is the "Terror." This is the terrible consequence we might have to pay if we do not learn important lessons from the behavior of our heroes. The terror is also what we might become during the act of worshiping them. We think they know something. Yet if their behavior becomes even more outrageous we might try to make excuses for it.

Achilles, the other great hero of the Classical Greek period astounded everyone during the Athenian/Sparta wars, he held great charisma, was a powerful fighter, deceptive when necessary and brutal as needed. He and Alcibiades encapsulated all the qualities of the killer or "hired gun" mentality. They have received great reward for their contributions to society yet as we become involved with these kinds of people their character often overwhelms us, much to our own discredit. For they will do as they please, take what they want and may even have a sanction by the state or a ruling body to receive these perks because they have contributed such great services to a people. However these heroes may switch allegiances if another offer is better. So they cannot be trusted and yet we give our hearts and souls to them for their efforts. At the same time we handle our heroes with kid gloves; we keep them at a distance and try to control their outrageous behavior. If we fail we become their victim instead of achieving our initial goal as their compatriot.

The personal oppression of Alcibiades was his inability to see he had something to teach and instead used his strength to dominate and satisfy his selfishness, and due to this oversight he eventually destroyed himself in the process-he could have been a great teacher like J. Krishnamurti who taught well in spite of efforts of followers to idolize him. He refused to lead[44] them in the traditional idea of "lead" and told them instead to find their own solutions. For this he did indeed become a great leader.

An extreme example of male oppression is the use of an initiation described in the book, "A History of Secret Societies." The author Arkon Daraul[45], actually a pen name for Idries Shah Naqshbandi, describes a technique used to create the Assassin cult of the Ismailis in 11th century AD Persia: "Hasan (the cult leader) himself takes up the story of how his fortunes fared after the flight from Persia. He had been brought up in the secret doctrines of Ismailism, and that in Cairo there was a powerful nucleus of the society. And if we are to believe the words of Fazal, (a personal friend) he already had a plan whereby he could turn their followers into disciplined, devoted fanatics, willing to die for a leader. What was this plan? He had decided that it was not enough to promise paradise, fulfillment, and eternal joy to people. He would actually show it to them; show it in the form of an artificial paradise, where houris (heavenly virgins) played and fountains gushed sweet scented waters, where every sensual wish was granted amid beautiful flowers and gilded pavilions. And this is what he eventually did."

Daraul continues "Hasan chose a hidden valley for the site of his paradise, described by Marco Polo, who passed this way in 1271 AD:

> *In a beautiful valley, enclosed between two lofty mountains,*
> *he had formed a luxurious garden stored with every delicious*
> *fruit and every fragrant shrub that could be procured. Palaces*
> *of various sizes and forms were erected in different parts of*
> *the grounds, ornamented with works of gold, with paintings*
> *and with furniture of rich silks. By means of small conduits*
> *contained in these buildings, streams of wine, milk, honey*
> *and some pure water were seen to flow in every direction.*

[...]he ordered that none without his license should find their way into this delicious valley, he caused a strong and inexpugnable castle to be erected at the opening to it, (the valley entrance) through which the entry was by a secret passage."

"Hasan began to attract young men from the surrounding countryside, between the ages of twelve and twenty: particularly those whom he marked out as possible material for the production of killers. Every day he held court, a reception at which he spoke of the delights of paradise [...] and at certain times he caused draughts of a soporific nature to be administered to ten or a dozen youths, and when half dead with sleep he had them conveyed to the several palaces and apartments of the garden. Upon awakening from this state of lethargy [...] he believed himself assuredly in Paradise [...] When four or five days had thus passed, they were re-intoxicated and carried out of the garden. Upon being carried to his Presence it was said: we have the assurance of our prophet that he who defends his lord shall inherit Paradise, and if you show yourselves to be devoted to the obedience of my orders, that happy lot awaits you."

"Suicide was first attempted by some; but the survivors were easily told that only death in the obedience of Hasans' orders could give the key to Paradise." This illustrates the problem with initiation and secret societies in general, is the lack of education for the initiates, and the general degree of ignorance that is maintained over them. (Remember Georgetown?) Mind control and the creation of a sanctified view of the world rather than one reached by our own personal experience and a life that is fully lived. This process requires the teachers who are often powerful members of the society to convince their pupils into a state of doubt about all conventional ideas, religious and political. False analogy and other manipulations of speech are used and the result is the student's complete dependence for answers from the leaders. Plus when the students were ready to receive knowledge, it would come to them. A vow of blind obedience was then made to one of the teachers with great fanfare and celebration.

The entry into secret societies reminds me of modern acceptance to clubs such as the Bar or engineering fraternities or other associations. Many Hollywood movies also idealize the secret society—the Star Wars and Harry Potter series for example. Of course the whole business is the same as our discussions about the requirements for survival. The fitting into a hierarchy in difficult times serves the greater good. In good times the structures remain non-adaptive and fear-based. Without preparation for the hard times, structures are like cement, intractable and conveniently invisible.

So how do we reconcile these apparently conflicting purposes to initiation? We all have within us gifts to share; yet we seek heroes or become victims because we do not believe opportunity is there for us. We want to believe in secret societies and special places to find meaning in our lives. Our own emptiness ties us to the "Hero" resulting in the total misunderstanding of power. The use of power is only meant to accomplish things not to separate one person from another-that is about authority and a whole other story goes with that. However authority is still something we agree to be bound by or are forced to accept just as we accept power abuses over our lives.

To provide some further evidence for the idealization of the hero, consider the effect of not believing that you have gifts within you. You will see yourself as incompetent, incomplete or overwhelmed and unable to make decisions. You allow others to make up your mind for you, and will not believe in any original thought of your own, or even believe you are capable of an original thought. You will perceive life as impossible to understand. Essentially you are lost. Challenging your fears is the last thing you might consider. You have become cannon fodder and easy pickings for dictators and tyrants alike and easily believe whatever they tell you. You have become child-like, innocent, and unable to learn the lessons your gifts have to teach you. You find yourself reduced to the condition of infancy. You have been made free of the responsibilities of an independent adulthood. You might be easily convinced that genocide is an acceptable component of conflict and be led to do it. You could be a time bomb set to go off at any moment with so many gifts lost to us all.

Such a great tragedy, lost forever.

When a people become tired or worn down by crisis, poverty or bloodshed, there is a great danger of the ghost of Alcibiades showing up as a champion. But if instead we face him, his selfishness and outrageous grandiosity, we realize what we have created out of our fear and exhaustion. We see there is no choice. We are not innocent nor are we without inspiration. We have to acknowledge the gifts within us instead. As Robert Bly says, "by eating our shadow"[46] and by learning from our depths, we become leaders of our own lives and free of the cunning and entrapments of others. Essentially we initiate ourselves.

Many of the initiations of modern society rely on young men and women to sacrifice themselves to the "Land of Milk and Honey" as in the "Land of the Ismailis" story which today is the computer game, or violence in movies or far away on some grand excursion, and our young ask themselves, "Where are my super powers?"

Of course acknowledging the accomplishment of an average man's good work is missing in modern society because his contribution is an expected behavior of his initiation, built into the role of the male breadwinner. He must know this in himself and not to challenge these standards. White males do not appear to need encouragement to overcome racial, cultural or ethnic barriers to opportunity, at least in the West. We accept white male failure or success as part of the "natural way" of things, even though white racial shame for the past treatment of minorities and other genders probably plays a role in today's multi-ethnic workplace. This book brings evidence that white males need support in a way that differs from traditional support given to others. Consumer goods, the annual holiday, a pension at retirement, glorification by the Church and State is believed to be enough recognition. But why do men kill themselves at alarming rates compared to women and why do males predominantly fill our jails? It goes to show that the male role is so much harder to fulfill than we might have thought. Is it too hard? Believe me, the comment on the street or from the boss man is "tough buddy, either accept the rules or get out" would be the normal rebuttal. How many men have not heard this from a boss or a father? Male oppression is everywhere and driven by survival anxiety arising from centuries of poverty and war. This was the way it was for our ancestors, does it still work for us? How about for our sons?

So what are your gifts? If you do not know, how will your children know theirs?

One example of an appropriate recognition for a man's contribution would be appointing a senior citizen or "wisdom officer" to the Board of Directors of every corporation. This person would have a revered place on the board and his opinion would be sought on critical issues. Another might be to appoint a senior citizen to serve on various government reform committees. The waste of the knowledge of our senior citizens is a tragic and avoidable loss. (This is a gift they have). Many seniors would serve if they were asked. Their own sense of invalidity keeps them from volunteering. How many other human resources are wasted in similar ways?

Other sub-cultures within white male society include highly oppressed males from other social spheres: the poor, the disabled, prisoners, the mentally ill, as well as seniors and children too. The question begging to be asked is: what do these males offer our society that has been overlooked? Have they been initiated in a way that is unique and valuable to our culture? How do we include them so they can contribute in their own unique way? How are they rewarded? Some might say consumer goods and a pension are a good trade-off for some. Yet this appears to be unsatisfactory or unavailable to many of the men in these sectors. They seem out of step with the great purpose of global consumerism. Somehow they missed out on the consumer party. It might seem to them the party is out of their league and unavailable. They might feel the party others are attending is even at their expense.

Could a part of the confusion be found in how we define a contribution? We hunger for something and we all have untapped talent just waiting to be used but is often overlooked.

If for instance, mentally ill patients were encouraged to speak on behalf of other patients, their contribution might be more easily understood than by referring to experts who rarely have 'personal' familiarity with the reality of mental illness. This is the wealth of the mentally-ill person: this sharing, their odd and wonderful sense of humor and unique vantage point on life and reality. It is not necessarily wrong, just different.

Could we deal with crime in urban ghettos the same way by including people who live there and encourage discussions about urban crime that in turn could influence police boards on policy and intervention? There are, of course, citizen boards at police stations. However, they could do so much more. A senior could ride in a police car and comment on issues as they come up. Could this be seen as a kind of wealth, one as valuable as a criminology expert, or a lawyer for that matter?

A further example in this line of reasoning is the use of circle sentencing—a recent development in Canadian Aboriginal communities.[47] circle sentencing uses local human resources to rehabilitate an offender rather than police and prison. This would appear to be a significant contribution but has been largely overlooked by mainstream rehabilitation programs. By finding more inclusive ways to better spread out the generativity of all our citizens without relying on the traditional hierarchies, we preserve much of the historically valuable experiences as possible. We create a greater opportunity for self-knowledge, community building, cross-generational as well as cross-cultural communication. More will be said of this later. The point is to not give up on people. It is no wonder elections are attended by few citizens when so little is done to include them in government or civil society. At one point a Canadian government program called Participaction[48] was formed to address this very issue. It was very effective at including people in civil society but seems to have reduced its reach.

Other important issues for all men include: the struggle to find meaning in life, the struggle to find love and friendship, how and when to give or take such as with the gift of philanthropy, the struggle for fairness in a community process (by using a mediation process to dispute resolution versus the traditional legal process), the specter of violence, and the drive towards democracy.

On reflection it should now be obvious that the history of humanity is not the history of men or of male behavior. Men's real issues are sorely overlooked in our society and worldwide. This is possibly due to the violence and aggression perpetrated mostly by males in a world that hypocritically seems to demand them to do so.

Many people who I have met while writing this book asked me what a men's issue was. Innocently enough they thought it was not getting laid enough or the stress of another man being interested in your wife. As important as these situations might be, they are only symptoms of a far deeper reality. Major men's issues include:

- freedom from non-stop wealth generation,
- acquiring healthy communication skills and
- appropriate education,
- finding the courage to care for rather than squash an opponent,
- freedom from requiring status,
- learning to listen,
- freedom from being initiated into believing violent competition as evidence of one's potential masculinity and the ability to see it for what it is—a separation from others and an admission, truthfully, of powerlessness,
- a failure to learn healthy emotional expression and an inability to acknowledge the emotions of others.

That is the short list. I could go on. My argument is that men's issues are specific to keeping men doing what they do. They must be appreciated in the same light as rape, racism and slavery.

There are many more that will become apparent throughout this book. Unfortunately, for men these issues are a long way from being seen as oppression at this time in history. The old roles have to be acknowledged and lived out until it becomes so obvious that they do not work any more. We are not ready to let go of the old ways just yet. This shows up in how we make up our civilizations and how we define wealth.

From the preceding discussion about men's real issues, a question arises as to how the initiations that told males to suffer in silence and alone were created. Also why haven't such obvious solutions such as circle sentencing and better communication techniques been used for centuries? They were available but not wanted because the male ideal that we were all taught to live up to was still the dominant archetype in our culture-essentially we were not ready. This is the major theme of the book and will be explored at much greater depth.

To conclude this introduction, is there a crisis in masculinity or is it possibly just another opportunity dropped in our path? In the media I hear it is a crisis. Is it true for all men or just a few? I will show the foundations for both views and how only one can be true. In reality, the truth about a crisis is that there are opportunities always hidden in the wreckage. We tend to not to see them. Instead we react as usual, by ignoring them. Just as we have been initiated to do.

Time for new initiations!

In the first chapter I will cover the construction of Western masculinity and document the events that cemented our behavior into a rigid hierarchical and rather sad, although very successful, institution that created the great wealth and power of many empires. This power and material wealth led the way to the establishment of other institutions whose sole purpose was redistributing this wealth and power to the rest of humanity. This is the real purpose of government. No small feat. However males are still enslaved in their own oppression and fail to see that these new institutions are paving the way for a greater creation-a new freedom for men.

Like all good stories, a little background helps to get this one going too. This is my story about men and our masculinities based on my own experiences. I admit to being a believer in the human spirit. This book is a small contribution to our overall maturing process. I believe we will eventually get it right. Even if it takes thousands of years and many lifetimes, we will get it right.

The only way I could possibly understand this whole process was to go back to the very beginning or at least a very long time ago and start over. I needed to forget everything that I ever learned about being a man as well as my own personal story for a while so the history could sink in as it became available. With my hard learned understanding that good things can take a very long time to occur whether it is personal or global, it was worth the wait and the sweat in the end. As the reader can see, my personal story has not been easy nor is it complete or perfect; it is evolving, as it should be. If there is a crisis in masculinity then it is about choice: crisis or opportunity. Is the cup half-full or half-empty? In the end our attitude is all that matters. The story of humanity continues to be heard with input from everyone, and in this book, the story of men, their masculinities and their contribution to the unfolding evolution of our species.

The
Foundations of
Modern
Masculinity

CHAPTER ONE

The First Foundation:
The Constructed Man

I sat on a rock a bit removed from the trail wiping blood away from my face with the back of my hand. The fall yesterday left one eye useless and the other swollen and painful. I knew that if I could not see, I would be left for dead by the rest of the tribe. There was no extra food for an injured and potentially useless dependent like me. I had seen others leave for similar reasons. While it distressed me at the time, it was soon forgotten as the hardships of daily life took its toll on everyone. Later the next day my fear of impending doom resurfaced as my face refused to heal. At that moment a small child bumped into my knee. I could see just enough of her to see her sweet smile and the light that radiated from her face. At first she hesitated then took a scrap of fur from her pouch and tried to clean up my bleeding face. Her mother happened by and swatted her on the back of the head, scolding her that I was to be shunned and should be left to die. She walked on, but the girl stayed with me, and I wondered what could I give her in return, or for that matter of what use was I to the tribe itself?

I began reviewing the last few weeks of our travel over the plains in our never-ending search for water and food. What could I provide now? I did have a talent for smelling out water in obscure places. The tribe did occasionally look to me when luck was against us. Was there enough of a need for water that the tribe would keep me alive? Would someone be my eyes while I recover what sight I might still have left? Could I make my discoveries more secret or restrict them to certain members of the tribe, say for example—the children? That's it! I would tell them where to find the water and the adults would have no idea how this was done. Word would get around that I was responsible for the children's discoveries. I would get the credit and be looked after by the tribe.

How often did creative yet injured, mentally ill or other different gendered members of early tribes create a need for themselves so they would be looked after and not be faced with abandonment and death? The above story of a water sourcer may have led to a position within the tribe as an early shaman[49] or witch doctor. These occasionally odd, possibly dangerous members often enjoyed positions of enhanced authority and prestige due to their unusual talents or disabilities. Their "magical" skills or quick-mindedness could morph into storytelling or myth-making. They had skills important to the functioning of early tribes and helped to maintain a cohesive sense of community between the members. As well, other oddballs, degenerates and loners found a place in tribal life, some much later than others. Yet many were cast out when injured or sick.

Even today, in wealthy Western nations some have yet to find an acceptable place. The urban poor for example, have not found a place. Those sitting in judgment of them assume existence in filth is a fitting end to those of an assumed weaker disposition. It is a rejection of their unseen value. Nonetheless we are seeing the slow acceptance of other-challenged persons within mainstream society in such areas as the Paralympics, creative transportation solutions for the disabled, sidewalks with dips to accommodate wheelchairs, traffic crosswalks with buzzers for visually impaired citizens, and many non-profit organizations set up primarily to assist these people. Something continues to include the oddball and the needy. As I have asked before, what is it? Is it just the recognition that skills are being wasted or that other humans are suffering needlessly that eventually brings society around? Could it be a concern about human rights? But where did that idea come from?

As further skills developed in pre-history and greater tolerance of exotic behaviors became commonplace, we see the establishment of hierarchy and the beginnings of the constructionist phase of our masculine heritage. We forget too easily that history has been winding its way for many thousands of years and we lose the knowledge of what happened in our father's generation and how that affected him differently from his father's. For example, in our grandfathers' day, it would have been a new idea to accept the possibility of rehabilitation of the mentally ill into functioning persons and to resist seeing them as wretched criminals without hope. Within that resistance lay the justification for their poor treatment. But the change had to be created by someone or something in order for it to happen. In our day, we have seen the acceptance of same sex marriages and the gigantic shadow of global terrorism. Two and a half million years ago it was something else. It appears to be part of a progression of some kind.

In more detail now we will explore this ancient and curious human trait of inclusiveness and generativity. Starting from the anthropological record we can witness the first stirrings of the future lives of men.

At this point about 2.4 million years ago early humans still lived in trees.[50] In the great plains of Africa began an expansion due to a drying trend in the world's climate. The forests that covered much of the world began to die back. In order for the early humans to survive, a major change to their lifestyle[51] was required. It just so happened that the human male was two times[52] the size of the human female, faster and not encumbered by young, soooo . . . guess who got to climb down from the tree and go get the bacon? You' re absolutely right—the guys!!! It just made sense; the environment demanded it. This was way before any choice was available in our gender roles. Even though recent research has shown that later in history, females often went along on hunting parties and assisted in the killing for meat, it generally fell to males to do this. Although females, proving their capabilities as warriors alongside males, probably stopped these adventures during childbirth, and no doubt choose for the rest of their lives to raise their young children.[53] For the male hunters in pre-historic times, not only was it hard work, it was also very dangerous. In those days, large cats and other predators roamed the plains. Many males were killed or maimed. Even with their large size, the males were very poorly equipped to kill game, as stone points and spears[54] had not been invented yet. Often the only fresh meat available was stolen from other predators or scavenged[55] from the natural deaths of prey animals. With other predators competing for the same food clashes occurred. That was the dangerous part. Lives were often short and brutal. There were no cell phones to call a paramedic in those days.

Thus began the tradition, an initiation, where we males came to see our role in society as defined by the level of risk involved in a given task. This defined us in its broadest sense, up to and including modern times. The male role models still in existence today as if they were the gospel truth, developed from this early beginning. This role model influenced the choices we made, as well as having an unconscious effect on the choices that were forced upon us. For example, the kind of work we choose can have a shortening effect on the length of our lives. The kind of women or friends we choose may severely limit or enhance the freedoms we experience in our private lives. We are still waking up to the cost of our survival from the past.

Ten thousand years ago early humans had evolved into the Cro-Magnon or as anthropologists prefer to call them now, Early Modern Humans.[56] They began to diversify into racial types. These included the Asian, Persian/Indian, African and Caucasian races. Some male cultures in these new races went in very divergent directions developing distinct initiations along their way. Hierarchy was in its very early stages and individuals found a place to survive using natural talent. Different cultures had widely imaginative methods for handling social power or prestige; it was an inevitable and urgent need of early tribal life. I will say more on this later.

With the development of many tools for killing and for preparing meat, the large mammals were largely wiped out. A new era was beginning and another forced change was coming. As with every major change in history, including living on the open plains and survival through difficult ice ages, the realities of life led to new requirements for survival. Without wild meat, many bands and tribal peoples were forced to cultivate agricultural plants and learn to domesticate wild animals.[57] Basically this change ended their nomadic way of life. They were evolving into something new.

But had their initiations changed? Not at all. If anything, new ones were layered on top of the old ones, although these early societies were often matriarchal or egalitarian in structure and substance. For example, women did often hunt along side males at this point. At the same time goddess religions[58] flourished. Men and women lived with equal rights and obligations, and close relationships were valued. This society had no need[59] for "Power Over" politics. Elites[60] however were beginning to take form. Changing initiations were beginning to establish precise cultures based on growing surpluses. In an absolute sense, if you have a full belly, you have time to think, to plan and to dream.[61] If not, your entire effort will be directed toward finding food: nothing else would matter.

Referring back to the concept of males judging their masculinity based on the risk in a given job, these new elites took the form of "warrior clans"[62] protecting the new surpluses.[63] The clans represented a major change in the way males of the day perceived themselves. As we shall see, this new identity came to be associated with, so called "healthy masculinity," where strength in battle, protection of women and children, and the cultivation of domineering and powerful instincts were desirable traits in men. Women and gentler men didn't stand a chance. Men's liberation was an unimagined luxury and would stay so for many centuries yet.

Hence the first signs of male oppression find its start in the simmering hatred and envy for the powerful and ruthless leaders. These leaders gave the initial shape to the generalized negativity that so often characterizes masculinity in the modern world.

This structured system recently called patriarchy[64] developed slowly. As women were often preoccupied with food gathering and raising children, the males focused on construction of shelters, hunting, protection of the tribe and decisions to move or stay in a given place. In early transitional societies these "necessary decision-makers" began to acquire power over others in subtle ways. They were not even aware it was occurring. It was more of an after effect of the need for these decisions to be made in a multitude of social, cultural, agricultural or defensive concerns. From his recently published book "Is There Anything Good About Men?", Roy F. Baumeister[65] writes that men at the time of egalitarian societies gradually created power structures because men are better at arms-length relationships or less intimate ones than women. For example, in a modern context, he says, men are better at business than women because they can make hard decisions about allocating resources, hiring or firing individuals. Women on the other hand view relationship as more important. His theory does shed light on how easily men created power structures and hierarchies. Men more naturally acted from the big and shallow relationships of business and the military, whereas women maintained small and deeply intimate relationships, generally with children and friends that essentially stayed the same over time. By focusing on close nurturing relationships women guaranteed the emotional survival of the species. Wealth, knowledge and power were created in the men's sphere fostering security and hope for the future and the continued wellbeing of the species.

James W. Messerschmitt,[66] Taking a more modern feminist view wrote "Capitalism, Patriarchy and Crime, Toward a Socialist, Feminist Criminology", states "[...] patriarchy as an ideology that arose out of the exchange of women, as simply being the power of the father, and as the sexual hierarchical ordering of society for political control." He defines patriarchy as: "[...] a set of social relations of power in which the male gender appropriates the labor power of women and controls their sexuality. This appropriation and control-in both the home and market provide the material base of patriarchy." In addition, "[...] patriarchal gender relations then, are similar to class relations in that they entail appropriation, control, domination, and conflict." He states further, "I use the terms "masculine" and "male gender" rather than "male" throughout the book since "male" behavior is learned[67] rather than biologically determined."

I am wondering if this analysis is useful. Does it help us to see clearly how history and circumstance led to the hardships and initiations that developed along the way to enable our survival? I find it confusing because it focuses on finding fault rather than seeing the circumstances, needs or purposes that led to these actions. It avoids finding clear-headed solutions and muddies the waters further with evildoers and their victims. I would rather advocate the creation of new circumstances so that domination of any kind is no longer necessary.

Messerschmitt states that all male behavior is learned; yet men are driven by a protective and provisionary impulse that almost all men know instinctively. Although both Connell and Messerschmitt pointed to the lack of evidence to support a biological urge in males, isn't the urge for survival alone a biological urge? Males historically responded to a clear need and provided food and security so others could survive because it was in them to do it. They had the strong bodies unencumbered by childbirth or the responsibilities of child-rearing, The lack of these things does not suggest a vacuous or selfish state. In fact it suggest a rough and ready can-do physicality that joyously takes care of all the other jobs needed to support the mother-child duo, or the elders or the wounded or infirm. Almost all male behavior is based upon this built-in response to threat or need. It may not always be the best response as in the example of the American response to the 9/11 attacks. However with greater gender equality, women's opinions may provide a different viewpoint. It is hard to say with confidence if women will provide a real alternative to traditional male thinking and acting. After all power is power and in the end women are still humans. Even research into lesbian[68] relationships has shown a high level of domestic violence between spouses and rates of mothers killing children[69] is also higher than one might expect.

Power then became more entrenched with the further establishment of male elites based on agricultural surpluses.[70] In more favored areas of the earth such as China and Persia, the need for decisions of how these surpluses ought to be distributed became an important social issue. It became clear that if a surplus of food was available then some people did not have to work, or at least not as hard as before. These people would then be free to do other kinds of work not directly involved in the production of food, which used to be a major part of everyone's day.

They could be the record keepers of the surplus or in the modern form, accountants. Then managers were needed to oversee the accountants. You see where I am going. Eventually all of these early societies that developed surpluses began the slow development of hierarchies in order to manage their surpluses, paving the way to the modern system.

As these activities advanced the new "bureaucracy" of males, cities were laid out with walls to protect the surpluses, guardians to defend from invasion, castles for ceremony, streets of certain width for transportation, aqueducts for water and sewage for sanitation. As these decisions were undertaken, males developed friendships and alliances with their co-workers who supported and promoted each other. Religion and social custom came to reflect the earlier social strata of males making decisions and occupying positions of authority. Women, less able men and outsiders (who could be categorized as the physically disabled, homosexual, blind or deaf, the mentally ill and other unwell people) were oppressed, controlled or killed if they tried to object to this new way of doing things.

These early leaders gave impetus to the class systems that separated human societies into haves and have-nots, or those with power and those without. A side effect was the separation of men and women into sex roles and stereotypes of what was expected of each role. Men in decisive positions became the ruling elites, further separating themselves from other men, bringing their families along into elitist neighborhoods that were often separated from the rest of society by high walls and armed guards. They knew what they had and would defend their right to power. The result was patriarchy, an unintentional hierarchy created by the brutal early requirements of survival. A deadly and necessary structure that remained unassailable for centuries.[71]

However much earlier in time and after crossing the Bering Straits to populate North and South America, Aboriginal societies took a decidedly different course in the distribution of wealth from the surpluses that developed in their cultures.

The First Nations of the Pacific North-West of North America developed the potlatch[72] ceremony to give away excess wealth accumulated by specific individuals. Many other Aboriginal cultures did so too, and still do where it has not been outlawed. Possibly early Caucasian (Northern European) tribal communities had similar gifting ceremonies. However the First Nations potlatch[73] ceremony survived into the twentieth century until made illegal by the white colonists. It has recently been brought back. This is an important cultural tradition to maintain for our human heritage. It is a "touch stone" of a different way of spreading the wealth.

In contrast, other societies, especially in the West developed philanthropy instead to direct aid to the poor. Private individuals fund worthy causes of their own choice. A weakness of this kind of philanthropy allows the donor to stay at arms-length and even remain completely unknown to the receiver of the gift. Consequently the receiver does not experience any sense of obligation to the donor, unlike potlatches and other gifting systems. The problem, as I see it, is that civil society is not improved by Western-style philanthropy. It would be far more beneficial if the donor and the receiver were to meet and experience the effect of the gift. The benefit of course is the building of community and the establishment of interdependent relationships built on sharing. Too much is done for us by community organizations and government agencies attempting to sanitize human interactions. Part of the problem is that our world has grown so large. With such great distances between the donor and the receiver, it seems to be easier to manage funds and distribute to the needy through a centralized non-profit society with a mandate to provide this kind of service.

Small towns still operate on the basis of the personal contact; this makes them vibrant and caring communities. Large cities have lost this connection and many people miss the closeness of knowing almost everyone they meet on a downtown street. Of course there are pluses and minuses to this. It might be better not to know the receiver of a gift if it might create a troublesome or pestering dependency. Still, many small town citizens would not change their closeness and prefer the occasional scrape with someone. They consider most encounters as positive and a betterment to their lives and their community.

Of course there are always exceptions to every rule. The Ophra's and the Bill Gates' of the world directly see the effect of their donations because they go where the money goes. A connection is made although they earn little or no obligation from the gift. While the gift is important so is an obligation in return. I'll explain further using a personal example. In my extended family, there are some significant income disparities between the in-laws. The well-healed few have been very generous with the others. Having been one of the receivers, I have felt dissatisfied that I have been unable to return the favor; even the preparation of a meal or doing errands is not quite enough. It is important to be able to return the favor somehow. This is true in community giving as well.

Anthropologists have documented many cultures relying on gifting and potlatching as ways to bind their cultures together. The Trobriand Islanders[74] of the South Pacific have over very long periods of time maintained and expanded their relationships with other tribes by another unique and different method. They use a cargo trading system referred as the Kula Ring. This trading system is not based on an economic outcome or wealth distribution, although economics and redistribution play a part. The Kula is a most elaborate complex of ceremony, political relationships and social integration for the purpose of promoting individual men above others by the trading of a simple red shell necklace and ornate white armshells. The better man is determined by the quality, size and color of the shells, as well as the pedigree of the shells' previous owner. The benefits to the better men are social prestige such as bragging rights to the best shells, economic favors and political rewards within the communities. The communities benefit as a whole by the histories and the stories brought back by the men and the social knowledge brought to the village by the ongoing trade. The odd thing about the Kula is that the red shells travel in a clockwise direction throughout the islands, and the white shells in a counterclockwise direction. These can be dangerous voyages as the men are in small open canoes for days or weeks at a time moving from island to island. There are many stories of sailors disappearing forever during storms or just getting lost. So, different yet inspired ways hold early tribal life together, and often continue to exist well into present times.

In Europe, wealth was seen in a very different light. As time progressed, agriculture like other trades began to see significant surpluses, animal husbandry, woodcraft, metalworking, and textiles. Even banking was created out of the surpluses of the trades. All of these areas needed management and tended to create even more male elites as societies became wealthier and more centralized. This huge construction totally rested on the surpluses created by the trades stemming from the surplus of food.[75]

Slowly, people began to accumulate things and value them as part of their culture. Ownership of land became common, and personal ranking systems continued to develop. As villages grew into towns, and towns into cities, competition for scarce resources, such as land and water, led to increased conflict and an even greater need for management. As Jared

Diamond[76] so aptly put it, armed conflict was now possible with a standing army supported by the stored surpluses. Not surprising the egalitarian system of doing things was replaced by this hierarchical system based on rank and now, on acquisition of property and other wealth through war.

Thomas Hobbes, who in 1651 published his famous work "Leviathan", suggested there was "a war of all against all."[77] According to Hobbes, it was always so and could only be averted by strong central government whose great power resembled a leviathan or monster. Hobbes believed that humans were basically selfish creatures who would do anything to better their position. Left to themselves, he thought, people would act on their evil impulses. Hobbes stated that: "Governments were created to protect people from their own selfishness and evil." However it is important to note that a powerful central government only focused this war of man against man onto chosen enemies rather than chaotic day-to-day struggles between free or lawless individuals. To prove his point, Hobbes wrote on what he saw as the three main principles of quarrel[78] in cultures where there was no common power[79] to fear such as a God, enforceable laws or a strict moral code. The first principle he spoke of was competition or invasion for personal gain, or the use of violence with the goal to be the ruler of others. Nothing is unjust and everyone is at war with everyone else. According to the second principle, quarrels often develop while one tries to defend the spoils of war, thereby creating other wars. The last principle relates to glory, reputation, status, or your perceived place in society and the securing of a memorable legacy.

Hobbes would say of the philosophy of the day, "[...] every man has a right to everything, even to one another's body. And therefore, so long as this natural right of every man to everything endureth, there can be no security to any man. Every man ought to endeavour peace[80][...] and when he cannot obtain it, that he may seek[...]all helps and advantages of war."

So the development of law and a moral code made sense for the times. It was essential, but not to all. Its implementation was extremely difficult. The realities of war and lawlessness still persist today in many parts of the world. Is Hobbes' interpretation of human nature correct? Remember Andrew Kimbrell's contrasting statement on Aboriginal cultures regarding male aggressiveness.

Much of the conflict and violence we see in today's developing world was similarly rampant in ancient Europe. Other than the recent past by which I mean the last thousand years, the Caucasian races have forgotten the brutality of their past. Every modern school child studied history, but can that knowledge be put to use in their lives? Maybe not much, as it appears most people need to learn their own lessons in their own time and in their own way. Sadly, it seems we all learn in different ways. For example the lessons learned in ancient China had little effect on the Middle Ages in Europe even though the philosophies of Confucius and Buddhism[81] had some impact on European culture with translated texts brought back to Europe during the eighteenth century by visitors to the East. Buddhist thought has been growing in the West ever since but it would not be considered a major religion. So learning lessons from afar takes time and these were not early influences by any means but were rather late in European history.

Following Hobbes' understanding of human nature, many of these early city-states developed a central government or king often with a huge bureaucracy supported by forced taxation. Taking stock of their new ownership and power, and the need to protect this wealth, profits from the sale of accumulated surpluses were used to hire permanent security forces or use the army to not only fight wars but to protect the King's property from the citizen's rightful rage who had actually created the wealth in the first place. (So a scoundrel keeps the wealth of the community from the community that creates it, and creates hatred and division instead of peace and prosperity) Of course this development cannot help but eventually lead to intense competition between individuals in nearby city-states but also through wars with other city-states or other scoundrels. The way was now paved for the never-ending wars of medieval Europe and the colonization of other lands to pay for these wars. China's economic collapse[82] at this time just made it easier. Europe is a fine example of these endless wars and subsequent global colonialism that culminated in the greatest war of all time, the Second World War, hopefully the last major colonial war. It appears for the moment Europe has put aside its Hobbesian atrocities with the formation of the European Union. It is a fine example and provides great hope for other areas of the globe now mired in constant conflict such as Africa, and the Middle East. Its current economic struggles will resolve themselves in time and the process of integration will probably continue.

To recap, men are increasingly being forced into different classes by the very engine that drives them: the drive for wealth. It would seem that within nations where the drive is the strongest and where real success is realized, great power would reside universally even though other nations with disparate cultures may wield it as well. By creating individual empires of wealth, we construct the hierarchy that separates and isolates us from other men.[83] Is it relevant to ask if this is what we want? It appears to be the way of the world, at least in these years. From increased centralization of industry and capital we lose the value of each other's company. Is this a fair trade? The wealthy and successful are sheltered away in their gated areas while the rest of the community has no access to the methods or engines of money generation. The culture is the weaker for it. It would appear that this process must be repeated until men have had enough of individual wealth creation and want to create something else.

Aboriginal traditions seem to have little impact on European thinking so what would this something look like? Even though men fought it out in this combative method of wealth creation for thousands of years, there was a kind of sympathy for women and children suggesting men knew that they did a brutal thing. What else was there to do? In English literature, paternalistic but well-intentioned and thoughtful husbands and fathers protect women from the realities of business and war. Examples abound: Jane Ayre or Wuthering Heights are classic. Try watching contemporary films from India or China and you will see the same theme paraded throughout. Somehow this protection seemed to be saying that men had to face this daily brutality but women could and should stay out of it, partly due to their more "sensitive" natures. Is it possible that what is really being said here is that men HAD[84] to face it. They had no choice. Whether they hated it (or loved it), it was the way of the world and the way of "men." Men's dislike of this way of the world would suggest men only saw hatred and brutality in the hearts of other men and of course, in themselves too. In contrast, they saw only beauty, grace and gentleness in the hearts of women. No wonder they desired to protect women so much from these dark energies and why women were so often portrayed in literature as their only "safe harbor." [85]

A similar area of concern to me is where men in Arab cultures refuse to allow women the same basic rights they expect for themselves. By way of example, some of these cultures refuse to allow women to drive a vehicle. I wonder if this reflects the seeking of a "safe harbor" of another kind where women are elevated to heroic proportions. As such, women are seen by men as "goddesses" where driving is actually beneath them, making driving a job men desire to do for women out of romantic duty or an unusual sense of chivalry. The men are invariably and understandably enraged when foreign cultures accuse them of sexism when their idolization of women is misunderstood. At the same time however, one needs to ask these "goddesses" if they prefer to drive themselves around or if this idolization by men is preferable. I wonder how likely this analysis is?

A tragic consequence for the male foolish enough to believe in these split roles has been well documented by other writer's of men's studies such as Warren Farrell.[86] Farrell laid clear the male reality in modern life that many males fall for the romantic fantasy. This is the idealization of women, as I did, but some see through it eventually. Yet they were a whisper of wind in a wilderness of hurricanes. Men were waking up but most go off to do battle every day and put up with the abusive boss, the toxic workplaces, the secrets, the conversations over-heard behind their backs and plots foretelling their down-fall, or worse, dying on some far away battlefield only to come home in a box to a woman expecting riches.

Of course these situations are complex and many current global conditions conspire to keep men doing what they have done for millennia. Only by a radical transformation of self-identity will men gain insight to this "civilization" they have created. However, it should be of no surprise to anyone today that women are now joining these ranks at breakneck speeds. Women are everywhere, in business, science and the military. The question must be asked: what or who is going to be the "safe harbor" now? Quite simply, it would appear we will have to create a safe harbor for ourselves. If we are to reassess civilization, what will we find? Maybe we would discover that the hierarchies and classes for people we created in order to organize our surpluses might actually be the engines running us now in ways we do not like or necessarily need any longer. In fact these surplus managers might even be detrimental to our progress as a species. The whole provider/protector/surplus thing might need a major overhaul regardless of the gender who is living out the myth.

We were talking about the beginnings of hierarchy and what eventually came to be known as feudalism.[87] In this system people worked for a king or a noble, who made sure that the people had what they needed to survive, including food, shelter, and protection in case of war. Wars happened often and many died. This led to great frustration and resentment. Yet people were supposed to know their place.[88] After all, this system had been ordained by God! According to who, one might ask. The answer to this question is clear: it was the powerful and their assumed role to protect us from ourselves. Or better yet, to protect themselves from us.

This period in time was the forerunner of modern individualism[89] (not to be confused with the Jungian term "Individuation"[90]) that has swept the world. As well, it was largely a time of innocence and blind obedience. Just as a child has no understanding of the parent, most people could not think of themselves as anything other than belonging to something or someone, usually a king or queen or the Church. Stepping outside these narrow lines of existence often led to death or imprisonment. The privilege of independent thought was unheard of and forcibly repressed as a threat to the established order. In many ways this ideology (of repression or protection, depending on your perspective) still persists in today's modern societies. Albeit it is a more hidden influence often implemented without the use of physical force. Just try not paying your taxes or drive on the wrong side of the road. The consequences are still tangible and unpleasant. Even more insidious is the unstated expectations. For example, public nudity is a freedom many people would like to experience. Yet archaic laws and morals prohibit showing taboo areas of the body. Really, are we not all nude under our clothes anyway? Just a thought, however pleasant or unpleasant it may be for some.

Hobbesian philosophy still has its hold on us, even in the more liberal West. Seven hundred years ago, the songs of the troubadours[91] captured the hearts and minds of people who yearned for romantic love. The tragic story of Romeo and Juliet brings to mind our "modern" expectations of love. This was one of the instrumental stories that shaped our concept of "free choice." Prior to this time the Catholic Church had prohibited love marriages[92], believing them instead to be socio-political arrangements[93] to tie communities together. All had been previously accepted in the Old Testament of the Bible. The fact that people wanted to choose whom they married challenged the structure of society at the time. Many cultures other than Catholic societies have practiced arranged marriages for centuries. We in the West have a tendency to view these cultures as restrictive. Yet arranged marriages[94] served as an essential link between families, tribes, clans and lineages. For many hundreds of generations, these "ties that bind" maintained peace and goodwill between diverse peoples. This is not to say it is the only way, but it comes with a long track record. If an arranged marriage resulted in an unhappy relationship, families tended to stay together because of the lack of any real personal choices. It created almost as many problems as today's tolerance of near total abandonment of relationship.

If laws and cultural traditions are seen as restrictive, new laws and traditions are required to replace the outdated ones. If the old traditions are abandoned because of ignorance or immaturity, the culture will suffer the consequences. I remember having to face the results of my immaturity as a young man; it was good to see that other people had gone this way before me and showed the way back to self-honesty. For example, many of the young women I dated could have made a perfectly fine mate if I was willing to do the work to sort out a responsible course of action. Instead I choose impulsive actions based on my impatience and their immaturity while ignoring my sense of loyalty and consideration. To be fair to myself, I was dumped for the same reasons by other women. It took me many years to learn we are not perfect creatures and that it takes time for difficult relationships to sort themselves out. However, throughout history people were often not allowed to make up their own minds; the Church reserved this special place for itself. With the weakening of religious practices came the explosion of the demand for individual rights and freedom of choice in our actions. In other words, I had to learn my own lessons.

Five hundred years ago the advances in plant and animal husbandry[95] had past its zenith. The scarcities and backbreaking labor created by agriculture's success would no longer be tolerated by the masses. At the same time, individualism continues to be embraced, and new methods of production begin to enter the marketplace. This new era was the beginning of the Industrial Revolution. It had a devastating impact on the extended family by encouraging policies that required a new type of highly mobile work force. This forced apart extended families[96] and led to the formation of the "nuclear family", the most isolated family grouping ever created by humanity. The consequences were severe to all levels of the family structure. Children were no longer educated at home next to their parents; they were shipped off to public schools in order to become adapted to the needs of an industrial society. Also, the elderly were shipped out too; they went off to nursing homes so as not to be a burden on their mobile children. Women were often isolated at home with young children and tied to the chore of household duties. As well, men[97] were far from home often in dangerous industrial factories, and not seen by their children for hours, days or weeks at a time. The emotional toll on the men[98] is written in the record books, filled with statistics on factory accidents, alcoholism, suicides, homelessness and an early death, not to mention the impact of their suffering on the families back home. The stresses on families were immense.

So was this new thing called capitalism[99] really worth all the turmoil that ensued? With the suffering being created it would be difficult to say it would lead anywhere positive. However people were beginning to question the authority[100] of the Catholic Church and the old ways. People increasingly used their intellect to interpret the world around them. The new scientific method began to eat away at the stone foundations of "Truth." People were very aware of laws forbidding them to think for themselves and the horrible consequences if they did. People began to demand changes allowing more personal freedoms. The elites responded with force, hoping to put people back in their place. However it was too late; the people had had enough. Even though it was not everything they wanted, there were some benefits to be had. People went after them with a passion reminiscent of a revolution.

One of the first changes to occur was in the sphere of business and religion. The term "traditionalism"[101] refers to the pre-capitalist working man who by his nature would not wish to earn more and more money, but to simply live as he is accustomed to live and to earn as much as is necessary for that purpose. Wherever modern capitalism has begun increasing the productivity of human labor, it has encountered the immensely stubborn resistance of this leading trait of pre-capitalist labor-that of the medieval man who lives in the moment.[102] In order to keep men working early capitalists thought high wages would keep these men at work longer, but upon reaching the amount each man needed he left until he had need again. This frustrated the capitalist because he wanted a guaranteed workforce so he could establish a product or a market for wealth generation. Then low wages were tried to motivate him because high wages did not increase production but lowered it.[103] As Peter de la Cour[104] suggests in Weber's writings, "the people only work because and so long as they are poor." When they were no longer poor, they went home. So theoretically, if you pay people poorly they will be more likely to come back to work for you. It would appear there is a modern application here: making the cost and variety of consumer goods attractive and pricey ensures that workers stay at work in order to be able to afford the goods. Again this fulfills the capitalist's desire of creating markets and the goals of the Church to get a share. At the same time the variety of new technology feeds on its own success creating even more exotic inventions to entertain us and keep us at work. A major fear of the early capitalists must be: "The Strike" where workers demand higher wages and better working conditions. Capitalists fear that upon receiving the increase workers will return to their lazy ways. Consequentially an understandable loss of power and control is felt throughout an industry during major labor conflicts.

Protestant ministers and capitalists worked together[105] unknowingly to motivate the "lazy" working man during the Industrial Revolution in order to complete two agendas. One is the mobilization of a highly structured and disciplined labor force for expanding industry; the other is the installation in people's minds of "The Calling"[106] along with a continued dependence on the Church. The Calling was the religious idea that one's purpose in life requires us to look "up" metaphorically to God. Originally this "Calling" was a call to serve God; it was later adapted to the modern era. These three directions (the original spiritual calling, the business calling and the motivation of labor) are possible within the goals of both business and religion with the overall effect of supercharging capitalism. The two "Callings" (the religious and the economic) show up in the Protestant work ethic.[107] The Church and business leaders did not work together in a conspiratorial way; the Church did recognize that the business of wealth generation and growing individualization of the common citizen demanded a new response, and could generate great new wealth for the Church.

For the Church, change included the establishment of the Protestant religions[108] apart from the Catholic Church, which opposed the Catholic claim of being the original faith. As well, the Protestants believed that people could interpret the Bible for themselves. This point is important for our studies, in that a new personality type had begun. This was the new era of the individual[109] and hence, the beginning of the modern Western style of masculinity where wealth generation or success was the key purpose and determinant of status as a man and as a citizen. This individual, now freed from the confines of the feudal system on one hand, began to turn skills once reserved for the king only, into profitable enterprises in the expanding marketplace. Specialists were no longer locked into a set role for life. Work became a means to acquire money that people hankered after with a real passion. As well, the more aggressive traits such as providing and protecting became even more firmly associated with traditional masculinity. These traits were encouraged to run free, and they did, setting the stage for the current domination of most of the world by capitalism. We were truly suckered by our own illusions of greatness. It seemed like a way to have it all.

At the same time, the European expansion created the first global economy[110] based on plantation labor in "the colonies." This ever-increasing pool of labor was now producing goods for an increasingly abstract, (or distant and diverse) world market. In feudal times, most goods were produced and consumed in the home. As markets expanded, people were forced off their traditional lands or (Commons) by landowners, more and more distance was placed between producer and consumer. As a result people became more and more distant from each other. Said in another way, the quest for power, prestige and influence became the "calling" of the individual and the tradition of the "religious calling" promoting God's glory was greatly lessened from its near universal dominance in earlier times.

Max Weber, in his book "The Protestant Ethic and the Spirit of Capitalism", observes that at first capitalism co-existed with the more traditional Church doctrine and eventually co-opted it. He has brilliantly mapped out this transition:

Prior to the Industrial Revolution:

- The world exists to serve the glorification of God and for that purpose alone.[111]
- Christians are to follow His commandments to the best of their ability.
- God wills that social life shall be organized according to "His" commandments.
- Christians share a social life with their labor and serve in callings that serve the mundane life of the community.
- Martin Luther's writings[112] refer to specialized labor in callings justified in terms of brotherly love (i.e., service organizations and assisting your neighbor). Is it possible this is the source of the term "the brotherhood" in modern unions?
- Then brotherly love,[113] since it may only be practiced in its original meaning for the glory of God, and not in the service of the flesh, is expressed in the fulfillment of daily tasks. Since it is a duty and a sign of salvation to have a calling, this clearly leads

us to the phenomenal effects of the Industrial Revolution: The fulfillment of this paradigm change from God's love to brotherly love assumes a peculiarly objective and impersonal character, that of service in the interest of the rational organization of our social environment. Hence, this makes labor in the service of impersonal social usefulness appear to promote the glory of God and to be willed by Him. Through the process of fulfilling this duty the Puritan ethic of hard work (or Good Works as it was called) developed. Self-confidence grew as the proof of salvation and the certainty of grace.[114] So the wealthier you were, the closer to God you appeared. Yikes! So God has been co-opted and the pursuit of wealth becomes the new religion. Another brick in the wall of institutionalized masculinity as provider. The result is a society being redirected into the rampant individualism we see in the West today as well as the almost invisible but growing isolation between individuals.

Based on Weber's analysis of "the Calling", anyone, with the simplest thought can see their work as a contribution to God's glory. Even though mainstream churches may not see it that way, the average citizen did come to believe they had value in their day-to-day activities. This was a subversion of the Church and its teachings; it is fascinating that it came about. I believe it is part of a process that has been unfolding for centuries where citizens take greater freedoms with varying results. Some experiments succeed, some fail. Others adapt and combine new with old and eventually what works will stick and what does not disappears—an evolution based upon free thinking individuals.

Of course to the wage laborer, a cushy job feels more God-like. If we all strive to avoid difficult or messy jobs who will do them? The answer is: the people that can do no other, the ones without training or wealth. It is difficult to escape this vertical job identification process isn't it? Fortunately for many of us in the West, unions (the brotherhood) have given us a decent wage to live on and a way up.

Being a landscape gardener by profession, I remember sweeping the road at some of my jobs. Occasionally I found syringes, CO_2 canisters for 22 caliber rifles and used condoms. Aside from the disgust I felt, it was in fact a service to the general public to clean up this mess. While it was a thankless job and somewhat dangerous to my health, it was important to dispose of these items properly. While I remember being slightly lowered by it, the experience was good for me to see the real contribution I was making in the community. If we take the time to think about it, all of our work can be seen in the bigger picture; we just have to decide to see it that way. We might also see that adding more skill to it or being more creative in how we do our work can improve upon some occupations. I found that continually learning new skills kept my interest in gardening alive and exciting. When I started out I mostly cut grass and weeded flower beds. Then irrigation became an interest. It took some time to learn all the skills that went into doing that well. Then I became interested in working with stone and rock walls, but not the mortared kind. A real challenge was the dry stacked kind that had to be built in such a way that each rock was locked in place by other rocks and would not budge. Then working with large standing stones drew me, especially the freestanding kind. I would search quarries and stone suppliers for the right height and textures, sometimes finding local black slates with beautiful veins of quartz running through them. I had quite a collection at home just waiting to go into the right garden.

So any career can be boring without some innovation applied to it. It sure felt like God's calling at work to me. Remember though I had to be the innovator. Messy jobs will exist forever until we transform them into spirit.

I remember talking with my son when he was nineteen and confused as to what to do for his work or career. He had considered professions such as chemistry and others that in truth, he was not really good at. He felt it was important to aim high. I agreed to a point but asked him what he was good at in high school. He stated that he was good at cooking, sports and music. He loved sports but not as a career, same as music. That left cooking. I asked him if he would look into the cooking courses at a local college, which he did. He enrolled and did well enough to see the potential for a career. He is now working in his trade with plans to work in Europe and train as a pastry chef. Curious how difficult it was for him to choose a career. Originally he thought it had to be hard and based on something he was not good at. Now he is supporting himself with something he is naturally good at and easy for him to do. We all have talents or "callings" already "built-in" just waiting to be recognized for what they are. The latest news though is he is thinking of going back to school.

Further to the development of the calling impulse, the huge upheaval that was the Industrial Revolution brought out some people who objected to the striving for material wealth. Their reason was that wealthy men would be distracted from their religious callings by too much relaxation or luxury.[115] Never ending relaxation was seen as a danger to godly men. These protestors, who followed the Protestant reformer John Calvin,[116] reminded everyone that only through activity was the glory of God increased, and if you happened to be a workaholic you created the greatest Glory to God of all people. You just cannot enjoy it.

Juxtaposed to this is the happy-go-lucky laborer who works for a short period and goes on his way; he is seen as the lowest of God's creatures because of his wanderlust. He may be happy with his chosen life, whereas the Church sees him as an inferior. Workaholism brought you closer to God and as a result, your own salvation was seen as inevitable. However, workaholism is killing many people worldwide. Do we stop or even consider these consequences? In the United States, the alienation of wealth creation from spirit has taken on the "character of sport"[117] where it no longer has any meaning, other than as a game. If we no longer feel a connection to spirit while we work we are surely automatons with no purpose to our lives. How many of us have inherited this alienation? It is probably now a global phenomenon.

Buddhists have pointed out "do right work[118]", and take the view that the function of work unfolds in three stages:

- to give man a chance to utilize and develop his faculties;
- to enable him to overcome his ego-centeredness by joining with other people in a common task;
- and to bring forth the goods and services needed for a becoming existence.

The Indian philosopher and economist J. C. Kumara[119] sums up the matter as follows: if the nature of the work is properly appreciated and applied, it will stand in the same relation to the higher faculties as food is to the physical body. It nourishes and enlivens the higher man and urges him to produce the best he is capable of. It directs his free will along the proper course and disciplines the animal in him into progressive channels. It furnishes an excellent background for man to display his values and develop his personality. How are we to find this elixir of life if creating wealth is the only show in our town? After all every man I know realizes that without some kind of strategy to create wealth, no reasonable woman will stay around for long. Even with greater equality between the sexes and a greater ability of women to cover the costs of a household an uninspired male quickly loses his appeal.

That is one side of male oppression. Another is that the fellow may be perfectly happy to downsize his life at some point, but his partner in life may not.

As time progressed, it became common knowledge of responsible citizenry that one was obligated to oneself, one's family and one's country to find a calling[120], be it religious or purely economic in nature. As well, as the new ethic became entrenched, Protestant clergy and the business community found themselves competing for the same "souls" as Weber has stated so clearly.

What we are discussing here is how we work and what drives our working relationships. This is based on three core ideas of work: the development of capitalism, the Calling and predestination. The latter two are from the Church. Hard work, the rational organization of time, self-discipline and thrift were the virtues encouraged by the new standard.[121]

Predestination or "man's eternal fate" had been decided before his birth and nothing could reverse God's decision. If his calling was a service to humanity then the calling could go hand in hand with the acquisition of money.

This impulse was basically irrational (not needs based). It was seen as a moral obligation to make profits. It survived the general decline in strong religious belief after the 18th century[122] and emerged as the deeply ingrained work ethic we have today. We work for very unclear reasons far and away beyond our real needs. The Biblical Book of Nature[123] (behavior based on nature) has been studied meticulously and copied in all its animal details for us humans to obey. According to predestination we have no choice in the matter. We must work as hard as we have been led to believe. Since we do not know our fate, as our ministers have said, who are we to argue? Have we not been told all of our lives that without goals and constant success we are useless to God, adrift in life and in danger of damnation? Meanwhile, God has already made up His mind about us. All we can do is work very hard just in case we happen to die on a good day whereupon He will send us happily on to heaven. Is this true? Is this definition of wealth creation saying that men of the Middle Ages were unhappy or unfulfilled before the Church came along and told them they were all damned?[124] This sounds strikingly familiar to the capitalist usage of low wages to motivate the traditional man to work. So we work. Martin Luther, the disenchanted monk, said work is good but not in excess, John Calvin, a French theologian, told us God just might be listening, so get to it. Calvin compared usury (paying interest on loans, more later on this) to paying rent on land.[125] To add to the confusion of the times, Thomas Hobbes said of the "Laws of Nature", that men should seek peace and follow it, or by all means defend themselves. For without laws or a god, we live in a constant state of war.[126] So life is a constant living state of hell.

A lot to chew on when we consider this is our Western heritage. The common man was eventually recruited into an economic machine that was not natural and created the often debated consequences and benefits that stemmed from this Industrial Revolution. Kimbrel in his "Masculine Mystique" says: "The separation of men[127][...]from the family may well be the most significant personal and social disruption men have ever had to face."

R.H. Tawney in "Religion and the Rise of Capitalism" critiqued Weber by commenting that: "The Protestant ethic, with its insistence on hard work, thrift etc. had contributed to the rise of capitalism, but at the same time Protestantism itself was being influenced by an increasingly capitalistic society." In "Capitalism and the Reformation-Problems and Perspectives in History", M.J. Kitch said: "The capitalistic mentality was so novel that an intellectual revolution was needed before traditional (lazy) attitudes could be replaced with the collective striving after wealth[...]. The desire for a large weekly wage earned by a commoner had to be created so that the Industrial Revolution could occur. The Protestant Revolution brought about such a revolution[...] unintentionally." In the end the desire to fulfill a daily need was slowly turned into a constant striving for material wealth and prosperity for all. An unintended development of the re-imagining of wealth as a "Calling" was one of the significant causes of the decline of the Church in industrial societies. Better off citizens now decided for themselves what was moral or just.

Have we created wealth but lost our soul? Sometimes you just have to step outside of your initiations and breathe for a while.

The early Church itself was much the same as tribal cultures were; they stifled the individual in favor of the collective.[128] The new definitions allowed individual expression to come to the fore and new ideas developed at an explosive pace. Many in the Church and other society watchers were increasingly worried that communities were becoming more and more impossible to maintain in light of the powerful market forces that teared apart individual from individual. Is Hobbes' war of all against all still on going? Communities were certainly changing in response to this intense marketing pressure. We can see the results today in my son's lifestyle. He is now twenty-one, spends many hours per day communicating with friends near and far about life and his work, and texting his girl friend thousands of kilometers away. They met on a game site years ago, communicated daily and finally visited only last year. He would say that it is a new era, less time involved in visiting except for planned get-togethers. He would say my worries about isolation in his room are the worries of my generation and do not reflect the values and beliefs of his generation. If he is right, and I believe he is, my concerns then will die with me. From his perspective my analysis may be correct but the concern is irrelevant to his generation. I will ask him again when his kids are literally living in some 3D or holographic game world. We will see what he says then.

However even my son would agree that in present times, if one does not "work their butt off", one will fall farther behind each year. The pace of change is so great and accelerating to the point that many families cannot fulfill the obligation to purchase all that new stuff. It seems that the economic system will run out of customers. However in the mind of a capitalist, there is still the developing world, Russia and China. So we have "boom and bust" fluctuation-based economies where consumers are manipulated to work like mad fools to purchase all the stuff manufacturers can pump out until they are all in debt and exhausted. The economy goes into recession and everyone freaks out that disaster is just around the bend. We blame the government or big business. Stocks go up and down, world currencies fly all over the place while we ignore real disasters such as Darfur, Somalia, and Rwanda. Eventually all that purchased stuff wears out or is obsolete. Consumers begin to purchase new stuff again and the economy recovers. The justification of global business rests on expanding consumerism to ensure continued growth in wealth everywhere. This of course would be the total triumph of capitalism. This might work if protectionist forces step aside. How we protect culture and local traditions from such powerful economic forces will determine if we have lost our soul or not.

Did the Protestant work ethic set us in the right direction where global wealth will eventually reach everyone or will we devour and pollute the planet and end up with no tradition, no culture and a questionable future? Maybe it too will be a passing phase into something else like many of humanity's inventions. This "something else" could be very interesting. As history shows us, change always happens. Few things stay the same for long. We will explore some of these later on. In the meantime, I wish to finish this short analysis of capitalism.

To recap, men were often isolated from their families for great periods of time while in search of a living wage. At the same time, enormous wealth was flowing into Europe from the colonies, as well as from other world trade. Nowhere was this truer than in the Netherlands. After achieving their independence from Spain in the 1500's, the Netherlands became a haven for religious dissenters,[129] who found a certain tolerance here that encouraged the pursuit of free enquiry. The handsome profits of Dutch traders led to the development of a major institution for the growing capitalist economy: the bank.[130] Banks existed elsewhere,[131] but they were controlled by the Catholic Church and were not allowed to charge interest on the basis that it was considered sinful. Capitalism is far from a simple wealth creation strategy. Some of its components when broken down were clearly seen as destructive when first proposed. One such component was the development of usury[132] or the charging of interest on loans, which bigger banks clearly favored against the wishes of the Church. This is important because it was the spark that started a major social conflict. Helen C. White[133] wrote that English preachers saw the delicate issue of usury in two differing ways. "What they saw was the world of small holders and independent craftsman, petty tradesmen, with their perennial need for capital to carry them till harvest to buy raw materials, to furnish the beginnings of a shop. And on the other hand they saw a host of prosperous yeomen, innkeepers, tailors, drapers, grocers, mercers and other successful businessmen with a bit to spare alert to any chance to pick up a little extra. In such a world, still of the small neighborhoods, they saw more sharply the misery which hard dealing on the lender's part might cause the unfortunate debtor and they felt keenly the destruction of neighborhood peace and amity that might ensue. So they clung to their Christian neighborliness of spirit that would prompt him who had a surplus to relieve the anxieties of his less fortunate neighbor without any thought of making his profit of the poor man's necessities."

However, capitalists believed usury was a magical way to create huge profits and expand the wealth of a community. Unfortunately the community did not benefit because more powerful banks and loaners competed with the owners of the local bank. As a result, the interest accrued from locally arranged loans left the small communities and made its way to the larger centers essentially bankrupting the smaller townships and villages. Certainly there was some benefit through the influx of the loan money for the short-term. However, any sense of community was lost on the borrowers and the lender. Hard dealing on the lenders part came to the attention of Church ministers[134] who frowned on wealthy individuals taking unfair advantage of their poorer neighbors. Thinkers of the time, such as William Perkins in 1626, complained that the poor could not become rich and be a benefit to the nation if the lenders charged excessive interest. In his 1626 book entitled "Usury, Capitalism and the Reformation,"[135] Perkins suggested of the reasons for taking above the principal were:

- That which the debtor may give in return, and
- That the debtor may give out of gratitude.

Otherwise it would be considered a sin to take more. So what happened? Not much except the loss of the local institutions to their communities.

The larger banks had by 1609 introduced loans to people who were unknown[136] to its depositors or owners. They continued to charge interest against the hostile response from the Church and other Calvinists. Calvinist ministers in Amsterdam actually denounced the most prosperous capitalists from the pulpit, and even expelled them from their congregations.[137] In fact, between 1581 and 1658, bankers were banned from taking communion.[138] Their wives could, provided they denounced their husbands' business interests. Thomas Wilson wrote that usury was "lazy" money where "lazy" refers to money that has not really been earned.[139] The Church's frowning upon interest taking may also be due to this "lazy" money being taken outside of a calling as discussed earlier.

Because this new class of business people was not going to give up its newfound wealth, the Church gave in leading to the establishment of the current usury system in effect throughout the world. Some credit card interest rates approach 28 % annually. Of course in modern times the Church has benefited enormously from usury charged on its properties and sales of its lands in spite of its attempt to defend the poor. By the condemning of interest, the Church attempted to preserve the old ways of the Middle Ages, and thereby protect the craft guilds and the large extended families from the coming industrialization. It was a hopeless attempt as everything was in constant upheaval; it may have been much more an attempt to stem the flow of money from the Church coffers to those very same banks.

I have often thought the small local bank was the initial mandate for the present day credit union movement. The profits from interest stayed in the community that generated them. In Canada they were rooted in the early socialist movements, such as the Canadian Co-operative Federation[140], that assisted farmers and the poor with low interest loans to start businesses. Savings would accrue interest to offset expenses. The hugely successful micro-credit[141] services being set up in the developing world are a modern example of this trend to localize wealth generation. On a similar note, philosopher John Ralston Saul[142] decries the loss of Canadian business to foreign owned and disinterested shareholders; he suggests we have lost our courage to keep what was grown at home at home. Other forces are probably at work here too, not just courage. Still, it is important to protect our homegrown wealth and the community it enriches.

Along the same lines of the supportive neighborly attitude of no or low interest loans have continued its expression to modern times by the good friend or concerned neighbor fulfilling the role of lender. However on a community wide basis it no longer exists. So where has this real philanthropic attitude gone? With no obligation forthcoming capitalists might choose instead to see their donation as a future benefit to themselves or their own community rather than one in real need. This is what Western philanthropy is all about—no reward collected. One wonders if we have become so hardened to life that another person's plight must be left to institutions or the state to deal with. Or is it that we have little or no understanding of how to actually help? There is also the attitude that if "I" can be successful then you can figure out how to do it too. I won't tell you how unless you pay to come to my workshop. At one time wisdom was shouted from a platform in the town square where you could agree or argue as you wished. The last time I saw anyone doing this kind of speaking was a fundamentalist speaker predicting the end of the world on a downtown street. Everyone ignored him. It used to be the only way of getting out information for many centuries. Now it has been replaced by the social network on your Blackberry. Maybe Blackberry's are better; just look at the Arab Spring uprisings throughout the Middle East.

By way of an example of my life I took advantage of social services in my youth so I would not have to work. I was searching for an answer for my way forward; there were no mentors or friends I could talk with, and all the counselors I visited offered nothing for my money. I learned slowly, but at that time, I didn't have a work ethic. I knew how to work and I certainly liked the benefits of working. However I did not like the work environments I found myself in. I believed in egalitarian and supportive relationships, and I loved physical labor. I found myself in heavy labor environments that often consisted of young and frequently angry or very competitive males who had a dark understanding of masculinity. In hindsight they may have been frustrated too and bidding their time. I often felt discouraged by them and their survival scripted lives. They liked to use bluffing and threat to get respect on a job site. It took me years to find a solution to my need for physical labor, and a friendly and collaborative work environment.

Up to that point I was a drifter through life, without much to root me to the earth or humanity. I was a man at risk. I saw an inner conflict with various kinds of work had been playing out through most of my life. I am not afraid of hard work. Writing is hard work, so is gardening. I had been so desperate to find work at times that I even considered hiring on for cruise ship work (really not for me) for a few minutes only—fortunately! Am I allowing the market place to determine my sense of self-worth? How can I fairly judge myself based on a desperate moment that could influence my decisions for a long time to come? The market place cares not for me, only for the input I give to it. So if I did not allow this influence on my long-term decisions what choices could I preserve in order to aid in my survival? Would I steal from the market? Would stealing debase me? I came close to actually stealing food one day while between jobs. Would I act parasitically by doing nothing and seek welfare again? I did this too, until I saw the possibility of starting my own business. Being self-employed gave me the possibility for an exchange to occur. I now write, work as a landscape gardener and I take university level courses when I can. Self-esteem is very relevant in these exchanges; at the same time the exchange builds even more self-esteem.

So what could I share and what would I want? If the deal is not satisfactory a new arrangement could be negotiated. The usual trade in market negotiations is greater return for greater responsibility. If I am going to trade my knowledge about landscaping, how do I share it? What do I do in return? First of all, is my skill wanted and where is it wanted? Do my skill and its participation have a partial share in the ownership of the work completed? I will say more about this part later. My work ethic is really only the part of me that wishes to improve my life to a standard that I choose for myself. Others might say it is also the economic forces that compel us to work. Those are the voices that will not take a stand and create their own economic reality-create their own initiations.

A saying comes to mind: "If you can get paid for doing what you like, then you will never work a day in your life." The difficult part is finding what you like. It's worth repeating that poverty is the greatest of all world problems and one of the easiest to solve. It is not rocket science, after all. It does need to be a focus of world effort. When we come to see that the tribe or the neighborhood is the same everywhere on planet Earth and that people are pretty much the same, we will finally grow out of tribal thinking. Having recently read "The Desert Queen" by Janet Wallach,[143] I was struck by the fact that the British were seen by many Arabs at the time preceding World War II as bringing a calming effect to the traditional Arab infighting and blood feuds. Arab thinkers believed their fellow peoples were not capable of negotiating an end to these bitter and often generations long bloodlettings. Occasionally we just need a friend to show us how to step out of the box we have been stuck in for a long time and see a new path forward. Arranged marriage might have been a way in the distant past to tie these tribes together.

By way of another example let's look at a more co-operative model that could easily help young people get ahead. Let's say I meet a young man or woman, who truly wants to start a business, but has no connections to capital, no savings, and no track record. I give this man a used piece of equipment I do not need at the moment and he goes off to find some work. Now say he gets work and is able to think of buying more tools but wants to thank me for the loan. He returns my tool and buys me and my family a nice lunch. Now what have I gained by this, just a lunch? What about knowing that I have helped a man to get on his feet? Have I lost anything? I don't think so. How we help a man get going is critical to creating a vision for men that was once commonplace.

Continuing on this line of thought, self-employment is possibly the only area of employment where individuals experience a relative freedom from hierarchy. Of course government regulation, taxing bodies and the established hierarchical order still persist in their reach. People who operate on the basis of trading their self-employed labor for goods and services are largely free of the money system. Do they offer much support to the general culture? Are they even aware of their hidden offering of freedom from employment hierarchy? Often self-employed work is much harder than the wage laborer or the modern office worker experiences. In some reasonable way a modern step to independence would be self-employment. It is really a simple step to do, although it takes a leap of faith or confidence that you can do it. There is almost always a "hole" or unfilled need to occupy somewhere in the economy. You just have to find it. By balancing your interests with your capabilities, you can generate your own income. However, with self-employment we have the choice to recreate the oppression of our fathers or to abolish hierarchy by staying as a business of one. We come into this life with nothing and alone, take and give as we need during our lifetime, and then leave this life with no bounds or ties upon us. Nice try, I'm thinking, but it is difficult to live this way in today's "fears of the future" ideology.

Since we no longer live in the perpetual present, as we did in the Middle Ages, fear of the future motivates and controls our every act. We forget the joy, beauty and peace of mind that can be found by living in the present. Everyone past forty is working for some far off day. We have come to believe no one will care for us in our old age and for good reason. Disposed of and by-passed in an impatient society too focused on their own success to care about us "has-beens." However, I predict that as our societies become even wealthier this fear may lessen to the point that we can live more in the present time without the worry of poverty in retirement. Depending on the country where you live and system of governance and pensions.

If I were not in a relationship I would downsize my life significantly. I like very small spaces to live in. A 12 by 25 foot cabin with loft is ample space for me. I have been meaning to ask a realtor why so few houses and corresponding lots are available in that size. Think about it, if all people on minimum wage could buy a small cabin say 500 square feet or less on a 1000 square foot lot they could build equity, feel like they were worth something and create wealth for themselves in the future. Would it be worth it to do this? I am actually working on this idea right now. More on this later.

Recall the earlier discussion on the demand for freer choices. New freedoms were increasingly tolerated because they were central to the new way of looking at the world—a view that seemed to bring considerable wealth. The separateness of individuals began to be recognized in small ways: single chairs instead of benches in the home, better mirrors[144] to have a better sense of what people looked like. In art, the self-portrait became common. This went hand in hand with the weakening of the ties that bound people together in families, trade guilds and communities. People no longer wanted to help the needy as they had been taught by Christian mores. The systems motto now was "Buyer beware"[145], and "there is a sucker[146] born every minute." Adam Smith said, "[…]the hidden hand of the market would regulate the economy."[147] The Future looked "very promising" indeed.

As the wealth and security of Western societies gradually peaked in the 1950's, the image of the isolated and single-minded sacrifice of the male provider and protector abated. He is gradually relaxing the control and letting go of the fears of an earlier era, allowing for the birth of a new society. As minorities and previously dominated groups join the work force, the isolated male can begin to reintegrate into his community. His job done, peace of mind is his reward. But he has to take his freedom, as it will not be given to him. Strange though, he is not taking it! He instead continues in his workaholism, his drug addictive behaviors and maintains his general isolation. What will it take for men to take their freedom from their initiations of the past? It would appear men believe they have not created enough wealth, and that they see themselves still relied upon as a protector by mainstream society. Some men cannot stop. This view is changing, albeit slowly, as each man has to reach this satisfaction on his own.

The anarchist view (more on anarchy later) that humans cooperate in day to day living versus the views of promoters of the individualistic lifestyle who see struggle as the natural process, gives men who have completed their biological goals (providing and protecting) greater choice for their future if they are willing to take it. Many men are unable or unwilling to make this transition and are stuck. As well, this life script has a deadly ending, since life for these men can become a life not worth living. So many men of the 1940's went to early graves from suicide, alcoholism, violence or disease.[148] They held the belief that since they were retired they were now expendable, and that they should self-destruct, and they did in huge numbers. Why are there so many elderly women and so few elderly men? Answer: the men are dead. See the Statistics Canada report by Jeffrey Asher[149]. July 1996.

As our societies become ever more isolating, only forty-seven years ago,[150] all of the productive work that used to be done in the home, was now done outside of it. This would include the making of tools, clothing, household goods and most foods. A major consequence for men and women was that they now had only each other to rely on instead of the much larger extended families people used to enjoy in the past. In this kind of home the husband and wife, often forced to work separately, lost the value of each other's company, and ultimately, lived even more isolated lives. I am not trying to idealize the extended family, only to see its advantages, and the consequences of its destruction. One could say the logical conclusion to all this individualistic and isolating behavior would be the complete separation of everyone within a short period of time, say by 2100 AD. Is it likely to happen?

Well, look at all the single parent families today; also look at all the single men, many of whom prefer to live alone or with other friends. With computers everywhere, shopping is as close as your keyboard; it can even be delivered to your door. In other words, why go out? Friendships live and die online, not actually needing to be in the others presence for years at a time.

I recently saw a film about a lonely robot that freed a society of totally machine dependant space faring humans. It is a disturbing but realistic portrait of the possible near future. It is a route we could go if we allow individualism to dominate our ambitions. However many forces compete for our attention and this bad end may not happen. These forces include the immense efforts going into the environmental movement, the new financial crisis, the growing human potential movement and the never-ending push for democratic reform. There are reasons to be hopeful but by the way things seem to be going individualism is growing ever more central to everyone's way of being in the world.

I know for myself that there is a limit to the amount of isolation I can stand. Because I have lived alone in the woods, only a few days would go by before I needed to visit with someone-even anyone. I remember having the flu once and needed to stay in my cabin for three or four days. As I neared recovery I could hardly stay in bed any longer, I had to go down to the village for a cup of coffee and see other people. Before I left, a few chores were to be done that included cutting some firewood and filling up the water jugs from the well. As I worked, some hikers happened to come by. I could not believe how excited I was to see them. I had to invite them in for tea and offer just about anything else in order to keep them there just a little bit longer. My experience must be similar to how it felt to see another person during pioneer times when people lived alone or on small family farms for months at a time. What a thought! I don't think I could stand that kind of isolation for very long. I suppose one could get used to it but I have read stories of settlers going stir-crazy in the woods and having what amounted to a nervous breakdown. This memory ties in with our theme by providing a first hand recollection of isolation and how the loss of companionship leaves one desperate, almost desolate. The effects on the population of a large city, if many live similarly isolated lives is significant. I believe many do, we just ignore them or hide ourselves away in our own cave. Maybe this is our life now. Great eh?

But is this the life I want?

What does the future hold for my children, or other people's children? Do we provide an example for our children or our neighbors of any community involvement? Do I make every effort to communicate my emotions effectively?

When I lived apart from society on my mountain top retreat, the singular thing that came to my mind was that the worldly struggle was actually a creation of human beings, not necessarily a creation of nature. It was a struggle for survival of some kind. It was self evident that property lines, fences, municipal bylaws were irrelevant here. Human interference was at a minimum. I could then learn from first principles how to live. First principles provide the opportunity to learn at first hand the consequences of living apart from human civilization. It is a way to escape from conditions not of my doing to conditions of another reality.

The rain comes down; firewood needs to be cut and dried for three days so I can have a fire to keep warm, stay dry, cook and to bathe. A step in the ladder up to my loft has broken and needs to be repaired, I can fix it with wood from the forest rather than a lumberyard, so I go to the forest and cut a piece to fit, it works fine. Who is gong to say it does not fit because it is raw unfinished wood. Who cares if I wake up, light a fire and have my breakfast sitting on the porch in the moonlight? After doing my dishes, then cutting some firewood for an hour, making my bed, I went for a walk. It wasn't yet 7am. I have had that experience of simplicity, the late night forest walks in moonlight, hearing footsteps near me and wondering what it was, dangerous or a harmless rodent or deer. People are killed in the bush at times in BC by cougars and bears although rarely, and here I was testing fate and feeling terrified yet enthralled at the same time. I could not believe how beautiful the forest is in moonlight, especially when alone on your path that you have memorized to the inch. I knew where every rock and root would be as I came to it on the dark nights. Then I was not so lucky to have moonlight or a flashlight and then it was really dark-pitch black, then I was nervous. Memorizing my trail to the inch got me back to the cabin but every sound warned of a cougar or a bear about to bite me-right now! This is the kind of reality that cities protect us and at the same time separate us from.

Eventually it was time to leave and return to civilization but my heart is still there in the moonlight.

I found a way out of some of my conditioning as a male through learning about first principles and then I recognized I was free to make new choices, free of the human education I had received. Without this I may not have survived. I could have followed my mother's example and commit suicide; however I'm glad I did not. Mental illness could have been my trap; an inescapable prison as real as poverty and abuse are for others. On a positive note many males come out of their prisons, real or imaginary, and make good adaptations in their lives. Unfortunately, some are still in real prisons or institutions or living in straightjackets with few choices.

By explaining how our civilization has been formed and seeing how our current ideas are not really based on first principles, we can see some of the errors in our way. What we experience of our civilization is only the end result of other people's lives-what they left behind for us to sort out and make some kind of sense for ourselves—or to ignore them completely and discover our own route through this life. It may seem as if all the questions have been answered but this is not true. They have only been answered for the people who asked them, not for you and me. We have our own questions and our own search. First principles come into play when you realize that your questions have not been answered at all or if you feel oppressed.

A modern circumstance many react strongly towards is the destruction caused by vandalism and what seems like mindless havoc associated with street gangs. They too are symptoms of a society where it appears all the questions have been answered. Gangs and vandalism are evidence of first principal questions not being answered. The work ethic has become a deeply entrenched cultural standard that replaces direct observation and questioning. Consider the idea that the non-stop work ethic we admire in chief executive officers can have a light and a dark side. The light side is the urge we all feel, to "do" something, no matter what so we feel that we have contributed or achieved a goal. That energy to do is constant and if frustrated and rejected enough, the energy can become the dark and self-destructive characteristics of gangs and criminal behavior. Is it possible that pressure felt in the average person to do "something" (without questioning it) can create a criminal act out of a deep and inwardly sensed lack of purpose, direction or "calling"? These urges must be expressed somehow. I think it is possible although the causes of vandalism and other social ills have been previously relegated to poverty, a bad childhood, mental illness and a patriarchal society. They are subject to many forces from society to conform to the attitudes of the current economy instead of being encouraged to use first principals to create an income within the legal economy. This is a dilemma in modern education where the needs of the individual are ignored in favor of the needs of the economy. First principals ask questions meaningful to the individual.

I believe we all want to feel motivated in our own lives. While admitting to being equally motivated, I can see other ways of living that are rewarding and life sustaining. How our contribution is defined depends on the culture one lives in or chooses to create. It is a human invention this "economy" and not set in stone, yet a certain level of economic prosperity is required to free oppressed peoples who may feel their lives ARE set in stone.

Angus McLaren, in his book "The Trials of Masculinity" refers to any males not living up to new standards of masculinity[151] created during the Industrial Revolution. Of course this new model was intended to fulfill the dreams of capitalists and the Church. At the time it seemed like a good idea, maybe it still is. However as McLaren points out, what it meant to be a man was hammered out in those latter decades of the nineteenth century. It was indeed based on the castigation of those males declared to be "unmanly." These unmanly males were the underdogs, sexual predators, mentally ill and the poor. A man in these terms was less than an animal and should be treated as such. Our deplorable prison system and welfare agencies are a testament to these early times and the masculine mythology that went with it. As was discussed with vandalism and gangs, aside from some mental illnesses, most of these conditions are rooted in a lost or perverted desire to contribute. This is the unacknowledged dark side to the unsatisfied and disconnected life energy some of us feel all the time—sometimes seen as a personal lack of motivation, depression or a dark time.

Here is a dumb question, but I have to ask it. Why do we continue to use the same assumptions for our rehabilitation programs hoping for a different result? The instilling of the work ethic, or what is referred to as "normalization" in our prisoners, mental patients and other people who might be disabled and do not fit in to the narrow definition of what our society demands is still seen as acceptable treatment or as a suitable punishment. Some highly marginalized people cannot keep up with demands placed upon them; yet we as a society expect them to do so. I suppose we have advanced somewhat; we no longer put them out in the snow. Pushed hard enough they will find a way to dispose of them-selves without our help. Their preferred tool, narcissism (or 'false purpose' as I like to think of it) is a place to shelter the lost soul, to teach them to be like the rest of us, a place to hide for a while, in bitterness, sarcasm and denial. Here egotism and self-deception are acceptable replacements to reality and emotional maturity. The most indoctrinated and damaged lash out in violent and criminal acts or take their own lives in a hail of bullets. This refers to a new kind of suicide called "Officer Assisted Suicide"[152] where police are set up by an armed gunman intent on murder and his own death. He could not kill himself so he found someone else to do it for him. He may even kill others before being shot by police. His acts now give him a strong reason to hate himself and hence allow his own life to be taken.

Is this man a monster who deserves death or a loud symptom of a society in deep denial of the responsibility we all share for the behavior of our citizens?

As time progresses, more and more people previously marginalized by disabilities, health issues and differences in gender find a way to fit in and create wealth for themselves and the greater society. No other time in history has seen the accessibility of so much capital to so many people. Democracy seems to be working.

Returning to our history now. The United States could be cited as the best current example of how far Western cultures have taken individualism as a lifestyle, The U.S. system idealizes passion[153], and is tremendously optimistic about an individuals' ability to move ahead and motivate their life. The opportunity to create immense wealth exists in this kind of culture. The consequences for the ones not motivated or who do not fit within this acquisitive lifestyle can be very painful.

Every culture has the right to define for itself what wealth is and how to create it. It would seem that the westernized nations have found a profound way to create wealth that does not seem to work for other nations, specifically nations of the developing world. The great concern I share, along with many others is best stated by Gandhi, when he said that "two planets"[154] were not available for India to develop the same level of wealth as Britain. Is it possible that the development of new technologies can keep up with the demand for essential improvements in food production, energy, environmental standards, and medicine as well as a host of others? Of course this does not consider the resources needed to create the wealth so one can afford these improvements. It may be true we all want the goodies no matter which culture we come from. They make life easier. Then again wealth has a very personal definition depending on who you are and the culture you grew up in.

In a relatively short period of time, I have become increasingly skeptical and concerned about the end product from the globalization of that potentially dangerous concept called "Individualism." In the west, it has been highly attractive to young working age males.

However with the immense changes in Western society, including improvements in gender equality, access to work for almost all able citizens and greater existential or community focused activities, males are being forced for the first time in world history to consider a different purpose for their future. As many societies become more democratic, community oriented individuals or ones searching for a broader role of one's masculine identity could see their own lives becoming a community investment for the well-being of themselves and everyone else. As well they would take care of their own best interests without an institutionally imposed hierarchy of morals and ethics to bind their steps. This might come easier for some and be immensely difficult for others. Some cannot easily dance to the beat of their own drum whereas others thrive in a solo or a kind of self-motivated and isolated environment. Individuals who require highly structured environments in order to function may experience intense anxiety in the coming Age of Globalization. It would make sense that various sub-cultures would organize themselves in order to shelter and nurture like-minded individuals outside of mainstream social safety nets such as clubs, associations and societies that cater to the average citizen. To be clear, many of these sub-cultural organizations will be highly attractive to poorly parented or alienated individuals seeking a safe harbor. Good parenting is the missing structural component to healthy life integration.

Poorly parented or alienated individuals might have serious difficulties with questions such as: Is it possible to live with someone that does something completely different from what I am doing? If they do not learn it from parents it will be difficult to learn it in later life. Of course many rebel from too tight a family belief system and many hang on tight to their cultural history.

In all these discussions of freedom and greater individual choice a flaw exists within our now global economic system. While it creates abundance of goods, it also builds into it a resistance to grant greater freedom for both men and women. Without a radical shift in our economic priorities both genders will be trapped in the never-ending struggle for the economic ability to shop. Is this all you want? Not me! As we have seen, the feminist movement is generally not interested in promoting freedom for all women, just the ones who are aggressive enough to either replace or compete successfully with men. I do not know about you but when I look around today, women are making similar decisions that men had to make when considering economic and family matters. I do not see a lot of new economic engines such as cooperatives or de-structured businesses popping up. The models are out there, but not used as well as could be. Women appear to have been co-opted by the individualistic system as easily as men, much to our loss.

Although many women do benefit from increased self-esteem from the efforts of feminist reform, only the radical fringe suggests a restructuring of the economic order to create a truly democratic society. What is needed is an alternative economic order that does not rely on the battles of competition[155] to create wealth. Rest assured, I do not suggest a violent overthrow of our present system. I suggest we add to what exists by thinking, as well as acting democratically.

I believe all individuals have merit and talent, maybe not economic talent but talent none-the-less. This talent is wasted in a competitive society by placing market forces onto art or public service in order to ascertain their monetary value. We must learn that replacing men with women and valuing competition above co-operation will create wealth to a limited degree only and mainly for the successful competitors. The ability to create wealth for everyone is rooted in the co-operative movement. I believe only through this, will men and women have a truly genuine freedom and universal wealth.

The solutions are not found in ideological beliefs such as communism and fascism that try to change human nature through the use of power and propaganda, or in its twin in Western cultures, media manipulation, which uses a similar process embedded in our education and market systems. For example, during the boom years (up to 2008) in the West, there was an extreme shortage in skilled labor, created in part because education leaders in the 1950's and 1960's discouraged students from considering trades by brainwashing a generation into seeing trades as inferior to academics. I know I was one. I looked down on trades thinking they were inferior and that only a loser or a poorly motivated person would settle for such a lowly position in life. Quite honestly I was only a marginal student at best, I just made it through high school. It took me till I was in my thirties to realize I was far more skilled with my hands than with my brain. Somehow I thought life had to be really hard in order to be worthwhile, doing something that was simple and enjoyable was beneath me. This was no easy adjustment for me to make, but like with my sons, doing it finally added some peace to my life. I could make a living, finally supporting myself after years of struggle in college. Learning the landscape trade was probably the best decision of my life.

Fears of poverty would be reduced if everyone felt valued instead of just high-income earners in academia or business. The unconstrained quest for power can create just more disaster for us. In a sense, the individual who craves this kind of power could be classified as mentally ill on the basis of their fear of being dominated by others, or on the other hand they could be truly altruistic. Regardless, their intense desire for protection and safety must be reassessed or at least questioned. Of course in a democracy, passion and the squeaky wheel are the motivators for change. Can there be no better way to learn?

If you follow my train of thought, throughout time we have been creating a civilization that incorporates all the qualities I have been discussing. We just have to take the next step, and the next and so on. The most important concept to garner from this discussion is the fact that our Western society is a constructed society, as is any culture, created by the people living in the time that they did and making the decisions they did in order to survive. It can all be adapted to new circumstances, or it will cease to exist. It is not permanent. It was forced on many of us but we can make a different choice if we wish. We can change patterns thousands of years old if we desire to. The development of democracy is a good example and in the process it can make the world a better place to live in as well. It really is our choice. Enough wealth exists for many citizens to survive without a "stand to the last man at the waterhole" and men can finally begin to ask the future of male purpose. Some of the answers men might discover as they explore their own lives might include:

- That they can finally be real equals with women; and by this I mean that men can help in the design of the interior of their homes, make important decisions about the family's diet and take responsibility for their own health. Economically, men can share the burden of creating wealth for the family without carrying it as a lifelong burden. Men's work and women's work no longer exist as purely separate roles.
- That they can enjoy male company without a nagging suspicion that the other men are secretly conspiring against them with tests and tricks to discover weaknesses or uncertainty.
- That competition is first and foremost a contest with yourself and nobody else. Sports can be a lot of fun and even a source of learning. However competition based on the comparison of oneself against others will result in an inaccurate conclusion. It is far better to base our assessment of our character or performance on internal standards than on external and non-personal ones. If we are living according to other people's standards we will never appreciate our own. Others can be guides but not our masters.
- That children are not our property. The tragic irony of this can be seen in many cultures where children are used as a source of income for impoverished families. This has more to do with poverty than the ownership of children. Yet the effect is the

same—entrapment. Children maturing in these cultural tragedies may never know self-worth of any kind, only victimhood. They make easy targets for prostitution, drug addiction or criminal and terrorist organizations. In the end they can become property to someone or something other than themselves.

- That power is only valuable if it has meaning in a community context and is used to build relationships rather than distinctions between individuals. Individuals who seek power as an end in itself may find isolation and suspicion instead.
- That women are our friends and not a source of obligation and duty.
- That discussion is used to negotiate all of our relationships.
- That what happened to you in the past was and still is tragic. Yet you could make a decision right now to find a new way to express those feelings instead of rage or self-destructive behaviors. For example, my mother's suicide was a tragic event in my life. I learned through a chance conversation with a stranger that if I wanted to, I could create a mother inside myself to care for me while I grew up. It was not perfect, but it helped. What can you do to help you through a difficult experience until you are strong enough to let it go?
- To come to an understanding about our historically constructed masculine sociology; how and why it was created and to allow ourselves unlimited expression of fearlessness and ferociousness in facing patterns of behavior that limit our growth today or deny our naturally expansive good will.

To conclude this chapter, everything that has occurred throughout history has happened for good reasons-mainly to bring us to now. What we do with it depends upon us finding the unifying thread that exists inside everything we have done up to now, and by doing so the path will be clear.

CHAPTER TWO

The Second Foundation:
Culture = Nature or Does it?

In general we can acknowledge that our species is still very young and that the natural world works fine on its own. However, it no longer provides us a behavioral blueprint to follow into the future. The Biblical Book of Nature was the template for centuries. Today however we need different choices, as we have done in special areas throughout history. An example is the development of democracy. As far as survival of the fittest goes, democracy is the antithesis to nature because it creates a totally human environment where existence is based on fairness rather than fitness. There have been attempts to destroy democracy throughout history, the most obvious example being the Nazi dictatorship of Germany. Yet democracy persists and the struggles to create fairness planet-wide seem to be growing. Education is critical to this process, and now today the remarkable social media network embellishes democracy even more.

Jared Diamond's important work "Guns Germs and Steel" covers a unique thread of our human cultural history. Diamond attempts to explain the causes of racism, heterosexism and war.[156] His ideas are compelling. For example, let's look at racism from his perspective. The historical guilt from colonizing other peoples has shamed the modern white race to an embarrassed silence. We have no understanding for this discomfort except that we "should" feel this way because many of us were born after the worst had past. In order to expose some of the historical causes for racism and its cousin, colonization, we must go back a long way. Diamond begins his search around the same time we explored in the evolution of power and hierarchy when humans were first making the shift from a nomadic way of life to a more settled farming lifestyle. This was about 10,000 years ago.

First of all, to get some perspective, let's think of the landmasses of our world. Many various shapes and sizes, some extending for thousands of kilometers north and south, while others extended for thousands of kilometers east and west. Some are fat in size, such as Asia, while others such as North and South America are skinny where they meet. Others are isolated in hot climates, such as Australia, while others are isolated in the cold, such as Antarctica.

Now consider people traveling around looking for food. People in Asia would have a much greater chance of finding what they needed than say those in Australia. They could travel from one corner of the continent to another; they could travel with the herds; they could travel to areas of great fertility. In Australia only a few isolated coastal areas could support sizable populations. In other words Asians had greater choice. In terms of clothing, and materials, Asia wins again with its great forests of wood, huge deposits of minerals, vast climatic zones that demanded variability and resourcefulness and included many kinds of plants and animals. Asia would also play host to many human societies that would develop new and inventive ways of living in similar or in challenging environments. This experience would provide by way of trade new technologies for other cultures to adopt these new methods and in turn to prosper. Along with this expansion of trade and technology would come territorial pressures, weapon systems, defense planning; and more copying would occur over time.

As well, many wild animals and plants could be domesticated and become useful to humans. One example is the horse. Within a short period of time humans saw the possibility for the riding of a horse as transportation and from that, for cavalry and success in war. Therefore, the ability to survive and do it well would be very good on such a continent. Australia did not offer such ample natural resources to her people and would remain underdeveloped until technology arrived from other continents.

Other continents such as North and South America would offer equally difficult challenges to travel back and forth. This can be seen in the narrowness of the Panama isthmus and the acknowledgement that crossing this bridge from either north or south would require moving from one cool climate to a hot one and back to a cool one again. The difficulties encountered would be immense.

So, what about places like China? China actually had the same advantages as Europe did, but due to an internal decision to isolate and seal its people away from the rest of the world, it never became an outwardly focused and expanding colonizer. However, China was and still is a potent force to reckon with in the South Pacific. If this isolation had not occurred, China may have actually colonized the world after a massive confrontation with Europe. Instead European colonists were left free to take all. And did they.

With all these developments the race that benefited most was the white race—by accident. As Diamond suggests, racism is simply out of the question as no inherent superiority is present, only geographical advantages. Citizens of favored nations assumed they were superior when in fact all races given the same advantages would probably have developed a similar sense of privilege and entitlement. Colonization occurred because of real differences in advantages. These real advantages are guns, germs and steel, and possibly other advantages we have not yet come to understand.

So culture is affected by geography, and Diamond provides more evidence with the following example. In some ways even more shocking and dramatic than racism is ethnic cleansing.

On the Chatham Islands[157], 500 miles east of New Zealand, centuries of independence came to a brutal end for the Moriori people in December 1835. On November 19 of that year, a ship carrying 500 Maori armed with guns, clubs, and axes arrived, following on December 5 by a shipload of 400 more Maori. Groups of Maori began to walk through Moriori settlements, announcing that the Moriori were now slaves, and killing those who objected. An organized resistance by the Moriori failed because the older tradition of resolving disputes peacefully took precedence. The Moriori decided in a council meeting not to fight back but to offer peace, friendship, and a division of resources.

Needless to say they were slaughtered.

The brutal outcome of this collision between the Moriori and the Maori could have been easily predicted. The Moriori were a small isolated population of hunter-gatherers, equipped with only the simplest technology and weapons, entirely inexperienced at war, and lacking strong leadership or organization. The Maori invaders [from New Zealand's North Island] came from a dense population of farmers operating under strong leadership, yet chronically engaged in ferocious wars, and equipped with more advanced technology and weapons. Of course, when the two groups finally came into contact, it was the Maori who slaughtered the Moriori, not vice versa.

The tragedy of the Moriori resembles many other tragedies in both the modern and the ancient world, pitting numerous well-equipped people against a few ill-equipped opponents. The Maori-Moriori collision grimly illuminates that both groups had diverged from a common origin less than a millennium earlier. Both were Polynesian peoples. The modern Maori are descendants of Polynesian farmers who colonized New

Zealand around AD 1000. Soon thereafter, a group of those Maori in turn colonized the Chatham Islands and became the Moriori. In the centuries after the two groups separated, they evolved in opposite directions, the North Island Maori developing greater complexity and the Moriori less complex technology and political organization. The Moriori reverted to being hunter-gatherers, while the North Island Maori turned towards more intensive farming. It is easy to trace how the differing environments of the Chatham Islands and of New Zealand molded the Moriori and the Maori differently. While those ancestral Maori who first colonized the Chatham Islands may have been farmers, Maori tropical crops could not grow in the Chatham's' cold climate. The colonists had no alternative except to revert to being hunter-gatherers. Since as hunter-gatherers they did not produce crop surpluses available for redistribution or storage, they could not support and feed non-hunting craft specialists, armies, bureaucrats, and chiefs. They could only prey on seals, shellfish, nesting seabirds, and fish that could be captured by hand or with clubs that required no elaborate technology. In addition, the Chatham's are relatively small and remote islands, capable of supporting a total population of only about 2,000 hunter-gatherers. With no other accessible islands to colonize, the Moriori had to remain in the Chatham's and to learn how to get along with each other. They did so by renouncing war, and they reduced potential conflicts from overpopulation by castrating some male infants. The result was a small, non-warlike population with simple technology and weapons, and without strong leadership or organization. In contrast, the northern [warmer] part of New Zealand, by far the largest island group in Polynesia, was suitable for Polynesian agriculture. Those Maori who remained in New Zealand increased in numbers until there were some 100,000 people. They developed locally dense populations chronically engaged in ferocious wars with neighboring populations. With the crop surpluses that they could grow and store, they fed craft specialists, chiefs, and part-time soldiers. They needed and developed varied tools for growing their crops, fighting, and making art. They erected elaborate ceremonial buildings and prodigious numbers of forts. Thus Moriori and Maori societies developed from the same ancestral society, but along very different lines . . . . The outcome clearly illustrates how environments can affect economy, technology, political organization, and fighting skills within a short time span.

Add in a few nasty diseases that the invaders are now immune to and you have genocide comparable to the European colonization of North and South America.

As far as the east-west trade routes are concerned, just think for a minute how much easier it would be to travel across Asia from, say China to Turkey, than from Chile to Canada. The difficulties are much larger in the north-south trek than the east west one. Why? Well first of all, one would go through major climatic changes on the north/south trek and would fall ill from diseases for which there was no immunity. Finally one would find unfamiliar foods and different kinds of animal dangers. Few peoples would be prepared for the unexpected dangers associated with this kind of journey.

As a result, trade would be limited across such a traverse and germs would not infect all of the peoples across this area eventually creating immunities in them but many would become infected and die. Domesticated plants and animals would not survive the journey from a cool climate through a tropical one to a cool one again. In other words everything would be locked in its own climatic zone.

Asia would be completely different, much easier to cross, with many familiar plants and animals along the way, and no surprises in terms of diseases or major climatic changes. Technological development was just a heck of a lot easier in such a place; hence Caucasian peoples were able to do what they did. I realize this is a very brief account of Diamond's book, yet it adds to the understanding of the phenomena he discusses in his book.

As I will demonstrate, the concept of masculinity is similar in that it appears relative to a given culture's influence. The Moriori valued hunting and peacemaking as their defining traits; the Maori valued war making. The two cultures could not have been more different; yet they came from the same original stock. Essentially this is evidence that masculine traits can be culturally defined as well. An important question is how a cultural definition of masculinity relates to instincts, sexual behavior, and male and female role models.

Another major influence on our expansiveness or democratic sense of fair play has been the development of science or more accurately a method of viewing the natural world. The earliest example I have encountered is the discovery from the early Persian Empire of the opposite tastes of "sweet" and "sour." [158] This appears to be one of the first intellectual concepts that may have led to the separation of the cosmos into "right" and "wrong", "good" and "bad", "male" and "female." This concept gradually develops into the more complex scientific method and continues to develop into a dualistic analysis of nature[159] as described by early Greek examples that observe rising forces (air, heat) and sinking forces (rocks, cold). We see an eventual conclusion with the twinning concept of "heaven and hell." This view of nature gave rise in Europe to "Natural Philosophy" or "The Book of Nature." The Book of Nature" was an interpretation of biblical writings promoting nature as the blueprint for humanity to follow.

A simple example might clarify the meaning of "The Book of Nature." If people were looking for advice on what role men and women were to follow, they should look to nature for the answer. Simply put if most animals rely on males to hunt and fight, then conversely rely on females to raise and nurture offspring, it follows that humans ought to behave that way as well. A questioner might ask if anyone considered that humans might possess qualities in addition to that of animals or that choice might play a role in human affairs as the pressures to survive relax. Anyone that did was probably executed.

The development of science has had a major influence on men, promoting the intellectual and emotional detachment from the experience of the natural world. This could be said to be the first rule of masculinity. Out of which came the justification and the enculturalization of masculinity. One of the first institutional developments to establish as a "law" for "right" masculine behavior came about through the development of the Scientific Revolution. Scientists and philosophers sought initially to reinforce the notions of hierarchy[160], power and authority basing their conclusions on Biblical quotes and observations of nature. However there is a problem with this science; it does not suggest any possibility of happiness or contentedness. It assumes its statements are correct and following them will bring satisfaction, and maybe security. In truth it is an illusion that entrenches wealth and power in the hands of the writers and the elite. Happiness in the average citizen is irrelevant. Clever eh?

In 1661 Robert Hooke[161] wrote that experimental natural philosophy, similar to a natural mechanical view developed by Sir Isaac Newton, was certainly the most likely way to erect a glorious and ever-lasting structure and temple to nature and thus to nature's creator. This melding of "naturists" and "scientists" attempted and succeeded at using scientific methods to promote moral and spiritual beliefs based on nature. This biblical/mechanical view of humanity worked on people like a well-oiled machine. Experimental research at the time was described as a kind of worship[162]. The English mechanical philosopher (of the day) was represented as a godly man, fit to celebrate divine service in the temple of nature. He was almost considered of equal status with ordained ministers. The title of this section asks us to question if nature and culture were the same thing. If we were to answer yes to this we would never escape the power of the elites because they would claim a dominant status and force the rest of us to accept a harsh pecking order based on their mechanical theories. They almost won but people rebelled against the elites and their hierarchies and gradually demanded greater personal freedoms.

Science from its earliest beginnings also attempted to distinguish reality from non-reality or chaos. Emotion was considered part of the chaos and was seen as inferior and not to be trusted. Hence the modern dilemma for men becomes visible as an alienation of feeling from any responsibility inherent in our behavior. As well this is felt through to the present day where isolation from feeling in men is a fabricated response arising from the nature-based necessities of hierarchy. Institutions such as the military, schools, corporations and many others carry on this ancient tradition. Feelings in males are actually counterproductive in a protector/provider or nature-based society. The protection of the waterhole demands fearlessness and even a ruthless attitude to one's own life as well as your comrades in order to safeguard the tribe or village. Herb Goldberg, an early writer on men's issues wrote: "The man who 'feels'[163] becomes inefficient and ineffective because he gets emotionally involved and this inevitably slows him down and distracts him. His more dehumanized competitor will surely pass him by."

While essential for survival at one time, this emotion-denial may be less of a necessity now and more of a hindrance to our present evolution beyond a nature based definition as a culture. Many philosophies suggest that humanity can only know so much knowledge,[164] that there is a limit to our capacity to grow and that we might be trapped in our biology. One source of this line of thinking would be the Biblical assertion to not question God. I am unconvinced that any limit exists. Other philosophies support this idea. Even human history gives strong evidence that we do not know what our potential capacity might be since it so consistently surprises and refreshes the understanding and the experience of our lives. The practice of meditation suggests we are all capable of profound understanding and even enlightenment. In the 1600's when this was being discussed it would be quite dangerous to admit to these ideas.

Science could also be defined as the struggle between an objective view of human affairs and superstition, which might be considered a catchall phrase for subjective and non-scientific views. Examples of superstitious beliefs or non-scientific observances include:

- Teleology—a philosophy that natural effects or events have moral meanings i.e., Thunder = God is angry.
- The rising of the sun as a theme of rebirth and hence the creation of sun-worshiper cults.
- A simple sense of being alive.
- Peace of mind, now how would you define that scientifically?

For us the consequence is that emotion and feeling are equally regarded as superstitious, unreliable and even unnatural. The history in the treatment of mental illness, of women and children, of sensitive boys and men, our views of homosexuals or any group that could be considered deviant is testament to the failure to direct our "Science" away from the "Top Dog" mentality. In effect it has been used to justify our fears and our actual limited vision for humanity. These are things that cannot be proven or explained scientifically so they seem unreliable or even threatening. The traditional fear is that open-minded people might lead to a tolerance for unconventional or anti-theistic ideas about the heavens or scripture or that culture is a human created process somewhat but not entirely based on nature.

Yet as Bennett Wong, a well-known West Coast therapist, has suggested in his book "A Manual for Life"[165] that "All feelings generated within a person are based upon that person's interpretations of reality. Nobody can make me happy or angry; I become angry (make myself) happy or angry over what I perceive and interpret others as doing. In this way I alone am responsible (but not to blame) for all my feelings. When I fully understand this, I can step out of the victim role and take charge of my emotional life, developing a strength that furthers my personal growth. In that process, the power inherent in the victim role is abandoned in favor of effective communication."

So by his reasoning and if his quote is an indication of emotional health then it must be true that fearful reactions to new ideas are the responsibility of the one who experiences those feelings. That was heresy during the time of Robert Hooke, but important and freeing for us today. So by understanding this what do we accomplish? By freeing culture from nature, we allow ourselves the right to create our lives as we see fit rather than by living out a script. However we need to understand how deeply embedded the script has become and who forced it upon us. This is the overall purpose of this chapter.

So what is the point of all this great construction of science? Is it the pursuit of wisdom or the engorgement of our desires, as in say, unhealthy fantasy, or that we allow science to go where it wants rather than direct it for humane purposes. Is the democratization or "across the board" justification of our desires[166] running rampant an issue of worthy discussion? No doubt religious or moral thinkers would agree, yet is it wrong or dangerous to conclude that our desires were to be experienced and learned from? How about as the constant source of an insatiable need for entertainment, of which science can take on the appearance of in modern media. So if we desire to hurt someone should we be able to go to a live killing of animals or people? If you feel suicidal, should you be able to hurt yourself without friends or family intervening? Should your suicide or that of others be televised into our homes? How far should the entertainment business go with modern technological developments, and what limits would you place on your desires and for what reasons? What do you consider entertaining? Conversely, what do you consider disgusting and immoral? Aside from outside influences such as church, parents or friends how do you know that something is immoral?

Experience and initiation are again important here. These are probably the only ways to know what is moral or immoral.

If we can trace how science has reinforced traditional or nature-based gender definitions and limited our experience in life, then we could see how science could encourage a greater diversity of expression as a healthy alternative. Males might feel freer to explore community service work as opposed to the providing and protecting ideologies. Hence the creation of a deeper experience for our humanity and a fuller sense of being can come into existence. Masculinity could expand from its traditional confines into something alive and evolving—something it should be able to do in a free society.

I will present in the following pages a chronology of significant scientific moments in time that I believe have influenced and supported nature-based philosophies, and over time helped establish the institutionalized masculinity that reinforced males' provider and protector instincts. Each item is a building block of a historically constructed masculinity.

This chronology is based on Steven Shapin's book "The Scientific Revolution." I could have started with the Egyptian or the Platonic dualistic views of the archetypes of the Greek Gods, but the Greek philosophers provide a better starting point.

I want to introduce you to the early Greek philosopher Claudius Ptolemy,[167] who in Ad 100-170 promoted the concept of an immutable (unmoving) earth around which orbited our sun, planets and stars. Here he established the human and earth centered worldview. He also wrote about the Greek philosophy on the nature of matter. He stated the belief that nature was composed of four elements: earth, water, air and fire, all of which had special powers or characteristics. Fire and air tended to rise therefore had heavenly properties. Water and earth had heavy attributes and tended to sink; hence they were associated with the underworld and darkness. In accordance with Ptolemy's theory, all the elements tend to aspire to be at their natural place.

A more modern interpretation of Ptolemy's theory is called "teleology." Teleology is an Aristotelian or goal-oriented philosophy. We might refer to such traditional views of matter as "animistic" in nature, or as having soul-like properties. For example, teleology tried to explain that rocks move as humans do, to be in their natural place, having weight, and rolling or falling. The lighter elements such as air and fire move upwards and away from the Earth, while the heavier or darker ones sank or moved towards the center of the Earth

If we are similar to rocks, could our behavior be predicted as well? If we had a depressive character would it not be easy to compare us to a heavy rock, and because of our "low" stature could we be seen as demonic, hellish or inferior? Light rocks are seen to be more reflective of God and therefore are given positive values. Science re-enforces this perception of a dualistic universe by assigning life roles based on these observations of nature. For example, Darwin developed his theory of survival of the fittest. Robert Wright in his new book "Non-Zero,"[168] recently suggested that co-operation is a far greater factor in survivability of human society than competition. So the moral of the story is that we humans seem to need to analyze the natural world and pin it down to either a co-operative enterprise or a competitive one. Life is not something that you can quantify and contain in a nutshell; it is a fluid thing and is forever changing. It cannot be nailed down. Therefore, for the rest of human history, new and contradictory ideas about life, nature and philosophy will come forth. While it is good to understand things around us, it might become commonplace (due to the pace of change) to develop a highly adaptable personality. This personality might resemble someone who consistently looks for the positive side of things, rather than exhibiting a specific philosophy.

It is easy to see how our past civilizations became convinced of what our "truest" nature might be. Do we possess a survival based (the need to know) drive to explain our universe, or is there enough of the good stuff to go around? Is this part of the human success strategy?

If we were to just accept our existence, as it is, that is, not to name or try to define it, what would be the consequences?

The problem with definitions is that sooner or later definitions go out of date. Essentially a given definition "evolves" over time and is at best only a temporary concept. It goes without saying that the concept of masculinity must evolve too. Yet there are powerful forces that do not want masculine thought to change; for some the change would be too frightening and disturbing.

So who is it that attempts to explain the universe to us? Do you believe we are ruled by a fear (survival/nature) motive? By way of example, consider this: Who has not experienced fear while being taunted about some less than manly act? Would this not influence your behavior about stepping out of line as a man?

One of my favorite philosophers, J. Krishnamurti[169] who I have quoted before, has said about fear:

> "What do we mean by fear? Fear of what? There are various types of fear and we need not analyze every type. But we can see that fear comes into being when our comprehension of relationship is not complete. Relationship is not only between people but also between ourselves and nature, between ourselves and property, between ourselves and ideas; as long as that relationship is not fully understood, there must be fear. Life is relationship. To be is to be related and without relationship there is no life. Nothing can exist in isolation; so long as the mind is seeking isolation, there must be fear. Fear is not an abstraction; it exists only in relationship to something."

The fear of course for the breadwinner and protector male is the possibility that he will not be able to perform his job. He might be disabled, lose his job, be seen as an outcast or even blow his hard-earned cash on an impulsive act.

The concept of hell is associated with fear and has been associated with the Greek interpretation of "heavy" and "sinking" as well, whereas heaven is associated with rising and lightness, or no fear. So we have a world split in two: the heavens, God and the afterlife on one hand, the earth, humans and at the core, hell on the other hand. There is no way out of this duality because humans were seen as unable to obtain advanced or non-dualistic knowledge. Hence limited lives produced limited choices based on limited self-knowledge. This resulted in limited horizons, self-doubt and fear of events after death. A philosophy based on unity was simply not available to Europeans until the Enlightenment.[170]

I have to ask what I, as an individual, believe to be my potential arena of expansiveness. To that all I can say is that if I limit my freedom or my thoughts to convention I am doomed; in other words, I become a victim to my indoctrination. If my individual view is part of the dualistic nature described above, what kind of freedom[171] and equality is available to me in this apparently limited universe? To repeat, many philosophies suggest that the universe is limitless; that it is only our unwillingness to accept expansiveness that blinds us to new paradigms. If this definition is too "far out", how do you account for any dissatisfaction or restriction you may be experiencing? Can your worldview become more expansive and adventure-like?

Albert Einstein[172] taught us that the world is a network of relationships that evolve over time. Thus there is no absolute background (or base point) and the properties (you and me) are defined by our participation in this network of relations. Science too is defined by constant change. Charles Darwin's[173] contribution to this discussion was to understand that there is a process called natural selection leading to the birth of genuine novelty by creating networks of relationships that are increasingly structured and complex. Einstein emphasized the relational aspects of all properties described by science, while Darwin proposed that ultimately the law governing the evolution of everything else was natural selection. What this means is that nature is never static and in a constant state of change. There is no right way to be. The social sciences are also relational and undergoing constant change depending upon the participants in a group and the dynamics of behavior occurring in that environment. Energies will rise and fall, change, and reappear in new ways and in new behaviors as the group evolves. So not only will men have to adapt, they will also have to conclude that no point in any relationship or singular personality is permanent and unchangeable. While this appears to create anxiety for the survivor type, it actually reassures the rest of us that every day is new and so who really knows what is possible. Nothing is set in stone, for even the stone erodes and becomes something new.

Let's take a look at Aristotle[174] who during his lifetime from 384-322 BC promoted the orthodox view that the sun and stars obeyed separate laws from that of the earth and moon. He felt the sun and stars were of a different nature. This strongly held view was the orthodox view for many centuries. It held the opinion that the sun and stars were perfect and unchangeable, everything moved in regular circular patterns. The earth and moon were changeable and imperfect, even the comets were assumed to belong to our zone. Much later in 1610 ad Galileo[175] discovered sunspots with his telescope, and it was considered a heresy and a challenge to the orthodox view. He was promoting the idea that the sun was not perfect. Therefore Galileo could not have discovered sunspots, since it was argued that he was actually seeing an illusion created by the telescope. Guess who won that argument?

To challenge the view of the cosmos such as Galileo did was an attempt to move science forward and it was not welcomed at the time. I included this note for reflection on how present day society and its institutions might try to deny our attempts to develop scientific thought especially relating to men's issues or any endeavor that attempts to influence how we might view our personal affairs. We are required to think in this life; failing this we become the victims of mass delusion.

Would you say that denial plays any role in your life? How would you know if you are or are not thinking clearly? Some signs might be: blaming others for life's troubles, not being able to walk in someone else's shoes, or being quick to deny another's point of view. An Arab saying has it that: "While pointing a finger at someone else's behavior you are simultaneously pointing three back at yourself." The thumb represents truth somewhere in between. So denial can also be found in our relationship to power. Assuming that power is something we all share, or are there some who have more and the rest of us wanting at least some of it? Is this a source of denial? Is your masculine identity based on the creation of an us/them dualistic world?

I asked this question because I have blamed the world too. When I am feeling unworthy, it is often because I am comparing myself to others, not remembering my own values and perceptions of who I am.

Sir Francis Bacon, who lived from 1561 to 1626, comes next in our chronology of science. He wrote "The Great Instauration,"[176] A passage from this book states that the "Pillars of Hercules" (Gibraltar) were not the physical limits of human knowledge as they were thought to be and much was to be learned beyond them. For many centuries a limited Mediterranean centered worldview had held sway and Bacon was rocking the boat. Any kind of privileged arrogance, false pride or deception whether it is individual or institutional is misleading to followers or vulnerable people. A temptation for men is to seek a monopoly of knowledge or influence in order to subdue the fear of vulnerability as well as to fulfill a role. I suppose the thinking is "the more I control you the less you can control or influence me." This of course is the fear-based thinking discussed in Chapter One. After all, power and influence are attractive to us men and to the opposite sex as well. Men of true inner confidence understand the difference between self-confidence and a given position of authority or a "collection of knowledge" in human affairs.

If one can take a broader view of the world today, one would find that many natural-mechanical based ideologies have persisted and they tend to limit the expansiveness of their adherents. Even our own "gang" has its rules. Who is leader, clown, loudmouth or troublemaker are all roles the members live out, just as wolves do. Expansiveness is not intended to pave a path towards permissiveness; it is more the attitude of consideration of all sides of an issue rather than a fear-based or impulsive response to a given challenge in life. It is hoped that wiser choices will be made by expansive rather than by linear or "inside the box" thinking.

Many men and women alike were influenced by persons who had authority or held sway at a critical time in our lives, and they may have set unworkable limits. These influential figures could have established restrictions for some, be too permissive for others, or demand even exceptional expectations that can destroy a more normal development for a child. Is it possible that the minds of those who did this are the same kinds of people Sir Francis Bacon was speaking about? That is, people frightened by change or evolution in their daily lives. Their thinking (initiations) requires them to insist on mental strategies to alleviate their own fears by controlling those around them.

Are we then mistaken about lingering memories from our childhood or were we just difficult children? If not, why do we allow people like this to influence our thinking? Obviously the simple answer to this question is that we will learn eventually or not, and through experience we will have to sort it all out alone anyway. Why bother indulging in other people and their opinions of our lives? Yet we seek opinions from others to help us make up our minds but in the process we give influential people and our political leaders power without demanding fair representation; for example, 5% of the votes should get 5% of the seats in Parliament or at least it ought to. We ought to say thanks for the offered opinion from our leaders or elders and then retain the right to make up our own minds. But do we? And yet again public referendums of everything to do with government can make a shambles of due process with the electorate sometimes destroying good legislation out of revenge for another failure by the government. Life can be difficult.

Rene Descartes said: "[…] There is no difference between the machines built by artisans (the fabricators) and the diverse bodies that nature alone composes."[177] Here he describes the new Natural Mechanical Philosophy. i.e., that nature is a brilliant machine (like a clock.) We humans are included in this machine design as well. We become more and more like a machine, in factories, on farms and all varieties of manufacture. This is the path to the creation of great wealth and great differences in class as well. Men come to see that being able to function like a "well-oiled machine" would guarantee them wealth, recognition, beautiful women and power. Natural mechanical theories flourished in a highly tolerant environment and were easily understood and accepted by the masses. After all, material wealth was very attractive. It is clear that our biological drives have been directed into wanting these things, and to base our esteem on what we can buy. The masculine identity has many bricks in its wall.

Johannes Kepler,[178] in 1596 wrote: "[…] that the creator God was a mathematician; the Creator had employed the principles of geometry to lay out planetary distances." Kepler had discovered the orbits of the planets corresponded to precise geometric shapes, i.e., cube, tetrahedron etc. He then suggested that since the heavens are mathematical and predictable, humans were as well. He is here crediting science and mathematics in order to limit human capabilities, personal freedom and creativity. More brick wall building.

The scientific revolution climaxed with the publishing in 1687 of Isaac Newton's "The Mathematical Principles of Natural Philosophy."[179] In it mathematics and natural mechanical theory were blended together to create a new definition of natural philosophy. As a result English "moderns" contrasted themselves with "ancients" by referring to the latter's written texts as "[   ] little more than a testament to human capacity for delusion and . . . gullibility."[180] The "ancients" were those that chose to believe in a non-mechanical philosophical approach towards life, such as the Druids, Celts and the ancient Scot and Irish cultures who lived a more earth and nature-based non-mechanical philosophy. Ritual and myth ruled the early peoples of Great Britain until the scientific revolution replaced these long held beliefs with "rationality."

So the separation of feeling and the intellect grew wider. This is not to say that many ancient superstitions and sexist statements such as "old wives tales" were not of questionable origin. However the effect of Newton's philosophy, and other forces such as our bio-cultural drives to provide and to protect taught people and especially men, to completely suppress emotion for fear it would overrun the faculties and thereby prevent them from carrying out their familial (scientific) duties. As a result we see the domination of earlier cultures and the loss to contemporary society of the inheritance from them. Not only does this include the Druids and the Celts but the nomadic peoples of Europe and Russia as well. This is nothing new. Throughout history conquering cultures dominated and suppressed beliefs, modes of living and traditions. Many absorbed and changed the meaning of popular myths or superstitions. For example, the Christian Church changed the horned god of wine and pleasure named "Pan"[181] into the devil. Could our fear of expressing emotion come from the fear of being overrun or of being somehow absorbed and diminished by expression of them? Is emotion devil's work? It appears this new scientific rationality is meant to save us from this danger we have been taught all of our lives. Yet the Church and science do nothing to remove this danger; in fact they rebrand it with The Book of Nature and natural philosophy[182]further suppressing emotion and making it even harder to understand our lives.

The Book of Nature[183] (also discussed earlier) as another of the "proofs" of our "true" human nature refers to the natural world as an unfolding tale of life, created by God, as "His Creation" or "Eden." It was considered God's other "Book" after the Holy Scriptures. Through this knowledge of nature, right belief and right behavior would follow. We are then to follow the Book of Nature and pattern our own lives after the models found there. Yet is this an accurate theory? To people of faith it does not matter. It was written by God therefore, it must be true. The theory suggests that "most" female members of various species spend a greater proportion of parenting time with their young, meaning that humans must follow this model too. It is obvious that this does not always apply in every situation. Among the Emperor Penguins of Antarctica, the father maintains the nest while the mother feeds. Even nature is inconsistent, yet that difference does not stop us from attempting to create theories based on inconclusive data. I suppose the author of the Book of Nature had not encountered Emperor Penguins at that time the book was "discovered." Other inconsistencies must have existed as well.

One of the best methods of discovering your truth in any complex matter is by basing your results on empirical evidence.[184] The view that proper knowledge is and ought to be derived from direct sense experience provides real learning. By looking back through the evidence for "right" living, it is amazing what can be construed as evidence. Any answer we wish can be created for whatever reason we desire. Does this mean we learn best on our own or through a more knowledgeable person or institution?

A notable quote on the topic: "When systems of institutional control are working without significant challenge, the authority of the knowledge embodied in the institutions seems similarly potent."[185] In other words fancy books or impressive buildings or uniforms may lack real knowledge but appear knowledgeable and reliable. So if institutions are not challenged repeatedly by the citizenry to maintain accountability their influence will remain as a mighty big shadow[186] in any given civilization.

But are you a rock, as Ptolemy suggested?

As science became ever more popular, as Steven Shapin informs us: "More and more gentlemen became avid consumers of a reformed body of knowledge," and "Writers close to the heart of European courts began to publicly urge the reform of learning, not just to suit it for the active lives of civic gentlemen but also to make learning a more effective arm of state power."[187] What for I ask? "Authoritarian states reckoned that matters of belief and its profession were their legitimate concerns. Individualism in belief appeared (as) . . . an object of anxiety. It was taken as a responsibility of the state, and the state church, to monitor and to manage belief in general."[188] Along with the growing interference of the state in personal affairs came "The New Atlantis"[189]—Sir Francis Bacon's plan for state power in 1627. In his book Bacon created a fictional state called "Bensalem" where all citizens were state officials doing research. The purpose of the research was for two ends. First was the development of "Natural Philosophy" or the study of (natural) causes discussed earlier. This is similar to the natural mechanical philosophy from writers such as Robert Hooke and Robert Boyle. The second area of study was the enlargement of power and therefore state influence in the Human Empire.

Bacon believed anyone who controlled natural philosophy controlled the world. From this book and other influential thinkers "[…] the codes regulating the civil conversation of early modern gentlemen warned against the intrusion of potentially divisive and disruptive topics. (This included) Ad hominem speech and politics, theology and metaphysics […]"[190] The Royal Society of London prohibited discussion of politics or religion. They were supposed to be focusing instead on this new mechanical philosophy (the human body as a machine). Bacon felt that "natural philosophy is after the word of God at once the surest medicine against superstition, and the most approved nourishment for faith, and therefore she is rightly given to religion as her most faithful handmaid."[191] This refers to science as religion's handmaid, or "right-hand man." Science and religion then begin to work together to collect the minds and souls of humanity. This is strikingly similar to Max Weber's later claim of capitalists and the Church during the Industrial Revolution being in cahoots to again hornswaggle the citizenry. Bacon later wrote in "The Great Instauration": "Humanity had through the fall from grace in the Garden of Eden, lost its original technological control over nature."[192] And, "some practitioners […] (believed, from The Book of Daniel) only when humanity had by its own efforts restored its original dominion over nature would Christ come again to rule the Earth for a millennium."[193] This is still quite a common belief among modern Christians. On one hand they fear it and on the other they recommend it as a final script. So is this then the real goal of modern Christians? To dominate nature so that Christ would return for a thousand-year reign and bring with him the promised paradise? I suppose that if the domination of nature brought enough wealth with it and if there was any habitable land left after this huge job was complete, it might seem like the biblical paradise. It strikes me as odd that mainstream religions do not support environmental reforms more than they do. After all it would be in their long-term best interest to do so. A clean place for this paradise to exist would seem to be expedient. Quite honestly, the domination of nature is a messy business at best. The destruction of nature is more in line with modern actions and modern churches than we might like to believe. How does the church rationalize this destruction? They appear mostly silent or ambivalent. Modern prayer gives thanks to God for the food on the table, but not to the fish that gave its life so we could eat. Therefore science becomes more justified to restore humanity's dominion over nature, and our own human nature, by extension. Feelings become stifled, sensitivities become muted, ethics become subjugated to reason, or worse to the glory of God and the supposed return of Christ. With a purpose like this, who cares that some Amazon tribe would like to be left alone? Progress is unstoppable—and as missionaries will so easily say, we really are here to help.

In addition, Descartes wrote: "We should not be so arrogant as to suppose that we can share in God's plans."[194] So we are not to ever question authority and especially science and religion. However our success in understanding nature has generated deep problems for understanding our place in it and indeed, for understanding human nature, partly because we have accepted the dualistic hierarchy developed by science and religion about nature. Eckhart Tolle, a very popular philosopher, suggests that you can hardly ever find the extremes of black and white in the world, sweet and sour and so on. Most of reality is shades that lie in between. Almost nothing is totally soft or totally hard, for instance. He asks: "How would you even define such polarities? No, duality has to do with not seeing the actual *wholeness of everything*—not recognizing that all is an expression of infinite *being*."[195] Essentially we are limited only by our understanding. As Krishnamurti suggests, it is about our relationship to the subject. Relationship is key.

So if science,[196] Descartes asked. "fails to report objectively on the world—it fails to be science—(That is) if it allows considerations of value, morality, or politics to intrude into the process of making and validating knowledge. When science is being done society is kept at bay . . . How else could properly scientific knowledge be produced?" With so many areas available to study, how is science directed? It would appear it is directed by the powers that be and the frame of reference at the time the study is being carried out. Hence science evolves too, and often has a heavy bias of some kind.

Charles Darwin[197]'s writings were also used to bolster the idea that those who won the race of survival were superior. This race of course could be anything, including the race against nature, the fastest submarine, or everyone else. Yet evolutionary scientists[198] eventually debunked the Social Darwinists' former grand ideals by saying he who co-operates will often survive far better. Maybe the day of the isolated loner who slays dragons for the helpless maiden is finally over. "It might be said that the success of natural science, (science without political interference) and especially its capacity to generate consensus, has been secured at the cost of separating itself from a practice[...]called philosophy and in particular the philosophy of knowledge."[199] In other words, how do you know that you know something, and is it worth knowing?

And finally there is a paradox:[200] "the more a (or any) body of knowledge is understood to be objective and disinterested, the more valuable it is as a tool in moral and political action."[201] Moreover these "scientific" observations could be used as justification for moral and religious values; it could also be concluded that a spiritual deity is male and not female or is asexual instead. Anything could be said to be true, even that thunder is God's anger. How do we sort out our own naïveté from what is true? It would appear that reality is more like the layering of an onion, that there will always be greater and lesser things.

Steven Shapin who wrote this chronology of the scientific revolution is hopeful "science" and "society" can be more supportive of each other. He said: "Science remains . . . the most respected component of our modern culture."[202] It just needs a little . . . clarification?

This analysis of the events referred to as the Scientific Revolution is an exploration of the impact of early discoveries one might call anthrodeterminism or the determining of the characteristics of humans based on science or the natural and wild conditions in which humans have been found and thus make predictions on their behavior. Can an animal be separated from its geographical location and still live like an animal? Of course not, at least not in totality. But for an intelligent and creative species such as humanity, it is hard to know precisely what our natural location is. Humans are probably not content to remain within constraints of any kind for very long, especially geographic ones. Short of death, humans are capable of a pace of change in multiple paradigms at a time, as the future will prove to be true. We are just beginning to free ourselves of the limitations of fear, such as the fears of others, and the institutionalized fear inherent in our societies by having the courage to ask our own questions and be capable to act upon our own answers, for ourselves, alone. Who is it, in the end that will lose out if you do not follow your own true heart?

I remember while growing up in Vancouver BC and attending church, there was always a philosophy of support for the downtrodden. However it was never suggested to challenge nature-based power structures in any way. In fact it was discouraged. My own mother became a tragic victim of public/medical ignorance and religious indifference. Through the "compassionate" efforts of psychiatry, she was electro-shocked and drugged until her nervous system was so completely destroyed that her life was unlivable. Our church slowly turned its back on my family. Probably her tragic suicide was wasted on "science" at the time. Yet I will admit treatments for the mentally ill have improved dramatically since then. Why should that be? Where do these improvements come from and why should it take so long and at such great cost? One gags at the lack of hindsight.

I heard no real answers for my personal questions from the Church, just different hierarchies with allegiance to "something" being the most important condition to follow. Even so it must be restated, probably again and again, that this hierarchical framework that I have so critically attacked deserves a round of ovation for creating the wealth and security we all enjoy and through that wealth enabling it to develop these new treatments. And yet, the cost, what a cost, my own Mother, a guinea pig, and in some ways, so are we all.

Granted a new paradigm is emerging: a lessening of the provider/protector role required by hierarchical structures to guarantee the survival of a people not yet ready for egalitarian democracy. We shall see if we are truly ready to create a new community-oriented society. The challenges are immense. As computers and the global economic system become more widespread, individualism will continue to be a preferred choice. We must give acknowledgment to the creators of wealth where it is due. An exploration of the source of that wealth and how it has been created is essential for men to gain insight into the making of new choices for the future. Yet due to the existence of domination and subordination hierarchies though, it may seem irrelevant to some to discuss the advantages of the market system and the ownership of private property because they appear to be part of the established hierarchical system, and therefore should be condemned. Regardless and while I agree to a certain degree, let's explore it to be sure we understand.

Today many trade laws, human and child labor regulations and government or environmental laws must be known and followed. With all this regulation great wealth can still be created and maintained by finding ways around regulations or in a more positive way, by working within these laws and guidelines. The current method around regulation is to manufacture products in countries where regulatory bodies are weak or do not exist. It is then a simple matter of shipment to the more regulated markets to sell the item. Very little information is available to consumers in regulated countries about how these goods are made and the consequences to host cultures or their environments. For example, in the manufacture of your gold ring, the mercury used in its purification might lead one to ask if the mercury was recycled or dumped into the environment after its use. Today, we know mercury to be one of the most toxic metals to our health. It is unlikely you were told this when you bought anything made of gold. Packaged foods are finally in the process of listing dietary benefits and liabilities, although they can still be greatly improved. Genetically modified foods are still not on labels and that is a real concern.

What is the solution? More education to business executives, better laws or a global organization focusing on quality of life and our health, and stronger regulation in how businesses are run. This is possibly something the United Nations could oversee, while encouraging governments to write better operating guidelines for corporations operating in their countries. Personal awareness, as in consumer purchasing power, is the final and only real challenge to corporate decisions and government authority. One cannot expect to change hierarchy from its dominating and subordinating traits in a few decades. This will take a few hundred years to accomplish; yet the forward thinking mind must continue to find improvements to the traditional wealth creation paradigm. These thoughtful individuals have been actively grinding away at hierarchical structures already from before the Greeks developed their great civilization. I believe we are already doing what needs to be done, although in a limited fashion. Corporations may not feel the same. In fact they may feel that government plays too big a role in their affairs. Some individuals who sell controlled items such as handguns or easily made street drugs should also feel closely watched. In the late 1960's for example, LSD was readily available on the street and although it was not illegal, selling it was. Now it is a controlled substance as are many others due to the dangers inherent in using them, and education in schools (in Canada) now discuss drugs. Further decriminalization is required here to bring all illegal activity into the light of day for people to consider the choice on their own.

As I think of some of the tremendous wealth creators I have met, I do not envy their non-stop work ethic. From "Haves Without Have Nots" James O'toole[203] quotes a Hungarian entrepreneur: "Under the (former) Soviet system, no one gets rich. To us, that is stupid. Under American capitalism, some got very rich, but others remain very poor. We don't think that is fair, but in Finland and Sweden, everybody gets rich. Now to Eastern Europeans, that sounds smart and fair!"

However we are still responding to manipulations by advertising and its development of consumer "needs" into products for sale. So where are we going here? There are real needs for some consumer products like toothpaste and soap etc. My point is that it appears that too much emphasis is placed on economic production and the generation of markets and their products as the only ways to improve democracy or, excuse me, create wealth! I am confusing spending with freedom rather than living as a reflection of freedom. How much of this need for spending and the prestige that comes with it are derived from our masculine history of the spending of our hard earned surplus? This deeply held belief or mythology demands a man work hard all of his life. If women no longer need to be provided for, or protected, what would be the purpose of all this male ambition? Would it be to work independently or as part of a team to produce collective wealth along side women? Maybe. Or worse, maybe we will develop a downward spiral into narcissistic greed and competition as many contemporary science-fiction movies portray our fate in the future. Men will have to rethink their reasons for working. It might be as big a re-think as adjusting to the agricultural revolution was in its time. Working half-time may become common with personal interests, exercise and friendships taking up the majority of a man's day. Possibly men will take on the mantle of stewardship of the environment. As well, women tempted by the same lures and similar pressures as men before them will discover the hidden costs of wealth creation.

Canadian writer L. Susan Brown quoting Betty Friedan[204] in her powerful book "The Politics of Individualism" suggests "modern liberal feminists see the liberation of women both as a problem of self-determination and as a matter of women taking their rightful place beside men in the competitive labor market." However women will not have the same pressures as men who cannot quit without social ostracization, unless of course they can retire. They will still experience powerful pressures, especially as the cost of living fluctuates up and down and worries about identity surface. Presently with two working parents most families still struggle to make ends meet. Women are no doubt finding that the competitive market place does not enhance self-determination as much as they might have liked but actually limits it in favor of market forces; the same ones men have faced for centuries. The imaginary freedom of the marketplace is replaced by "wage slavery." And in a sense, we prostitute ourselves by the selling of our labor. We unintentionally recreate a relationship of domination and subordination. Really, wasn't feminism supposed to "free" women? In fact, the freedom women have gained might just be the oppression men need to quit. In truth, this is impossible but men can relax somewhat more than prior to 1920 when the female vote was finally legalized and women took a stronger role in civil society.

So what is freedom?

Again we do the long loop back to the original thesis of this writing. We place individualism and the individualistic lifestyle ahead of an individuated one by choosing to live as isolated units with our own thoughts, in our small little world, struggling to get to the top, just as The Book of Nature wanted. We unknowingly think the same thoughts and have similar aspirations to the same goals of wealth and accomplishment as almost everyone else. In the end we are not individuals at all, just a manufactured customer with an insatiable need for the products of a manipulated market.

So you tell me, what is freedom?

On the other hand, people who have considered individuation over market individualism find many of the market lures unappealing for the simple reason that they are designed with the sole purpose of enhancing market individualists in their collective war with everyone else. Some people actually want to find common needs based on quality of life rather than the created comforts appealing to market individualists. Still we all need a certain level of wealth for health, learning, developing friendships and deeper relationships or having children.

Another way to look at individuation might be the ability to recognize one's responsibility to create a free society however you may define it, and the commitment to live it out. A small example might be suggested by a family outing. Along the way everyone stoops to pickup some litter and take it home. A large example might be the executive who reduces his/ her salary to purchase some needed safety equipment for at risk workers, or start a profit sharing program for employees, or teach employees how to run the company. Another would include twenty families purchasing recreational property where everyone gets two weeks per year. These are examples of community-oriented thinking.

I place so much importance on this community concept because I believe many of us have gone down the market individualist path and need to stop and take a look at a bigger picture. It is becoming clear to me that this error in thinking is caused by basing our quality of life on the consumption model rather than a human one. Economic models must have come about as a result of various kinds of oppression such as poverty, religious persecution, slavery or war. In the act of escaping the oppression experienced elsewhere we unconsciously recreate it in wage slavery and addiction to the latest consumer products in order to protect ourselves from our painful memories. Could it be said that Post Traumatic Stress Syndrome[205] has found a home in all our market individualists, and you just have to say "Ouch." These economic "heroes" are waging a never-ending battle with isolation as their belief system struggles against poverty or perceived powerlessness as if these realities were theirs alone. The need for friendship and intimacy is felt as a deep unmet need, never acknowledged or addressed. Sometimes we forget to ask if we are satiated. Would we even know how to answer the question?

So as men we are now beginning to see the consequences to our health. We are learning that we have choices to make and some are taking the brave step to walk away from the individualist lifestyle. There are few at this point but the current is becoming more visible, as some men tire of ladder climbing and take a less stressful position or decide to spend more time at home with their children.

It is difficult to know what freedom is. How would we know a freer society if we were looking for one? After all, humans have for centuries been forced to live under intense colonization or economic slavery whether it is totalitarian fascism or manipulation by consumer advertising. We don't know who we are apart from what we should buy and how to get it. The West is so-called free; yet we are inundated daily by market advertising that attempts to define us and run our lives. We say it is our choice, but they are the choices that the economic establishment wishes us to see. The resulting list is called freedom of choice. Our daily lives seem to reflect hierarchical structures established in early farming cultures that set individuals apart from the general population. We all seek that same public prominence and markets seek to satisfy that urge. In reality we are all members of the general population yet somehow we seek to be more. The societal expression of these phenomena is class politics, where class is descriptive of your character. A higher class is preferred to a lower one that reflects an underdog status.

In the area of ownership, Brown suggests (which can be included in the discussion of freedom[206]), competition between self-interested owners of real property (real estate) and property in the person[207] (our bodies, as capital or labor value) can never result in the freedom of all because it inevitably results in relations of domination by the owners of real property and subordination of those who only own their human bodies. This confrontation is the direct result of the fear-based and market driven urge for separation from others and falls into the arena of the old surplus management based masculine role. The clash of our bodies versus capital continues and we refuse to let go. Many individuals refuse to detach themselves from the corporate umbilical cord and try something truly self-actualizing. Their fear of failure or of change keeps them trapped forever as subordinates of others, and not as our real potential suggests we could be. Surplus strategies were essential to the development of wealth and with that surplus we can re-think it as community wealth instead of corporate wealth, which one could say is what taxation really is. It is made available to the community through the examples of Health, Education, and Infrastructure spending by governments, donations by individuals and organizations to worthy causes. We must remember that it took many centuries to force the powerful Instrumental interests to think in an entirely new way-that they have responsibilities, and that they will not be allowed to think only of their own self-interest.[208] It is a balancing act played out over centuries and must be maintained by the average citizen. Unions have been largely responsible for this vigilance, and paid the price for this to occur.

As Jean Jacques Rousseau[209] suggested in his First and Second Discourses, our first property was our body and as we lived in a primitive state of hunter-gathering we were happy and free, yet as soon as one of us saw the advantage of having provisions for two, or a surplus, equality disappeared,[210] property in land was introduced and labor became necessary. I have spoken about this before regarding the role of agriculture and it begs restating here. As Soren Kierkegaard[211] has said "a singularity versus a life in the universal" suggests as soon as a surplus was created we were caste out of Eden, we became a singularity no longer fighting nature but each other. When an individual asserts himself in the singularity, he sins, and only by acknowledging this can he be reconciled again with the universal. Another way of seeing this might be when we think of ourselves first, we sin and only by reconnecting with community can we be healed. Again I refer to Hobbes on this idea too.

Through seeing the advantages of a surplus or it could be considered a hoard, men became filled with a consuming ambition to place themselves above one another where they often came to harm. Competition and rivalry, the opposition of interests, and the desire to profit at the expense of others are the evils of property. Yet the resulting inequality led to an awareness of suffering which spurred the development of the Democratic movement leading to attempts to confront the contemporary views of the evils of Man. The Church cast doubt on all Human activities yet democratic reformers believed in the goodness of Man and set about to prove it.

Our imagery is of some perfect lifestyle free of the stresses of contemporary life and peace of mind. We cannot know, really. It does seem the Church is suggesting we return voluntarily to a hunter-gatherer society in this life. Is this true? Why wait for Christ to return? How many of us could do this? The back to the land movement of the "Sixties" seemed to be listening to this unusual message. The only way for this to actually occur the world over would be for millions to die.

In Western industrial nations, markets for new goods and services are often created by advertising agencies for the manufacturer. Consumer preference determines which kind of bikini or sports car is successful. Women did not decide to wear bikinis since they were sold on them as the modern relaxed thing to do. It also makes some women very attractive to men. Is there a possible link here? Nah! Who would stoop to sell sex? In the 1990's men's skimpy bathing suits were becoming a precursor to the objectification of their bodies too. Many manufacturers might say that women's bodies were objectified, so why not men's. Some consumer choice! So who are we apart from what we buy? Do we vote in order to buy more?

Even under ideal conditions, where wild capitalism is controlled and the economy achieves a certain self-regulation, markets have a limited capacity to generate what a society needs. One such need is readily available public education that is non-dogmatic. Yet markets could never create non-dogmatic education, as markets would adapt education to serve its needs, and markets need educated persons in order to operate. However markets have their own motives and they are not to educate you, but to sell you and its products. Ideal conditions only mean that sellers and buyers interact in accord with prices whose fluctuating levels keep goods, consumers, and laborers interacting productively. At best, this only secures maximum economic efficiency in producing and distributing hard (durable) goods. Nothing else. Advocates of laissez-faire or "savage capitalism," a term coined by Solzhenitsyn,[212] claim that they have achieved far more, especially for the successful, and therein lays the problem. In "Jihad vs Mcworld", Benjamin R. Barber states: "In the international economy, for here sovereignty vanishes and aggressive transnational bodies pursue market strategies in the absence of any countervailing regulatory bodies whatsoever."[123] Real freedom is undermined, as we become the addicted customers of the multinationals. Any cultural components that do not make money are tossed out and forgotten, so who are we without our culture? We have been reduced to a culture of shoppers.

Robert Kuttner, the author of "The End of Laissez-Faire", thinks that although "global intelligentsia may think of itself as stateless, and global capital may see nation-states as anachronistic encumbrances [ ] the state remains the locus of the polity" that "[ ] remains the structure best suited[214] for counterbalancing the excesses of the market." Far more today than in the nineteenth century, the workers of the world need to unite to offset the exploitative consequences of monopoly capital on a global scale. Yet never has there been less likelihood that they could do so. Is anyone awake or are we all paying off credit cards?

We're too busy working so we can go shopping.

In conclusion, science and markets work together to provide the material or intellectual comforts we crave. Long ago none of these were provided and life was harsh. We kept working and struggling and fighting to create the products and wealth so we could be happier. Really that is what a market economy is all about. If we were to take away all the labor saving devices and the comfort inventions and the books, what would be left? Well, our culture or what remains of it. People might start helping each other again, yet human cleverness to make things simpler and more comfortable would just reassert itself and the process would start all over again. So this is in reality, a paradigm that seems unchangeable, but not entirely non-adaptable. People want the fancy things, yet the environmental movement is one example where rampant consumerism and waste is being redirected in a positive way. The environmental movement shows that we have the power to influence our cleverness and guide what it does so it does not run us. It may seem like a constant but necessary battle. The path here is clear. We must continue to help each other, encourage environmental products instead of more wasteful and dangerous ones in order to safeguard our health, wellbeing and the planet itself.

Freedom is the tool that allows us to do this job. It gives us the clarity of mind to think things through, to plan and organize ourselves as well as others in order to create change. Maintain your freedom because the danger of corporations disregarding our most treasured cultural inheritances will not occur if consumers consistently place a high level of expectations on them. If corporations wish to stay in business, they will be forced to make the products demanded of them by an informed population. After all we are the ones who buy all that stuff. We really are our own worst enemy here. Corporations only respond to requests from consumers or to demands the corporations have managed to create in us. The struggle between nature-based ideologies and people based and evolving ones is a long battle that plays out in our fears. So we have to stand up and make a choice.

CHAPTER THREE

The Third Foundation:
Objectivity = Survival of a Kind

In chapter two we were discussing making a choice, so how do we actually do this, this making of choices?

Firstly we need to return to our initiation discussion again and remember how powerful they are in shaping our thoughts and future actions. We have been taught to think primarily about achievement in individualistic goals for consumer acquisitions. Note that the vast majority of real improvements in our civilization have not come from these acquisitions but from altruistic ambition instead—people who sacrificed to improve the lives of others, sometimes at the cost of their own lives. In the previous chapter we looked at the creation of the consumer society. Here we will look at the creation of how change occurs. We need to take a look at how altruistic actions are created and why they are so important for any future we might wish to imagine.

Susan L. Brown's book on individualism defines two significant poles of identity.[215] Although she does not intend to focus on males, her analysis does fit the call. She defines two items "existential" and "instrumental" individualism. Existential individualism is characterized by freedom as an essential end or driving purpose in itself. It depends on social respect and co-operation; it follows that all must be free if one is to be free. Freedom is inherently valuable in and of itself.

The opposite pole, instrumental individualism, views freedom as a means to achieve individual interests. Freedom is not valued as a desirable end in and of itself, but rather as a means by which to justify competitive self-interest or the nature-based hierarchies we discussed in Chapter Two. Seeing freedom merely as a means for individual self-promotion destroys any possibility of ever achieving real freedom as an end in and of itself. Instead it leads to relationships of domination and subordination, which then levels an attack upon the existentialist commitment to self-determination and deters any possibility of genuine liberation in a given culture. An analogy could be seen in comparing non-profit societies with corporate business models where the corporate model of ownership of land, minerals and capital leads to further social stratification, and gives a distinct advantage to some citizens over the average. While instrumental individualism needs existential individualism in order to come into being through establishing democratic institutions, instrumentalist behavior ultimately annihilates existentialist ideas because freedom for one or the few (wealth and power) can only occur with the subordination of everyone else. Instrumentalist individualism proposes a siege mentality as found in gated communities and promotes this lifestyle as a kind of freedom for only privileged members of certain classes. In reality all are limited by instrumentalist individualism because class structure enslaves everyone. None are free since it is only another misunderstanding of freedom. True freedom has no leaders or advocates or specific locations; it is something you carry inside your very soul.

An important component of this intellectual conflict is recognizing the consequences of knowing that instrumentalist individualism has its roots in Bacon's natural mechanical views on nature. He attempted to spell out clearly what constitutes the bounds of human nature based on The Book of Nature suggesting human behavior should follow a natural example. Existentialist individualism points the way to what constitutes human freedom and how that freedom can be expanded. Clearly a different kind of agenda unknown in nature or biblical writings is expressed here and is precisely what is desired in existential thought. After all, as Friedrich Schiller states: "it is only through beauty that man makes his way to freedom"[216] and so we can realize our noblest destiny. Eden could be this "beauty" or similar projections such as democratic ideals, or a religious experience or a compassionate society. This is a significant departure from more conservative views about our inherent nature supposedly based on competition for scarce resources and the survival of the fittest. The more optimistic existentialist view even suggests a way forward for a new masculine mythology based on generativity and stewardship.

To conclude, the existentialist view of the cosmos would suggest a less hierarchical orientation and more value could be placed on the experience of the culture as a whole rather than on the experienced and accomplished among us. The effect is a society that values individual effort without unfair status. Now without sounding like too much of a left-winger, I want to add to the earlier discussion about heroes that our fascination with them is a serious pitfall in our hierarchical society and continues to add to our own experience of oppression and powerlessness, even though we can learn from their examples. Heroes are made by an overwhelming agreement within a given culture to raise up exemplary behavior to others less accomplished. We are not honoring the teacher within the "junior" to know what is best or what is right from his or her own sphere of "genius." I have heard that we are all geniuses and what we lack is the opportunity to develop it. Leadership has its place, but too much focus on the hero removes the value of the follower, creating a judgment of inferiority and therefore a loss of initiation towards better outcomes. An obligation of the leader is to get out of the way and lead by encouraging exploration and new ideas that will only come from the hearts and minds of the young or the inexperienced.

By way of an example, I just happened to come across an article in the Globe and Mail about a major clash between environmentalists and clear-cut logging practices during the 1990 Clayoquot Sound[217] protests in British Columbia. A subsequent search of the web found more on this topic. In late 1997, MacMillan Bloedel's new CEO, Tom Stephans, invited leaders of the most critical environmental groups to his home to discuss their concerns about clear-cutting. He was convinced that MacMillan Bloedel needed to change the way that it operated in order to reclaim its "social capital" in B.C. Nine months later the company announced it was phasing out clear-cutting in favor of more sustainable harvesting. From that beginning the company became a leader in sustainable forestry practices and completely stopped logging old growth forests. The Globe and Mail article[218] passed on the fact Tom Stephans discovered the company had made more money doing business this way than using the old clear-cut methods. Here is a way for leaders to get out of the way metaphorically by listening to feedback from the public on company practices. It was clearly a win/win for both sides. Mining and oil sands companies and other forestry companies are now contacting Stephans seeking advice on how to deal with environmentalists in their sphere.

When we have to deal with power and authority issues, Robert Paul Wolff, the author of "In Defense of Anarchism" felt that authority is the right (or the earned right) to command as well as the right to be obeyed. It must be distinguished from power, which is the ability to compel compliance, either through the use of or the threat of force.[219] The article on Clayoquot shows that power and authority were intentionally put aside in favor of reconciliation and community building. MacMillan Bloedel's CEO used his authority to enable changes in his logging company operations; by the same token, he may have helped to alter oil and mining companies' view of public criticism of their businesses. Many civil confrontations in the past would have been met with armed resistance from police or worse, the army. We now have a model for the way forward. I recall many job sites where the employer had not earned the right with me to use authority so he used force or the fear of what he could do to me as motivation. One day I even had an employer kick me in the behind because he felt I was going too slowly. It taught me how to go faster but it was not on his earned authority.

In comparison, another employer came out of his office and into the warehouse where he would often talk with me about life, his hobbies and relationships. I became fond of him and respected him as a person. I wanted to work hard. Of course, the other employees felt I was getting away with something and would pick on me. Their jealousy became too much once (as I mentioned in the Preface) and I told them all to f—off! It seemed to work since they left me alone after that. Isn't it odd how even the employees preferred the classic class separation of labor and management to an egalitarian relationship? To me it was the way I liked to work and why should I not be a friend with my employer? Many other companies would probably disagree. They believe it is better to maintain a separation so that the lines are clear. This belief stems from the fear that a subordinate will take advantage of the relationship and be less productive. This brings to mind the idea that class separation is more about keeping the experience of authority to the upper classes in order to maintain a level of unconsciousness in the general population. Keeping the average citizen ignorant of how the other half lives is key to disempowerment, as employees that have no access to management experience will grumble about their bosses without having the slightest idea of how their bosses live. The resentment stalls the interest of workers to learn about management and they remain disempowered.

One could say that there is a separation between mentor and apprentice but does there need to be a class distinction? I think not, so why maintain the difference in the work place? Other institutions such as the military, police forces even doctors and nurses maintain a divided work place. Not much growth here. Without growth there is no responsibility or innovation.

Now we come to a term often misunderstood and feared by contemporary society, and that is anarchy. Anarchy[220] and existential individualism are very similar concepts. Both hold personal freedom and self-actualization among the highest of goals. Anarchy has become associated with violent protest and a skimpy political platform. Many protesters who call themselves anarchists are actually quite violent. As well, the picture it presents to the average citizen can be very unappealing. To the educated masses in the West, violence rarely attracts much support unless the state is involved or if it is meant as an entertainment. Examples include Iraq, Panama, The World Trade Center or legalized and glorified violence such as some sporting events or police chases and finally, the violence seen in many comedies. We love to watch these things. Whereas true and responsible anarchy is a culture based on mutual respect and an equal dose of self and societal responsibility. It is not about the overthrowing of anything. It has been confused with fascism or chaos, of which fascism is a brutal form of revenge for the atrocities of a ruling elite or the social deconstruction favored by the Nazis. Chaos is the removal of any and all systems of civility leaving all citizens in danger. If we seek revenge, we create the desire for revenge in our enemy, and chaos creates a power vacuum. People cannot function guided by such ideas as fascism. We are left always at war, never at peace. Is this how we make our lives better? Anarchy is a genuine attempt to give individuals equal power and genuine respect in all civic duties. In modern times though, the term, anarchy has also been pointlessly used by protestors calling themselves anarchists. In the end the fearful public reaction they get helps no one. It just drives a wedge between the worthy cause and an uncertain public.

Our collective struggle throughout history has inched forward hopeful of peaceful resolution of conflict. We have moved from the chieftain to the king and then to democracy. Our level of maturity is still in question as we continue to resolve our problems with war making and denial of accountability for how the world's nations create hatred in other parts of the world. The World Trade Center attacks in New York produced only anger, sorrow and revenge. While appropriate for a while these actions must be replaced by the inner looking self-reflection of a mature person or nation. When will the war-mongering stop and the self-reflection begin?

Reading the local paper on September 10, 2002 a year after the fact, I was impressed by the idea that some American citizens[221] are saying that there are people in the rest of the world who may not agree with the

American way of life. A few of these speakers went so far as to suggest that Americans ought to try to understand these foreign views as counterpoint to their own. I think this is a very mature and important philosophy to undertake. It cannot be stated enough that it takes two to tango, and two to make peace. Is there something amiss if we attempt to seek out a root cause to terrorism? In a similar vein of thought, do we lash out when our partner makes a personal slight against you, or do you seek insight as to the root cause of the slight? Of course some people can be just plain mean and must be challenged or ignored, however we must consider the actions of others as meaningful and try to understand. After all this is what we want for ourselves, to be considered, appreciated and consulted where our interests lay. In finding common paths with others we work out our day-to-day problems and concerns.

Democracy in its least mature stage of development combines only a semblance of equality of persons. Governments are elected based on a system that grants power to whoever wins the most seats or ridings, rather than a fair percent of the vote through proportional representation. Never mind all the posturing and promises made on the podium. Citizens looking for role models find only the emphasis on winning and promoting one's own agenda instead of co-operative models that can provide healthier and more responsible examples of how leaders act and promote their policies. After all it is a shared world. If we seek fairness and consideration in our personal lives, our nations ought to reflect similar values too.

From his book, "In Defense of Anarchy", Wolff states the situation clearly. If we are autonomous citizens, we cannot in good conscience agree with some policies and laws made in our name without our agreement or consultation. Further, "On what grounds can it be claimed that I have an obligation to obey the laws which are made in my name by a man (a politician) who has no obligation to vote as I would, who indeed has no effective way of discovering what my preferences are on the measures before him?"[222] In addition, "If autonomy and authority are genuinely incompatible, only two courses are open to us. Either we must embrace philosophical anarchism and treat all governments as non-legitimate bodies whose commands must be judged and evaluated in each instance before they are obeyed; or else, we must give up as quixotic the pursuit of autonomy in the political realm and submit ourselves (by an implicit promise) to whatever form of government appears most just and beneficent at the moment."[223]

We have to face the fact that we are left with those two choices: either we become autonomous beings or we submit to a greater authority. It would seem that most of us have submitted to the authoritative model of culture that supports the market individualist view because it is deemed correct by the elites. Additionally we now have the right or the obligation depending on how you think of it to participate in the survivor/surplus paradigm with all its individualistic wealth and privilege and of course those shopping trips. What happens to those that do not wish to participate? Are they the homeless, the mentally ill, the drug addicted, the criminal? If it were true that humans are prepared and willing to move towards a more autonomous world-view then power-over others and the survivor paradigms would become less of a distraction. Individuals would cease to seek power in addition to their inherent skills and the value of each person would be honored as a gift. Some have learned this and hopefully more will; but it is not enough, it must be global to be effective.

The fear that erodes this process is the deep hurts and rejections of the past as reflected in the institutional, corporate and cultural taboos regarding trust, intimacy and cooperation. Being realistic, trust issues must be addressed one person at a time. What is often forgotten is the recognition of beauty in a simple device such as a trust exercise and how it could lead fearful but curious groups of individuals to a more open experience. If you have ever been in a circle of people where power, place and striving are missing and inclusion, cooperation and peace are present, you may be experiencing a trust exercise or a different type of democratic process. Imagine that the people or person that organized the event cannot be distinguished from anyone else, that there was no evident hierarchical structure and yet a task was before the group. Let's say all the participants had agreed to be neither a leader nor a follower for carrying out the task to completion. What is occurring here? Have you encountered this process before? You may doubt its possibilities but you now know what a trust exercise is from this experience. Through this understanding, you can take the next step to transform your daily life into valuable and intimate encounters by including trust-building processes in your relationships. Your children, love partners, employees, friends and strangers will also notice this about you. There will continue to be people that gravitate towards power and authority; for example people who have doctorates in a given subject and somehow believe this gives them complete authority to talk over everyone else present and will not be silenced. The common man has his view worthy of consideration too.

The educated can be useful in many applications, especially where only one person can make a contribution due to specialized knowledge. Here specialized knowledge is not the problem; the problem lies with this individual and his or her relationship with the non-specialized general public. Aboriginal societies in particular have struggled with academia to have their voices heard. If the general public feels confused or alienated, there is no relationship established. As Krishnamurti said, relationship is the key. True democratic processes are the best medium for relationships that humanity has created. In this light, some humans fight oppression because they have a different kind of nature. They seek relationship in a global sense. Possibly we have a multi-polar nature where anything goes, even fascism. It comes down to choice and what we want. So if we choose to improve society we will eventually employ trust building processes and other anti-authority means.

On their own, these techniques are ancient and yet are proven ways to democratize society. They were originally used to describe wealth-sharing processes among Aboriginal peoples. They may have been developed in order to find a way out of escalating conflict, restore peaceful co-existence within families or a given culture and to slowly take away power from the elite. As more and more wealth is developed and immense numbers of global citizens get to shop and learn about freedom-there is that comparison to shopping again! To be honest, shopping is one of the first activities to happen in our existing paradigm. It is a creator of great wealth and power for many people but again mainly for the elite. It has allowed the affluence of the Western middle classes but a fairly large segment of global society is still left out at the bottom. Volunteer dropouts of this system find survival on the fringes very difficult because most people have given over to whatever shopping philosophy is currently popular. This is a false trust building phenomena we believe will eventually produce a fair sharing of wealth. We forget the strings being pulled behind our backs by marketing specialists always looking for the next big thing.

One might say gambling is a form of shopping as is investment planning. What about the underground economy, are they relationship building or trust exercises? Shopping so you can shop more. Because we do not make the products ourselves we have lost the connection between the need for something and the satisfaction gained from actually making it. We have traded this satisfaction for money creation schemes so we can have more and more stuff. Most of us want this ability in our purchasing power yet a loss of satisfaction in western lives may be related to the isolated money schemes we create in order to be a consumer. Since the industrial revolution we have been told, taught and manipulated into this philosophy of life and sold a bill of goods. Men exhaust their lives in order to shop more. (Have a look at Warren Farrell's books for a lot more on this topic) This has been the male role if I must say it; the creation of wealth in order to shop.

Most western governments would prefer not to inculcate in the individual or the greater culture a strong desire for greater freedoms because men as surplus managers maintain hierarchy and power relationships that benefit the elite, as well as their communities to a lesser extent. However as governments or individuals appear to be occasionally autocratic, as the economic meltdowns in 2008, and again in 2010 have shown, the citizen may feel isolated from an upwardly spiraling ambiguity coming from government and other powerful institutions or individuals. It would appear democracy has failed to protect us. Of course this is seen as something for others to create, definitely not us, and definitely not something we would even aspire to, or is it?

Now when faced with ambiguity from government or a mind fettered with fear, a deep cynicism or nihilistic apathy can overtake the individual. By retreating into a corner, the person effectively evades responsibility for the success of his own life and may not survive. Because we are "unfinished beings"[224] there is a lot of room to make an ethics that truly reflects our own values and beliefs. Nothing is set; nothing is permanent. We often use the saying "That is the way life is, get with the program!" It is not so. A key message of this book is that nothing is fixed and that nature-based solutions attempt to fix life into a concrete cast that never changes. We ourselves make it fixed by assuming all the questions have been asked, and that we are foolish for thinking otherwise.

We continue to associate human potential with Bacon's nature-based model of culture that suggests that hierarchy and status are natural for humans. The consequence is that we are being trapped in an endless loop of the fear of others, fear of scarcity and fear of the unity with our basic reality—fear of life itself! We insist on confusing nature as defined by the biblical Book of Nature with the human development of democracy. We believe they are the same, yet they are very different. Democracy as we know it does not exist in nature; it is a totally human made reality. This yin-yang conflict of religion-based versus human-based philosophies will be with us forever and like the realization that even the most isolated individual has a contribution to make, there is value, even in this struggle.

Gradual public education about rights and responsibilities of living in a free society may eventually help. In the meantime we must work with all people to find the best solution possible. A possible compromise might start with an understanding of our fear. We can acknowledge that easily, yet actively dealing with it is something else again. Relying on Krishnamurti's quote on fear, we see clearly that fear is about relationship or rather a lack of one with the feared individual or situation, which in this situation is honesty with the public. Clearly relationship is the missing component here to help in the understanding of the issue. Mediation can be used to find many common solutions. To me this is a simple and appropriate way to resolve problems preferably before hand rather than as an after-thought. The moral is that we have to build relationships in order to prevent fear.

A couple of examples may help to illuminate where I believe we are headed as a species. We seem to be creating over time a decentralized and self-regulating society consisting of a federation of voluntary associations of free and equal individuals. The current mania about terrorism is a real danger to this development and could actually reverse human cultural evolution. We see examples of this in current films such as the Terminator series where the world as we know it, has been destroyed in a battle between technology and people. The robots won and humanity is struggling to survive as an underground resistance movement. The danger here is that we will decide to believe only continued public scrutiny and surveillance will protect us. As Krishnamurti wrote, it is relationship in the end that life depends upon and without relationship there is nothing. So what kind of relationship do we want? There are two choices: one of control and manipulation to secure our needs, the other of mutual support and cooperation. We seem to be leaning more towards the former. We now know that some people do not like what the west has done in the world and they are angry. So we respond by shutting down the lines of communication and making it harder to cooperate. The male protector raises his shield and out comes the sword. However dark the near future is, many people are working towards the goal of greater transparency and openness. They want the good to win out, but we have to rein in our fears and keep the dialogue going or this will not happen. We love watching those tomahawk missiles way too much.

Democracy is the main tool that the common person has to control the self-motivated individual or a corporate reach; unfortunately this tool is rarely used, and if used at all, it is used poorly. Often democratic ideals are manipulated by elitist forces that attempt to lead the common people into the latest scheme of another ambitious social climber. Slowly true democracy is being formed and reform is ongoing. At the same time the process is surprisingly slow. I fear we love and need our heroes too much, criminal or not we adore exceptionalism. Our inadequacies glare brightly in the light of day. We are fools, led by the nose off any number of cliffs, and we go gladly.

We can see that an expanded democracy is a useful philosophy to deal with unjustified social controls that are defended by powerful hierarchies, corporations and governments. A compassionate dictator might be heard to lament when will the people make up their collective minds. Yet people in positions of influence and power occasionally become respected philanthropists. They have useful skills that can be redirected for purposes other than to dominate and isolate. It is the average citizen's duty to challenge these favored individuals or corporations and to help direct the philanthropic effort. Often the average citizen is too busy making a living or raising a family, have lost confidence or have no driving vision to challenge the wrongs in society. Many give up because they feel invalidated by the political process as well as sensing they will not be listened to even if they make an effort. The stronger ones get listened to, not because their ideas are better or that they have better solutions, but because they are stronger than their contemporaries and will not be defeated. It is simply a matter of persistence; the last man standing wins. We give up, give in, and walk away from decisive moments that reduce our freedom.

In a personal growth setting, you become the person you settle for in the end. If you believe in instrumental individualism, you will progress only as far as your culture allows you to expand. You are a victim of market capitalism, and you may see more open-minded people getting in your way, trying to stop you from achieving your personal goals. However if you believe in existential individualism you will have no boundaries other than mortality, and you may choose to challenge governments, corporations or individuals that promote an instrumental and market-based individualism.

Community vs. individual, individual vs. community.

The choice is ours. Yet humanity has a hard time making up its mind what the real purposes of life are about. It is time to cast aside the philosophies of separation, distrust, and doubt and seek unity in the struggle for fairness. The day will come where divisive philosophies will be seen as immature and selfish, a childish transition to be tolerated by adults. I hope the day will come when our similarities are apparent and appreciated, the differences tolerated and accepted, and human behavior is embraced as one large culture. After all, what is the purpose of democracy anyway? Where is it going unless it is to greater harmony and inclusiveness? Could it lead to a mass enlightenment?

CHAPTER FOUR

The Fourth Foundation:
A Purpose for Life, Resolution?

Make a commitment to create unity in your life and to grow
in your own understanding of "The Great Illusion".[225]

According to its adherents, religion and philosophy have for millennia attempted to show us this very message: unity[226], the whole being, or unity with God, or some kind of completion in one's existence as the final and only true goal of life, other than just the biological act of procreation. According to these beliefs anything else is really part of an illusion and as well, human life has a higher purpose. In counterpoint to this is the non-religious community that sees the betterment of humanity as a worthy purpose alone and this betterment will also lead to unity. Is there a possibility of a crossing over or a blending of these two vastly differing philosophies?

The idea of seeking unity seems to be an almost universal urge, a desire for completion and peace of mind. Unity also leads us towards a greater inner understanding and self-knowledge. These apparent contradictions may not be so different although some insist only one way is correct. Yet the secular and the religious have existed side by side for thousands of years. Humanity has progressed in some important ways because of the tug-of-war between the two although we have suffered many unnecessary wars based on minor differences in these beliefs. It is central for men to understand the concept of duality or disunity because we so firmly believe unity does not and cannot exist. We believe life is hard and conflict is never far from the door. According to traditional attitudes we just have to suck it up and get on with the job. The belief that unity cannot exist shows up through a close inspection of history-in divisions between sexes, classes, or racial stereotypes. It also manifests itself in sports teams seeking to win rather than work toward mutual learning. Recently I saw a jersey worn by a weight lifter that stated "No Goal, No Glory." We have not yet learned competition might bring out the best in an individual but doing things cooperatively brings out the best in our species. We insist on dualistic methods of organization because we believe that some people deserve more power and rewards than others. We are in this all together, but that concept is way too big to be easily accepted by the common citizen, at this time, that is.

The idea I am suggesting is already happening; we just refuse to see it. Almost everything we do is a work in progress towards something on the good side: the good does win out. Does it matter if a supreme being or a philosophy or just a natural urge towards betterment is the cause of it? It does appear that history and our ongoing attempts to humanize our societies are showing us that our actual struggle is the creation of this very state of unity we have been discussing. Who or what is doing this? Again, maybe it does not matter.

If we are responsible for waking ourselves from this "Illusion" or for that matter "The Many Illusions," what behaviors in our earthly life might resemble a more unified existence? Is it possible to determine this, while living in our current situation? One thing that helps us is the fact we might know inside that something may be unjust and that it must be corrected. Moving the scale forward are democratically motivated initiatives by individuals working unanimously to improve conditions for all, not just for a select disadvantaged group. All humanity is in need of this, not just the victims or the disadvantaged. Plus we see more and more collaboration with religious and sectarian efforts to produce change.

So building on what men have done for centuries (protecting and providing) our emerging role may be the continuing integration of humanity. We need to do what we have been doing forever, no more, no less, although there is much more room for a creative and personal solution to masculine purpose. Even though I wrote about the effects of science on male thinking, many more people have been working behind the scenes to deconstruct the evidence that scientists like Bacon and Aristotle promoted. Unfortunately, many of these reformers as well as average citizens have paid with their lives for promoting a more accurate interpretation of the cosmos and human capability.

There are a few concepts that must be understood. One is the capacity to make new choices based on the recognition that nothing is fixed and that everything is in flux, including masculinity. The term "thinking outside the box" or actually getting rid of the box entirely is very relevant at this precise moment in history. It suggests our fear of non-dualistic philosophies feeds the urge to maintain hierarchy or fear based thinking without thinking about the huge loss that we experience to our real freedom. Remember that hierarchy was created in order to guarantee survival in a hostile world. Maintaining an unnecessary hierarchy in a wealthy industrial culture such as ours can only be supported by fear-based and restrictive thinking. Second, in order to challenge hierarchical thinking and institutions, we must face the fear of the democratization of these existing power structures if we are going to move forward at all. Many attempts have been made; yet the structures remain, although somewhat tamed. Three, we must question the truth we hear from powerful individuals or institutions because however genuine they appear to be their words may just be a deception in order to maintain their power over us. They may not even know they are saying it, since social climbing can become such an ingrained and habitual behavior.

How do we continue to level the existing power structures and ease the fears of those entrenched within them? Consider for a moment the different culture that would exist if the non-dualistic view of our nature continued to evolve.

One of the first things to disappear would be the need to be right! Another would be moving away from individualistic economic striving towards community economic planning, thereby supporting everyone. We could also just decide to let the world described by The Book of Nature be and base human affairs on choice rather than on nature as our template.

The treatment of mental illness, criminality and self-destructive behaviors are also slowly emerging from barbaric practices. At one time even eminent doctors believed these ailments were caused by demons, or pressures in the head. People were even tested to see if they would float in order to determine if they were witches and therefore deserving of execution. Since our understanding has evolved over time, how can we be so certain a given conclusion or interpretation is correct when in fifty years it might change yet again? It appears as well that the speed of change is increasing. By the next century nobody will be able to say anything conclusively because within an hour or so another interpretation will be announced that nullifies the earlier solution. In a thousand years that speed might be every second, then what? How would it be possible to incorporate all that knowledge? How could we even function?

To bring this discussion back to earth, I have heard of a logical solution for the future of computers that may work in this challenging time; it involves the use of continuously updateable server computers[227] that are located in a central area, where public users will have only a keyboard or voice interface, and pay a monthly fee for access. This solves many headaches. Firstly computers cease becoming obsolete because nobody owns one. Secondly electronic trash is greatly reduced. Finally the actual performance is magnified many times by instant wireless access to information using the latest updated search engines. This is one of many possible solutions to the great challenges of way too much information in the near future.

However, our interpretation of truth is based in large part upon our particular vantage point and time in history. For men then, masculinity is like seeing that the beauty of a rose lies truly in the eye of the beholder. We have choices to make. Where are we going to put our energies? All these choices are just shades of "The Truth." Or is truth something else?

Is there another way for the independent thinker to proceed? Consider the events that have occurred. A significant portion of the study of history could be seen as a compassionate overview of the human struggle to improve life for all humanity. To be clearer, we are living a dualistic existence of our own making and it is within our grasp to accept the unified system, which actually exists, if we wish. It appears to be happening anyway so we can add more to it or not, it does not really matter; it is up to each of us to decide. Duality only exists because of our fear; the unified system is what is actually true.

From these insights and others we might justifiably conclude the human race might be getting to a decisive awareness at long last, or that every moment is special or precious. Could this tie into the Christian view of what Jesus said that by going through him you could enter the Kingdom of Heaven? In effect, the illusion would be swept away and you would see clearly or in other words be unified. You would be one complete person, not a sea of contradictions and unmet needs attempting to survive in a power seeking and hierarchical society. If we can imagine it, we can create it. Many great teachers down through history have said similar things such as the Buddha and Mohammed. Many people have listened. It is interesting that there are new teachers speaking today and more people are responding through avenues such as social media about democracy.

Another example of the illusory world I refer to is the world of fantasy created by Hollywood, but also by those with any kind of an agenda: the salesman mystique, the hero mystique, the multi-tasking mother mystique, the warrior mystique or even the victim mystique. Hollywood promotes the never-ending fantasy of perfect love and rewarded accomplishment. Life is not like this. The effect of such illusion is to encourage a society to be forever dissatisfied and under-appreciated. Hollywood teaches us to see that our happiness depends on extraordinary effort, or the good fortune we seek can only be for the royal born and thus granting of notoriety without effort. We seek the worshiping response of others rather than the recognition of our responsibility to learn our limits to dependency. In other words we have not really matured into fully functioning adults. We rely too often on the opinion and support of our culture or the greater society before we act or to know how we feel about ourselves. How many of us believe in the "magical quick fix" such as lotteries for example?

So if we rely on others to fill that "hole" in us we will be forever dissatisfied because they cannot do it. Many will try or attempt to pressure us into performing their own little idea as if a push will get us on the "right" path. In truth, all we can be certain of is that somewhere under all that illusion lies our true nature that can possibly be revealed to us through meditation as well as the ongoing democratization of our societies that create the foundation for our continued experience of freedom.

In the West we are nearing the end of the male dominated economic system and the risks and opportunities for others to find a voice are being created. Males are completing one task of their role and the time to find a new sense of purpose is already here. Even though corruption, greed and environmental destruction are rampant, the previously oppressed groups are beginning to find economic sources other than continued reliance or dependency on males. For example, women's financial situation today is a major departure from the early 1900's where government regulations such as minimum wage guarantees, child labor laws, environmental guidelines, taxes or unemployment insurance plans did not exist. As liberalization of labor laws occurred including work place safety, a shorter workweek, higher wages, and benefit packages, profits may seem to have been seriously eroded. But is this true, or have the costs just been passed on to the consumer in the form of higher prices? Profit margins[228] for many businesses have remained relatively the same even with the demands of labor.

Does this in turn drive the demand for higher wages and even more reforms? If this is true then great wealth is still being made but the difference from one hundred years ago is that reforms have created a large and politically powerful middleclass—not to be left out, the working class also has its access to many of these benefits including education and health care. It appears that the wealth creation impulse of males and the corresponding use of democratic mechanisms have allowed the creation of the broadest wealth base at any time in world history. This is a good thing and it is still growing, but is it just?

What do I mean by just?

The term, "old money" refers to money made a hundred years ago or more and is often seen as an example of one of the last remaining accumulations of wealth not subjected to economic reforms. Many will say not to touch it, although in some countries inheritance taxes are substantial. Other areas of concern are offshore bank accounts, excessive property holdings, and of course criminal money exchanges. These things are possibly unjust and in need of reform.

In the next chapter we will look at inheritance, private property and alternatives to the Western economic model that have worked elsewhere and are slowly making their way into Western thinking. The purpose of this is to encourage an evolution of thought and to consider the work ahead.

CHAPTER FIVE

The Fifth Foundation:
The Evolutionary Process

"[…]all human beings are worthy of a kind of unqualified respect by virtue of a capacity they all share: the ability to set the course of their own lives as individuals, to be self-determining or autonomous beings"
Immanuel Kant. Critique of Judgment, 1790[229]

Up to now we have considered reforms that have been achieved and are underway in Western ideas and cultures. We have not covered areas still requiring reform and how they can be approached. Each generation has its own reforms in mind. It is almost as if the new feisty energy of the young is born to address certain issues. Although I am not saying it is fated; yet it is sometimes eerie that each generation finds a cause. However several issues are consistently avoided, possibly too big to be dealt with properly because of their complexity or inherent dangers, or are fundamental to the way our hierarchical and dualistic society operates. These are the ones I wish to cover in this final foundation. To a major extent these issues have been the engines of our prosperity and security and who in their right mind wants to toy with something that works? The problem is they work only so well and could be made to work even better with reform.

This final foundation attempts to lay out the future of masculine activity as the emancipation of women, gays, First Nations, the disabled and prisoners are finding equitable relationships within the existing economic environment. With men no longer needed as the principal breadwinner, I want to remind men of their substantial historical contribution to democracy by encouraging them to move towards the egalitarian and philanthropic sectors of society. Aside from economic activity this is the other good men have always contributed to. Much good is still to be addressed. The naturally good man shines in this work and finds there is no other place to be. The topics in this chapter are areas I believe are essential for good men to focus on with the purpose of expanding the wonderful democratic institutions we enjoy today.

The beginning of this exploration is with private property. Up to the present time contemporary thought rarely touches on the private ownership of land. The only recent discussion I have seen in the papers was the gratitude people had for the outstanding profitability that owning land might produce. For most average citizens it was the only way they could generate wealth for their retirement, with many putting their entire life's work into their homes and lands in order to prepare for this distant but inevitable reality. Unfortunately, not everyone can.

So let's go back to a time where privately owned land did not exist, and was free to who ever passed over it—a natural process for some and a nightmare of chaos for others. However it did exist for thousands of years and ended with the start of the domestication of plants and animals about ten thousand years ago. At this point humans were forced by a changing climate and population growth to stop their nomadic way of life. The arable land all around them became invaluable to their survival and they slowly began to cultivate the wild plants that nurtured them, but now in fixed locations. Thus they were permanently settled on the land and new rules to govern them had to be created.

John Stuart Mill[230] said the moral basis for private land is the result of what nature created plus the effort you put into it. You have created a value that did not exist before and you are therefore entitled to a benefit for your labor. In support of this Pierre-Joseph Proudhon said in his book "What is Property?", if one clears land then one alone should enjoy the benefits.[231] When land was available and not densely populated, one could settle wherever one wished. Good soil and reliable sources of water were everywhere. However as the population and values shifted the easily tilled soil and accessible water became an issue of conflict for the new settlers. How was land to be shared, by what rule should we proceed? Apart from royal or military control of resources it became common that the original settler had ownership and rights of an heir. With males, their main purpose was to create wealth so they became the heirs thereby disenfranchising women, gays, youth and seniors. One could say property is the central pivot around which oppression revolves. With a more equitable distribution of property, much of our planets history could be radically different.

But if I am a small landowner intending to create greater wealth, I can make a profit off the production of a helper because I have appropriated the land as mine alone. Thus we see the start of capitalism where exploitation of the worker and the general public is standard procedure. Unions and civil rights groups had to be organized in order to demand some level of fairness from landowners and the growing business classes who attempted to capitalize on the growing needs of society and emulate the example of the small landowner's success. This span of time of which we are talking about is of course thousands of years. It was no picnic for workers who often experienced brutal controls put in place by pro-business governments, dictatorships or monarchies. Workers often died in great numbers usually in unsafe work places and through the use of toxic chemicals or harshly disciplining masters. This is still the norm in many developing countries where labor and environmental standards are either minimal or non-existent.

From an alternative viewpoint, Proudhon suggested, if an employer chooses to give fair payment to workers who help to bring another piece of land into production and this payment includes a portion of land or shares in the farmer's company, exploitation of a worker can become almost non-existent. The original owner of the land maintains his ownership of the original tract but benefits in a share of the profits from the increased production that the available labor has provided with the new land. This is an uncommon practice even in developed economies.

Seeking an explanation Proudhon asked why have we stopped the further development of democracy by not liberalizing this ownership of land? He feels it is because of the old regime,[232] which he describes as follows: "Formerly the nobility and clergy contributed towards the expenses of the state only by voluntary aid and gifts-their property could not be seized even for debt-while the commoner, overwhelmed by taxes and statute labor (their obligation to serve), was incessantly tormented, first by the king's tax collectors and then by those of the nobles and clergy. One whose possessions were subject to mortmain (a death in the family) could neither bequeath nor inherit property; he was treated like the animals, whose services and offspring belong to their master by right of accession." This old regime still exists today as "old money"—the substantial inherited wealth of private individuals, monarchies, dictatorships, private property and the realities of class warfare and the assumption of privilege. He goes on: "Yet we see that nothing seems more just [...] than the despotism of their sovereigns; that with the ancients and in the opinion even of the philosophers, slavery was just; that in the middle ages the nobles, the priests, and the bishops felt justified in having serfs; that Louis XIV[233] thought that he was right when he said, 'The state! I am the state'; and that Napoleon regarded it, as treason to oppose his will. This is no small matter, it is world encompassing, its consequences deeply misunderstood, and the prime human insult is that this is a legally enforced control over our lives."

Proudhon suggested that the purpose of profit sharing or labor ownership of a product is based on actual common sense. The farmer, the homeowner, or the city that might have tendered a contract to have a bridge built has had its future security enhanced for many years by the hired man's labor. If the hired man is only paid in wages, his future is definitely not as certain and he must go from job to job possibly receiving only a subsistence income (unless he is very frugal). Receiving a portion of the land or the product or share of the profit is fair and just. Proudhon further said: "[…] this preparation of the land and manufacture of implements for production represents what the (business owner) owes to the producer and what he has never paid; and it is this fraudulent denial which causes the poverty of the laborer, the luxury of idleness, and the inequality of conditions. It is this above all, which has been so appropriately called the exploitation of man by man." [234]Even though as we saw in the earlier study of the beginnings of the Industrial Revolution, capitalists tried paying workers good wages but workers would not come back to work until they were broke. This caused production problems and shutdowns for the owners. Owners tried low wages instead and found the workers came back regularly because they had to. The one thing owners did not try to do was to actually share the business with the workers in order to create a sense of ownership in the worker. The owners got hung up on their fear by seeking to hold their wealth too close to themselves instead of generating wealth across the board within their existing culture. An opportunity was missed for a win/win wealth generation system due to fear. Truly, fear is humanity's biggest issue.

Gerrard Winstanley[235], the leader and main writer for the Diggers during the English Revolution, suggested to Oliver Cromwell "that the only way the revolution could achieve true liberty would be to carry it to its conclusion by abolishing private property." Our justification for property rights is that it gives everyone who can afford to play in the game an opportunity to create wealth. In fact property is probably the fastest and safest way we know of today to create wealth for the average person. This is why it is still in existence today. Through this discussion though the consequences to the very poor and the alienated is telling, as Winstanley attempted to address in the 1640's, and that not all can profit from property, yet economists and financial planners are telling us that they believe property is still the best way known to create wealth with the least hardship on the citizenry. But again there is that section of society that gains nothing from this plan and in fact they subsidize the wealth of others by paying high rents often to subsidize the owners mortgages and the poor live a marginal existence on their own with no way to create equity. It is our collective responsibility to help end their alienation. We are duty bound to find democratic mechanisms that address property issues. To that end, it would be an interesting experiment to attempt a universal ownership of land so everyone could participate and create wealth. One way this could be accomplished would be to reduce the size of a lot so that smaller and more affordable homes could be built. This would also allow builders to get out of the pressure to build largely unprofitable rental accommodation too. Someone just has to do it.

A possible goal could be to eventually ban all rental accommodation except units for temporary workers, visitors such as professors, migrant labor or military personnel. Rental apartments are actually a step backwards as far as generating wealth on an individual basis is concerned and should be limited in use. If there is a fear of ownership in low-income buyers, the rules could be simplified to make the squeamish more comfortable with purchasing instead of renting. Imagine all those currently renting apartments, and many live in them for decades, if they could turn over their keys to new owners and get a check for one hundred thousand dollars or so instead of what ever is left of their damage deposit. Even with their balance to pay off they will probably be ahead by far.

We have an opportunity with this kind of property reform. Let's expand the concept a bit: consider that small parcels of land such as twenty-five by twenty-five feet could be purchased by people who today can only afford to rent apartments. Their dire situation is largely due to the difficulty these people have in coming up with a down payment for a standard size property. Generally this is about five percent of the purchase price. If a standard size lot of 125 x 50 feet could be subdivided to accommodate twenty-five by twenty-five foot lots or 625 sq feet ten lots would be available. If the lot was worth $200,000, divided by ten lots the total lot price would be about $20,000. If a 400 sq foot house (two floors = 800 sq feet) could be built for $30,000, an affordable home could be bought for about $50,000. If the down payment was $2500 or five percent, a person making $10 per hour or $1600 per month could afford to buy a house with six months savings. Mortgage payments of 30% of income or $480 per month would also be affordable; the house would be paid off in ten years. Current rental rates could easily accommodate this plan. In fact rents in Canada are comparable to mortgage payments any way. With a mortgage equivalent to rent payment, a decent structure could be purchased for one or two people; it can help them create wealth too.

A comparable system is the condominium. However, it does not go far enough to lower costs. Even with this proposed reform of property rights for the poor the enslavement remains and expands to all of us. We are the servants of property and the demand it takes on our lives is almost endless. It is no wonder that the term "mortgage" means, "engaged to the death." We must, in order to continue our reform of the remains of the King's land institute democratic processes as described above or alternatives similar to them or remove ownership completely. If nobody were to own it who would? The State? But then we might find ourselves back in a command economy driven by State imperatives and not democratic ones. That is no way to go either.

We have not finished with property yet but maybe if we expand our horizons a bit further it might help us clarify the issue even more.

So let's keep looking. In a non-agricultural setting such as a steel mill, how could fairness be made to work? We consider the start of a business by a single person and let's say the business becomes successful. This person can no longer keep up with the demands of his customers unless he hires people to keep production going. He must work as part of a team. How would we organize this team in a win/win way so that management and labor are not adversaries but collaborators? The owner's reward for this would be the increase in profits earned from improved productivity, of which he would get a share because he is not wholly responsible for the creation of it. Team members would deserve a share proportionately to their production above their wages. The more they produce, the bigger their share. Now say the owner wants to retire. He would sell his share to the other workers. The workers would then determine the products produced, their price, their components and design, and then would build them. The ones who would deserve a larger share of profits would be the ones who would create the most. The producers direct the sales team in ethics and the quality control of the business. No single individual would own the mill, since it is owned by everyone in the form of individual portions or shares of the actual production. The share can be bought or sold by vacating workers or by new ones arriving. A share can be paid for by a deduction in wages over a period of time, say a year or longer. Why this business model has not been put into place is baffling.

What about a builder who hires many trades to build a home for a family? The builder pays the wages of the trades, yet all employed in building the home own the value they have added to the project. If this were a large building, a ship or a major engineering project like a dam or a bridge, the list of people owed a portion would become a nightmare to remember. How could it be done? One solution would be to pay off all owners at the end of the job based on their wages and share valued to the overall value of the project. Wages as well as profit sharing are owed to the worker. Owner value could be retained in the finished product and paid regularly with interest or dividends paid. Smaller enterprises could maintain substantially smaller lists over long periods of time without collapsing in mountains of names and totals.

Since the employer cannot promise to employ the worker forever,[236] the only fair solution is a division of the property or business. Then all conditions will be equal, and there will no longer be either great capitalists or low-income workers. Individuals may squander their wealth; yet they are interconnected in so many ways with others and may own shares in many parcels of land and businesses that they can sell or trade them. As a result, poverty will be much reduced if not eradicated. Of course there will always be those who are unfit to work, but that is another matter to be looked at further on.

One clear observation can be made about this entire discussion: good land or rather arable land is now scarce and for that reason there is great competition for it. This helps to explain the unwillingness of current societies to abolish ownership regulations for all land. That said, a new relationship with land could be imagined much like our relationship with air or the oceans. It cannot be owned since it is a community property and as a finite resource, it is essential and must be protected.

Although it is also clear that if it were considered to be immoral to own arable land but that everyone had a right to occupy it but only when they needed to be there (like using the air or the oceans; a license might be required to use it). It is possible that if arable land was recognized as scarce and of critical importance for certain uses such as food production it would never be used for construction of cities or industrial structures, because the average citizen acting as owner would not allow it. It would be similar to protecting oyster beds or spawning streams for salmon. Notice the outcry that often occurs today of a plan to destroy a spawning stream for a mine but we hardly raise an eyebrow when arable land is destroyed to create a sub-division. Housing should only be allowed on non-arable or rocky land. Proudhon adds "[…] but land[237] is much scarcer than the other elements and so its use must be regulated not for the profit of a few but in the interest and for the security of all. In short, equality of rights is proved by equality of needs." So when abolishing the Emperor's land, if it had been offered to every individual and that their labor was considered a value in addition to their wages the reality of property law might be quite different today.

It might appear, that to the suspicious, private ownership is based on the fear of others, what someone might do to me, my family, my belongings, or what they might not do, so for safety sake we will isolate ourselves. Or, for example they might just ignore me from their vast expanse of land or I can ignore them. Maybe we have lost our tribal sense of responsibility for each other. The benefits of privacy and hence large tracts of land may bring a relief from having to exist so closely with so many people and in other times and places always being at the service of your King or Chief. Yet most of us in the West have become like isolated elites living in gated communities or modern compounds we call cities. We learned by watching our Kings and Warlords as they claimed large favored chunks of land and kept us out, then watched as they gave other nice parcels as rewards for service and what left we could try to hack out an existence for ourselves. Out of revenge we have been taking back the King's land ever since. We removed the King only to find we have become him. We judge the homeless and the infirm as unworthy so we give them what the King gave us-virtually nothing. We blame them for their anger and their disconnection. However they are beginning to demand a share just as we did in our time-funny how this works. We think that if they work as hard as we did they too can have a piece of the King's land, but again we forget all those people that helped us up when we needed a hand, or who trusted us to do a job for them—who is trusting the homeless? That is just the start of the list. It also includes people with criminal records, the mentally ill, the physically or mentally challenged, the aged and the young. It is all about fear—a fear of scarcity, on both sides. The disenfranchised have a set of fears too and are stuck in them-really it is a mess. We have to let go of this idea of craving to be Kings, as our intention has made clear by the 1950's statement "a man's home is his castle" but all the obstacles and institutions that exist are the cement maintaining this old illusion. Just as we have learned about men and the institutions that maintain a survivalist hierarchy, the disenfranchised suffer in the same way; it is the same institutions in effect that maintain poverty, criminality, drug addiction and for that matter, political corruption—and we bought into the idea that they would provide a good example. I have witnessed police cars crossing double yellow lines, doing u-turns in downtown streets and a group of police motorcycles tailgating and speeding behind passenger cars, all without sirens or lights flashing. This sends a message to the young that it is cool to break the rules, and they flaunt the rules because they can. Our current financial mess is another example, while we are finally charging white collar crime with appropriate jail time, my trust for corporations is at an all time low, as well as our shameful treatment of first nations people which ought to be resolved by now. I have been hearing about first nations issues since I was a kid, fifty years ago. As we come out of our survivalist identity though and choose a new life for ourselves we will find a better way, free of land and free of the King, and in time free of fear. This is the very real promise of Democracy, but it must have teeth in order to maintain the expectations we have of corporations, institutions and the traditional ways things worked in the past. If we truly are a mature species then the right hand must know what the left hand is doing. Or Labor must know what Management is doing, and vise-versa.

The most devastating injury maintained by institutions is the lack of any feeling or responsibility inherent in their actions. They base their actions on the guidelines established by other earlier institutions that mimicked the nobility and kings. They have no real vision for their own behavior. They try to convince us they are accessible to the public, yet they remain unchanged and unwilling to incorporate democratic mechanisms because such mechanisms would essentially destroy their power over us. We like the image of a strong edifice in which to store our money, our insurance, our faith and so on. We think slow progress is a good thing because it appears resilient and not impulsive. In reality institutions are resistant to change and only change when they are forced to. Proudhon would call this kind of change a progress of a kind[238] because institutions are attempting to develop modern attitudes. It is not however a revolutionary change. Revolutionary change would require the removal of the safety net around these institutions and make them accountable for their actions to the general public. That is, every individual that is employed there would be responsible to the public as individuals rather than as a corporation. They would not have a choice because they would be completely accountable to their customers and not only their Board of Directors or shareholders. They would not be able to hide behind legal guidelines or traditions. Corporations as persons should be a thing of the past.

Confronting this problem of privilege is not only an issue for institutions. It is also an issue for individuals to resolve. This belief we are more deserving than others may be clarified by considering another illusion elaborated by the early economist David Ricardo. His ideas were also based upon the growing social awareness of poverty and the public demand for solutions. Many redistribution theories began springing up from North America to Europe seeking a solution to poverty. Ricardo saw it as a problem related to owners of wealth. He was writing during the Napoleonic Wars of 1804-1815 and noticed the rising price of grain due to the conflict. At the end of the war rich English landowners demanded a law that would maintain the artificially high grain prices well into the future. These laws were called "the Corn Laws" and created mass riots when imposed in 1815. The average weekly wage of agricultural and factory workers at the time was almost cut in half. Ricardo building on the earlier work of John Locke believed this was wrong. He developed the theory that any artificial increase in prices should go to the state to be distributed to the needy. He felt strongly that unearned income fueled the purses of the wealthy. He also illustrated his view that increases in property values, also an unearned profit, should be owed to the society in general and not the owner.[239] Many held views similar to contemporary attitudes that any increase in property values should go to the owner rather than the society. As well, we have this feeling that all the income we have created as individuals is the direct result of our intention alone and that we have had little or no help in achieving our successes, outside of maybe our families and close friends. However, according to some writers, most of our present income is not based upon our efforts. In fact it relies heavily on the knowledge, skills and technology that we inherited from the past. According to Herbert Simon,[240] "[...]a person working today, working the same number of hours as a similar person in 1870—and working just as hard (and no harder)—will produce perhaps fifteen times as much economic output." This increase is entirely due to inherited assets and suggests we as individuals are deeply indebted to, as Simon suggests, "[...] an enormously productive social system"[241] which we have taken for granted, hence our illusionary sense of privilege.

Jared Diamond's previously mentioned work on privilege is also very relevant because advantages in technology and other pluses give some cultures the belief they are inherently superior. If anything, we ought to respond with gratitude for the incredible wealth we so easily inherited from the past and which we did nothing to create. For example in Canada today all people enjoy the right to vote. In the past it was only men who owned property that could vote. All the rest of us, men and women alike, had to wait until 1920 to get that right for good. We take for granted so much and so easily. We are obligated to return something to society for these many gifts. Many wealthy people have learned this critical lesson and created vast charitable organizations to give back something of the advantages they received from society. Many more could give, but do not.

As real property became available, the determined individual saw opportunities and room was made for this to happen although often at the expense of the poorer citizens. However, Murray Bookchin argues that equality is inextricably tied to freedom.[242] Together with the recognition of the natural inequality of individuals, the establishing of a culture and distributive system based on compensation for the advantages of this natural privilege had to come into existence. Yet this recognition does not give the naturally advantaged individual the right to rule over the rest or to buy and sell us as a commodity as labor often is. It is obvious that this understanding cannot be achieved in a system where individuals own, buy and sell both real property and property in the person (or labor), or where the ambitious instrumental individual constantly destroys the freedom of others by denying the will of others by their endless self-interested struggle to get to the top.

The early feminist writer Emma Goldman refers to property[243] as that which "means dominion over things and the denial to others of the use of those things [...] and [...]. It is private dominion over things that condemns millions of people to be mere non-entities [...] who (through their employment) pile up mountains of wealth for others and pay for it with a gray, dull and wretched existence for them-selves. It is conceded by some thinkers that the fundamental cause of this terrible state of affairs[244] is:

1. That man must sell his labor, apparently,
2. That "his inclination and judgment are subordinated to the will of a master."
3. Further, "The Liberal believes that individuals own their bodies and the associated skills and abilities, and the 'labor power' that accompanies their bodies. Liberal thinkers consider the right to buy and sell labor power as essential, just as they affirm the right to buy and sell real property. In liberal thought, there is no practical difference between owning property and owning one-self" or someone else for that matter. C.B. Macpherson[245] the noted Canadian political scientist recognized in Liberal thinking that: "political society is a human contrivance for the protection of the individual's property in his person and goods, and (therefore) for the maintenance of orderly relations of exchange between individuals regarded as proprietors of themselves."

Labor can be viewed as energy, but is this energy your property that you can sell or barter to the highest bidder? If that is the case then you will never be free of domination and subordination hierarchies[246] because the selling of your labor creates its own hierarchy. We assume that we are freeing ourselves by employment, but actually we are instead creating further dependence on hierarchical financial structures. In order to free ourselves of this process we must consider alternative economic systems that do not involve the selling of our labor for a wage, unless for example, we are self-employed where we control a much larger portion of our destiny, and can demand a much higher wage as well. So if we don't own ourselves because we have sold ourselves in order to get employment, where are our safeguards? Where is our fair compensation? We have sold ourselves down the river for a days work.

L. Susan Brown's writings depict a never-ending struggle for dominance and wealth creation as an individualistic calling rather than a cooperative venture for all citizens. In a major way creating wealth for the individual has created wealth for the many, but is it efficient? Regardless it may be the only way it can happen for now at least.

It might seem that property ownership is probably the only way to guarantee individual ambition or collateral in business. At this historical moment property laws of Western capitalist countries may be one of the few ways or even the only way to create wealth. Many gifted, deserving and hard working people have never figured out a way of acquiring a piece of property for conversion into capital. Take for example people who love their work but get paid less than they would like. Some would suggest that they are happy doing what they want, so they should not seek greater things. Yet they are still poor and not benefiting from all this opportunity and so called freedom. Freedom to be poor or rich you say? Yet there probably are many ways lenders in the West can assist low-income people to create more wealth in their lives. Of course banks will only do it if a profit is available to be made. I say to the banks, consider micro-credit, a system developed in Bangladesh by Mohammed Yunis who saw skills being wasted for want of a small investment in a citizen. It has had the effect of enriching the whole community. Small groups of women negotiate loans, which are given to group members in the most need from the Bangladesh Central Bank. The women are expected to go through training in their proposed enterprise and in financial management. The loans are repaid in fifty equal installments, and the repayment rate is above 94%. Similar micro-credit schemes have been set up throughout the developing world, and have been enormously effective, not only in alleviating poverty and improving child nutrition, but also in increasing the voluntary use of contraception.

The ideas presented earlier by Proudhon on shared ownership of land and based on every individual's effort are significant and worth considering. As we move further into the future this inherited mass of knowledge will grow with the contributions of our own generation and leave more potential wealth to our descendants. They will create even less of their overall real wealth than we do today and this will progress into the future, hopefully forever. After all, this is what we want, a better life for our children. This is the major motivation that families for thousands of years have based their energies upon, and this accumulated knowledge is the basis for massive wealth creation in the future. It is our natural inheritance unrelated to family or place or class. While risking repetitiveness, this suggests we do not need our familial inheritances any longer and while it might be easy to say, what we have received from the past is far and away several magnitudes greater than what the average person could inherit from family. However, I could use mine-but then I am not a wealthy guy. Could it be relative to our standard of living, and that it might be hard for even the best off to just hand it over to the public purse? Tough choice, yet an essential debate is needed on an international level.

In many economies of the world, knowledge, technology and skills are not easily incorporated into wealth generation. The process is hampered by the existing relationships of domination and subordination, tradition and secrecy, which stifle further wealth creation. According to Hernando de Soto, author of "The Mystery of Capital",[247] the reason the Third World is poor while the First World is rich is due to property laws. These are the laws that have established clear ownership and therefore responsibility for property, mainly real estate, inventions, stocks and bonds. His proof lies in the recognition that many Western entrepreneurs use their homes as collateral in order to back up a bank loan, whereas in developing countries this is largely impossible. An example of De Soto's view of property[248] ownership in the developed economies followed by the inherent difficulties creating wealth in the developing world:

Developed World:
- Regulated, legal, property can be inherited, and can be used as collateral for loans.
- Impersonal; no ties to community, maintains isolation of wealth.
- Creates wealth quickly.

Developing World:
- Property ownership is known from interviewing neighbors, relatives, and friends, and through oral traditions.
- Bonds individuals together in their histories.
- But limited growth potential due to inaccurate history, and therefore the uncertainty of ownership exists; it is therefore

difficult to encourage a bank to use this sketchy history to grant loans.

- There are huge obstacles to overcome for obtaining business licenses so many people go underground to get the money they need.

For countries such as Egypt, if the human impulse is to create a more democratic society they must see the outcome of their version of a restricted Capitalism before they can do anything else, they must prove to themselves that it is unworkable to create great wealth in such a tradition based society. Indeed this is a long-term project for all of humanity everywhere, but we really are so very young and creating wealth is only the beginning. Also the developing world has seen tremendous inequality and its citizens are starting the process by which they will create wealth for themselves—in some situations by taking it from us and in others by maximizing their own creative energies—they are on a road to self-discovery. Hopefully they will stop us from exploiting them, and they will write their own environmental laws when they can, and their oppressed minorities will be given equality when and if they demand it and if the society can afford it. Freedom depends largely upon the individuals in power listening to their people.

We cannot expect humanity to instantly accept a classless society and create wealth without exploitation or the loss of personal power until they have tried all the alternatives. These include the most barbaric and disgusting of human depravity. Only by going there, if one is driven to do so will they have even a chance of discovering for themselves the error of their ways. On a personal note I have rarely learned anything really valuable when someone told me to do this or that thing. People are like this they learn by making mistakes. Many might not care for our conversation here until they had discovered something significant about their own life that might make them question their present day reality. There are many scripted blueprints for a good way to live yet most people are too busy living out one or two prevalent ones such as the "Hollywood Life" and its opposite the "Great Victim." For some it is one or the other with no in between, they cannot see the multitude of scripts available to them.

Mr. De Soto's research shows that the developing world's citizens are far from poor. In fact he has estimated the actual property value of all enterprise in the developing world at $9.3 trillion U.S. This is an astonishing figure—three times the current U.S. GNP. This valuable resource is not available as collateral for loans because of the difficulty in obtaining accurate records of property ownership as stated above. Months of waiting and hundreds of forms are required for these simple certificates. De Soto's message to the developing world's governments is to include enterprises in an easily accessed legal property system similar to Western capitalist countries. These legal enterprises can then borrow against the market value of their properties in order to expand their business frontiers. Some observers are calling his book an important key to growth in Asia and elsewhere in the developing world while others are worried capitalism will destroy their culture, and for good reason.

This is not to say the West is totally liberated in its capital availability, far from it. Some of our hesitation might relax further if ways to create wealth were brought out in all cultures, and not just the developing world. An international discussion is needed to find blockages that are systemic to all economies and not just discussions held by The World Trade Organization where the average citizen is left out, hence the riots wherever these closed-door meetings are held. Wealth can be created without destroying cultures or the environment, but the facts must be put on the table too, and include the average citizens concerns.

In order to deal with the huge gains in prosperity in Western nations, demands for the sharing of this wealth took the path of taxation based on income, but still maintaining the institutions of control, thereby effectively keeping wealth generation in the hands of the elite. Other writers and economists along with John Stuart Mill, Ricardo and Locke began to notice increasing gaps between the rich and poor and began to suggest this situation was still unfair. They began to notice that individuals in the wealthy classes benefited from many unearned and therefore undeserved opportunities to create wealth where ordinary citizens and the poor did not. So not only did they receive this vast inheritance, largely from the past, and created by others, they also kept it to themselves. There are many examples, including education, their inherited wealth, knowledge, technology and important social and church connections. Mill felt that based on purely Lockean principals that these surpluses belonged to the state and ought to be distributed to all.[249] Knowing how to do something is as important as wanting to do something. The "how" was often lacking to the poor. Many schemes were proposed such as Social Credit[250] in Scotland where a percentage of national worth was suggested to be distributed to each citizen. Some were actually enacted upon to level the playing field at least somewhat such as the "dole", or welfare or universal health care. These changes were never enough though and the wealthy continued to move ahead of everyone else. By creating more jobs and support systems such as academic or trade training governments say they are making an attempt to encourage more and more citizens to claim greater access to land, and therefore to wealth. However this is still based on an inherently unfair system of acquisition. The cards are stacked against the poor man.

It was proposed by Simon, "[—] that in the present day economy taking into account all the skill, knowledge, and technology that has been passed down to us essentially free of charge constitutes eighty-five percent[251] of our income". It was proposed that a portion of that eighty-five percent, essentially a free "gift" from the past was owed by us to society. So as a result of these reactions proposed solutions surfaced including greater taxation to fund a monthly universal cash payout to everyone regardless of economic situation, payments to the poor only, or as an alternative, make improvements to many government services, such as free health care, education, pensions and care for the elderly and disabled. Even with all the advantages given to them the average citizen would stomach only so much taxation to fund these programs.

These plans and programs are still at arms length and excludes discussion and accountability. The attempt is made to spread the wealth around, but in a highly impersonal way, with no connection between giver and receiver. European and Western distribution proposals have involved the command economy and its opposite, the market economy with many versions in-between. The Europeans, Americans and members of the British Commonwealth pursued the market economy allowing individuals to decide what to do with their inherited income whereas Russia, China and others followed the command economy where their governments felt itself was the best dispenser of inherited wealth-different attempts to deal with the same reality-how to make the costs bearable for the extremely privileged while giving something to the average citizen. Funny, that a narrowly avoided nuclear war could have obliterated the planet over competition and rivalry between the two systems. However let's be real here—both systems murdered millions of people in order to maintain their chosen wealth creation-distribution schemes. The market system did it with slavery, unsafe work places, disease and war; the command economies did it with all the above plus severe social repression of their own people. They were not friends experimenting with alternate economic systems. This was a fight to the death for both of them-and it almost ruined both-and the world as well. Yet that is what happens when we think we are right—a big lesson here if we choose to hear it.

Here is another funny circumstance: In the western choice of market driven rights, which create economic "freedom" something is amiss. While it appears western citizens have free economic choices the disparity between the wealthy and the poor is substantial and it would appear that the call for a new discussion on the correct sharing of this inherited wealth is required again. It must be continually addressed or it will be buried in our minds, and like the issue of property forgotten forever. We forget again so easily about the inherited wealth from the past and its requirement to be distributed because we did nothing to earn it-we have no right to claim it as ours. Many governments do attempt some control by refusing corporate donations to a political party when the firm might benefit from an awarded contract, but this is only a small step to actually dealing with it. A guaranteed annual income might be one way to deal with it.

As well, the world of copyright[252] is complex and sometimes difficult to understand, it is essentially a temporary protection for the inventor. Many inherited ideas are considered general knowledge and no copyright is associated with their use. For example, the shape and function of a hammer, whereas the exact shape of one manufactured hammer might be protected if copied too closely. The shape and function of a hammer is knowledge passed down to us and we have no claim on it, although we can use it as a template upon which to develop new ideas or improvements to the original. Our modern world is full of literally millions of these inventions from the past that can be freely used and adapted. This is part of the wealth we have inherited.

In addition to the design and function of a hammer is the knowledge and skills used in the manufacture of it, often using complex tools and methods, which can be copyrighted and are similarly based on earlier and simpler methods and tools that are no longer copy write protected. Then there is the packaging and marketing as well as the economics needed to develop such a tool. These issues can be enough to block many inventors from acquiring a patent and bringing a new product to market, and is major unseen block to wealth creation in the West. So it can be seen that the great quantities of indispensable knowledge we acquired from the past is required to do anything new today-if we can get access to it. With our wealth largely based on this past knowledge we cannot claim to have done it, "my way." This is evidence that we are not alone in this life and sheds light on our insistence to maintain the illusion that we are.

This area of "general knowledge" expands over time as improvements are made to the hammer and the term of a copyright on the improvements comes to an end. The sooner an improvement becomes general knowledge the sooner it can be improved upon and how long this period is depends upon government regulation and property law. The inventor of the improvement deserves some compensation for effort and expenses so a temporary monopoly is allowed for a set period of time. This time period is monitored carefully by regulatory bodies, however some inventors have managed to maintain a monopoly on their products for very long periods of time and are often accused of anti-competitive practices and could be forced to relinquish their copyright or even pay fines for not allowing innovation to occur. A balance must be struck between the benefit to the growth of civilization and the right to profit by the inventor. Many writers today are increasingly worried about this relationship between government, the civilization it represents and inventors or corporate power. The fear is that corporations are becoming far too powerful in their influence over copyright and monopoly and they might be seeking to diminish the right of civilization to use general knowledge as an improvement to their societies that will lead to difficulties in the evolution of future skills, technology and wealth itself.

The only real control possible over the actions of corporations is an enlightened and cautious population. It must be demanding of corporations for accountability and it must protect vulnerable children, the environment and cultural values from detrimental influence. An example is public protests aimed at making the general public aware of important issues corporations might prefer to keep quiet. An example might be the ongoing whale hunt by the Japanese and the protest group The Sea Sheppard Society who is attempting to influence our opinion by harassing the whalers in full public view. The only problem here is that a non-profit society has to do the dirty work of exposing actions by corporations whose actions should be under the watchful eyes of public regulatory bodies or international agencies such as the U.N.

From the book "The Corporation" by Joel Bakan[253] he suggests several changes that could assist in better corporate monitoring that include the development of a strong public awareness of issues by improving the political voting system that might encourage citizens to vote more frequently. He suggests proportional representation as a needed alternative to first past the post systems that are in use by many governments today.

So regulatory bodies must be maintained.

Many structural impediments have somehow crept into western market economies, often without the public's knowledge. I have compiled a few impediments to wealth creation that upon examination are actually protections for inherited wealth, knowledge and technology profiting owners that did nothing or little to earn or deserve them.

An additional difficulty for wealth creation by the wage earner is the lack of supportive institutions that could encourage the development of new inventions. It is exceptionally difficult unless you have a large disposable income to finance a prototype stage, let alone the developmental costs later on. A major engine of invention comes straight from the worker who uses tools on a daily basis. Yet he has no opportunity to benefit from his discoveries since his employer often claims ownership. This is a good example of where partial ownership of an invention ought to go to the actual inventor. If he is self-employed, he may not have the capital to invest in his ideas. Who is it that misses out? Certainly not the corporation who hold the previous but less advanced patents, but both the inventor and our entire society miss out on his new idea. Personally I have talked with many friends with ideas that could have become inventions if they could only build a prototype. The obstacles stopping them included a lack of time, the ability or the capital to invest in it. If I were a rich man, I would help fund these prototypes.

What is our purpose in developing these emerging ideas? Is it to create wealth for the inventor or is it to bring needed products that might help reduce an environmental footprint or decrease our energy usage or make a tool more user friendly? In the past the answer to this question often involved whatever the inventor could sell to the public; often filling a real need such as washing machines is what drove the market, whereas today it seems many purchases are driven by a new morality such as this next story of how the bikini was first marketed.

The bikini was invented and launched almost simultaneously by two French fashion designers: Jacques Heim and Louis Reard.[254] Heim was a swimsuit designer who had created a two-piece suit to be sold in his beach shop in Cannes. He marketed the swimsuit as the "Atome" (named for its small size and meant to be compared with the atom, the smallest particle of matter known). The same summer of 1946 in which Heim was introducing his "Atome," Louis Reard was creating his own similar two-piece swimsuit. He named and marketed his swimsuit as the bikini, proclaiming that it was "smaller than the smallest bathing suit in the world." Both of these designers created sensations wherever the suits were displayed. Shocked and mortified commentators the world over reacted to them as immoral and scandalous. Heim and Reard helped to foster in more tolerant attitudes towards nudity and possibly helped to start the sexual revolution of the 60's and 70's. They created a need rather than filling one.

If unintended good can come from corporate leadership and inventions, risk is also possible. The breakthroughs in the understanding of the genetic code have opened a very dangerous door that could lead to engineered humans, plants and animals that might be used as deadly weapons by terrorists or unethical governments. We must be ready for this and not wait for it to get out of hand. At the same time we really do not know if one invention will be good or not until it is projected on the world stage and the consequences are noticed.

As well, new and pressing environmental concerns are forcing the change of the older survivalist paradigm into a more need-based system. Yet we keep fighting with this old paradigm that attempts to conceal information and manipulate the markets. Instead of building barriers that protect fear-based wealth creation we could build enlightened access and support to ideas and markets for a more integrated life that includes business, culture and a healthy world in which to live in. This ought to lead to greater wealth creation because opportunities will be more visible and where innovations are supported in the communities they originate in.

A second impediment to wealth creation is an educational system designed to create workers, managers, and leaders based upon wealth in families, friends and connections. Corporations do not generally look to the radical fringe to find inspired individuals who might be exceptionally creative and have fresh ideas. The talent is out there we just have to have the courage to engage it.

Recently I read about a man whose purpose in life was to make people smile. He stood on a street corner in downtown Vancouver B.C. waving to people and telling jokes to any who would listen. He became a fixture. He died recently. The news article celebrated his life and those who knew him. Yet he was never acknowledged in any official way, although everyone knew him as "the King of Cassiar"[255] named for the street corner he panhandled from. Here was someone who had a special gift that had not been put to a greater purpose. Imagine if he had been hired by the prison system to cheer up guards about to go on shift. Do you think it would make any difference to the inmates if their guards were happier? I bet it would. Or what if he had been hired to cheer up cardiac patients before heart surgery? Would it help them get through it? It is worth a try. So many places a person like him could be used to improve society yet wasted because of a lack of imagination.

I remember years ago when I lived by the sea, there was an elderly woman who frequently swept the sidewalk for several blocks around where we lived. I do not recall if she was ever thanked for that. Regardless she deserves something for that act. There are countless thousands of similar deeds of kindness given freely every day that go unacknowledged. What if they were acknowledged somehow? One effect would be to make these people more visible.

Another lesser direct effect on wealth creation is government restrictions on Crown lands (Canada for example, probably most jurisdictions internationally). At one time there were squatter's rights[256] and easy access to land for settlement for those who might wish to create wealth in a different lifestyle than what is considered normal. Opting out of our current system was easier to do in the past than it is now.

To highlight the easily confused terms "wealth creation" and "freedom" I had originally placed this last item together with the wealth creation list, it really is an issue of freedom although anything that impacts freedom also impacts wealth creation. Possibly wealth creation is far more important in the West than is freedom even though we believe we are "free." We are freer than the rest, but not totally free as we could be and still be considered civilized and responsible. This issue is our "first past the post" electoral system constitutes a major block to improved democratic processes because the political party with the most votes regardless of any actual percentage of votes forms a new government and effectively shuts out the opinions and ideas of everyone else. This is tantamount to dictatorship ruling over us until we vote them out, only to be replaced by another dictatorship—we call this democracy. A much fairer system of government recognizes each vote has a point of view and deserves to be heard. In my home province of British Columbia, a proportional representation system was put to the vote and rejected twice by the electorate.

People have got to want freedom in order to get it. Hiding under a rock will not get it. A popular civic issue is gaining support in British Columbia; opposition has mounted against a tax increase. We can find the backbone to say no to something, but to get us to say yes about a much-improved voting system is impossible. Wouldn't it be interesting if we were all willing, for a day, to be guided by one rule: to say yes to everything. Jim Carrie, the comedian, starred in a film, called appropriately enough "Yes Man." It is an interesting experiment to try, as the blocks we normally use to limit our involvement in life are pushed aside by a potentially new adventurism. Doors open into new areas we have never experienced before; it could have a way of reinvigorating our lives in the most positive ways. You just have to say yes.

The problem overall is structural and not really repairable in the context of the systems we use to create wealth because we are locked into it by our habits and fears. Since our economic system is primarily based upon managing surpluses, a more productive system involving a new attitude is required and that attitude is fairness. Our current level of democracy today has been obtained at great expense in order for the surplus management system to work better, without however any attempt to change our way we actually create wealth. It cannot be much improved while living within this kind of management system, although it is interesting how the role our justice system plays out in it. Fairness after all exists as a counterpoint to simple surplus management. Justice is relative to fairness since even in the West, it is occasionally based on privilege, that is who you are and what you own. However fairness is still the driving force behind the democratic change we benefit from today and without it there would be no change for the good anywhere or at any time. There are of course many kinds of justice or fairness efforts such as unionization of the workplace, which would never have been able to create safer working conditions for millions of workers without a sense of fairness driving their vision.

Watching Supreme Court judgments and how their decisions come down is also very interesting. Democracy is strengthened by many positive judgments of the Court. But can we actually hope for continued improvement if we fall back onto the surplus driven economy we live in today? Fairness is important here; it will continue to play an important part of the development of our societies.

We are left with these impediments to wealth creation and obstacles to fairness where many people cannot afford to buy a home, let alone arrange for a mortgage to invest in a business. Property law is however a major step in the path to creating wealth for many marginal economies, and for maintaining wealth in the West. However as we discussed earlier, property issues remain to be challenged democratically in order to bring out even more wealth creation potential based upon greater fairness. It seems wealth is still far more important on its own than fairness. Until fairness is the more important driving force, we will have oppression and hierarchical institutions that attempt to rule us and enforce rules of behavior on our lives.

Having failed to make this transition to a fairness-based economy, we continue to try to make our current systems work better so that the good that is left in men's lives is not totally thwarted. A lot of this blockage is made by habitual modes of behavior that limit freedoms. Many reforms are needed. It is mostly our personal habits and the ease we have of saying no to change (such as proportional representation) or new ideas that combine to create an attitude or mindset resistant to change or creative expression, and therefore to freedom. But what is fairness?

Within a system based on fairness, there are levels of contentment for each individual regarding wealth. Who is to say what is a reasonable amount of money or possessions? Some may be satisfied with very little material comforts; yet others need immense properties filled with beautiful belongings. Our culture has idealized the materialist side of the equation along with many proud announcements by the owner. At the same time the monastic or frugal side of the coin as in the idealized opposing image of the monk in Asia or the wilderness survivor such as in the American series, Lost, is revered. The underlying social understanding is that the austere life is by far the least desirable we are taught it is unfair or hard. Yet certain segments of our culture believe that having great wealth is the hardest of all positions to manage, and many complain they want to give it up. This must be based on the idea that fear of its loss and suspicion of others grows accordingly to the size of the purse, let alone the responsibility of its use. A retreat in Britain for executives at an ancient monastery[257] deprives the visitor of all external stimulation including watches, cell phones and newspapers. The attendees hope to clarify their purpose and maybe make a major change in their direction. This temporary isolation from others and the total emersion in one's own emotions can be a powerful example of what the hidden costs of the seeking of power can be-we can lose who we are because we have been so focused on managing our wealth. So fairness and freedom are intricately related.

The exploration of a consistent male identification with power along with the study of wealth creation is fundamental for men to grasp if freedom from the abuses of and desire for power is to be achieved. After all, is it power or is it ideas that change people's minds? One of those great ideas we can encounter in life is a crisis of thought. Example: the discovery of a freedom to act independently versus having power or judgment over others in order to get what you want. If we agree that power is an important issue to study, then we must be cautious when we listen to existing leaders and we should resolutely maintain our independent perspective. After all leaders who do not step out of the way and encourage others may not know how to follow or how to support others to lead. They can be a great inspiration but they can also lead us blindly to an unclear goal that is part hysteria and part hero worship. The earlier discussion about Alcibiades is a clear warning of this kind of relationship. We can easily fall into it without considering that we might be replacing our own real needs for a temporary external stimulation based on some previous trauma we have forgotten about. People who seek power over others for influence are clearly not acting independently and need to be questioned as to how their power over me (or us) will enhance my ability to act independently and affect my own life goals and visions. For example, by giving you power does that reduce my personal power or does it enhance it?

Religion is one of the great callings for men who might seek power or influence over others; call it service, i.e., the power of God. Ministers and other clergy stand apart from the congregation (this is key) and tell the people gathered what the truth is. It would suggest people drawn to this occupation strongly believe in controlling the masses by using methods and tricks that exploit our thinking and by teaching us to obey rather than think independently. We are then expected to believe what we are told and dismiss thoughts or ideas contrary to orthodox policy. I suppose I could just walk out of the service if I do not like what I am hearing. For many this choice may not always be possible or safe. Many wars and millions of deaths have had to occur before people had claimed the right to think for themselves. The recent democratic protests in the Arab world are a good example of the costs involved in building freedom. Many long-standing and even habitual institutions worldwide still maintain a dominant role in the behavior of the populations where they exist, and people are willing to die to challenge them. Even though attendance in churches has been on the decline recently, many people still look to religion as a solution to life's worries and as a salve to the stresses of everyday existence. Even though the world's church's attempt to do good, I am suggesting that many people are vulnerable to these experiences, such as the choice of words used in religious language and the risks of the potential harm coming from supposedly carefully trained spiritual leaders. Let's not forget about the very real sexual abuses coming to light recently within all the mainstream churches, and it begs the question: what is it about the priesthood that attracts these kinds of men who abuse children, and what is it about institutions in general, and this includes the Church, that feel they have the right to ignore or protect these abuses from civil prosecution? We can see clearly in this example the dangers of hierarchy and the search for influence over others.

To be fair, all institutions have been implicated with abuse of one kind or another: sleeping around to get to the top, putting up with an abusive boss, being sexually abused by your hockey coach, and being sent to prison by unjust policies in proportionally greater numbers if you are black or of First Nations background.

We forget the real message of religion though. It was supposedly about fairness. Jesus was in the historical sense, a revolutionary of his time. He was the visible spokesperson of the struggle against Rome, or in the ideological sense, tyranny and oppression. Today the leading churches may seem to preach a "New Life" in Christ, but often they seem teach conformity to consumerism, hierarchical power questing and a future good life in some other dimension. Whatever happened to modesty and humility? Where are the followers of Jesus who demand and are willing to lay down their lives for fairness as their leader taught them to do? He was the example Christians pray to. Of course this spiritual "good life" is not only taught in traditional churches, it is to be found in almost every new age bookstore, alternative religion, and business seminar room in the Western world. Their motto is "build your own empire" and who cares where your opportunities come from or who you hurt. "Create wealth from Real Estate" that is, from foreclosures. Or, "Sign up for our Free Trial Offer of a New Weight Loss Product" and only pay the shipping and handling charges for the one free container. However, the small print tells you that you will be billed on your credit card for two extra containers at the regular price of $79.99 each. One of the very worst is the calculated and practiced exploitation of friends, associates and relatives by criminally minded members of one's extended family in ponzi schemes.

The wealthy and the clergy should be on their knees daily in the town squares of the world thanking all of us for buying their products and believing the words that gave them their riches and their influence. But no, not much gratitude is to be found there. In actual fact, we own them because we have financed their positions. We have given them the money and influence they wanted; it was a contract supposedly between equals to deliver a service. But did we get our money's worth? If not, where is the complaint department or is there a money back guarantee?

Instead of leading world opinion, the contract should have stated the main focus is the creation of wealth or power for the wealthy, the clergy, and their followers. This is why the less powerful and the hungry would like a share without the pretence and deception. In religious communities more business gets done on the steps of the parish church than just about anywhere else.[258] There is nothing wrong with this as long as everyone knows about it and can get a piece of the action. Often you have to belong to the "club."

Another ridiculous modern religious tradition still places the groom at the head of the household in the marriage ceremony by announcing the new couple to the assembled guests as Mr. and Mrs. "His Name." This is a completely unnecessary embarrassment for the bride since I doubt that the groom really needs that kind of structure in order to create wealth.

Of course at one time it was important to support the husband's attempt to support his family. If it is used now, then it is used only to bolster any character weakness the groom cannot hide or to puff him up. Is it even conceivable that this ritual is used in order to chastise the bride who may be so egotistical and self-centered that she needs to be humiliated in public so that she will be a productive and reliable partner? Again this must be highly unlikely. So why would any modern woman or man regress to such a conservative and archaic announcement? It seems riddled with unwanted consequences and platforms that will have to be dismantled. What could motivate anyone to subscribe to a process that is demeaning to women, not necessary and is potentially restrictive for her continued wellbeing? Faith you say, ah yes the great excuse. How many atrocities have been committed in the name of faith? The only possible reason I can think of to remove a woman's first name from the bridal announcement would be to make a public statement removing the woman from the ranks of single and therefore available females to men unaccustomed to taking no for an answer. Essentially then, at least in an archaic and primitive society, this public announcement would hide and protect the woman from abduction or rape, a security ticket that primitive women needed in a violent survivalist society.

Today this is clearly unnecessary and a restriction to the women that at one time it protected. Women may wish to be seen as giving themselves "away" to their new husband. The consequences to her and the husband are great expectations potentially trapping them both in future hurt and disappointment. The husband may not be able to live up to her expectations of being "protected" (read "money" provided) and she may not fulfill his "needs to protect" (read power and influence). It is all quite deceptive and dishonest, yet this is still a reality for many newlyweds. In safer societies women do not really need protection just the sense of it and men do not really need to protect but that they can be there if needed. I remember dating women who put themselves in danger or were "acting out" in ways that suggested they actually wanted saving but more from themselves than any external threat. I have witnessed men who so dominated their women they could not breathe, and vice-versa. It was kind of sad; all this chest beating and weakness faking has to occur just so we appear attractive.

Somehow we humans still confuse wealth creation with power, and education with class. To repeat, we think we have created all this alone and since we believe this, we alone are responsible for its generation and thereby its use. We can buy not only things but favors, prestige, influence and people too. We believe there is not enough self-confidence to go around so we hoard as much influence and power as possible. We do this by symbolically refusing to share center stage with others. We have no sense that we are obliged to others in any binding way. We believe we are isolated and alone. We seek solace in drugs, sex, even violence, but mostly a self-deluded sense of our own importance. We believe our cultural enclave, our profession, our language, our masculinity is the only true reality. We do the full circle back to the magic world of Hollywood and worship at the feet of our God, Alcibiades, secretly wishing to be him.

In reality though, we are part of a complex web of life that supports us and nourishes our very existence. We could consider humanity as a living organism existing throughout history. As we die we leave behind for those who come after us, something not unlike coral. In the day-to-day scheme of things we are individuals. Yet if we are part of this creature, we might resemble a tiny synapse or some unique incandescence building towards a fulfillment, towards our own transcendence. We see we are not alone or irrelevant. We are in the end, indispensable and essential. Just like everyone else.

So what happened to the church? Or rather, what happened to true spirituality? In day-to-day events it has been transformed into a corporate pseudo-religious calling in order to create wealth, to centralize power and to maintain hierarchy. This is what it is, after all, all one has to do is look at its structure, and as soon as any group can cut itself off from the majority of the members they become an elite often making decisions for everyone else. This is the slippery slope human's fall into; we fear the unpredictability of non-hierarchical existence so much we cannot allow it even in our most sanctified places. Our religions and spiritual centers have for centuries used executions and torture to run everyone's lives based on the assumption they knew what was right. Again, it was based on what men learned when the agricultural revolution created the first surpluses of food; they realized they needed to organize all the citizens in order to safeguard this surplus. They did it by establishing arbitrary power in a hierarchy backed by a standing army and run by committee. It should be of no surprise to note that churches played a major role in war by maintaining the image of right cause backed by the hierarchical transition to Heaven. Often both sides had their own "true" religions that spoke their version of reality and were willing to send young men to their deaths in support of this surplus management scheme. Funny how when using plain language and taking the clever power saturated words out of the description the meaning changes and we can see another truth easier.

So what do we do now? Do we continue with our old identity or do we change it? Are we up to it? If so, what's next?

Is it possible that globalization is the evolution we have been waiting for, or is it the evil oppressor so many have predicted? Is global wealth creation the problem or is it the way out of poverty? Can humans be persuaded to try less hierarchical methods to create wealth? Will we eventually get "there" through the trial and error changes like we have used in the past? Probably the protesters who demonstrate at World Trade conferences might not demonstrate so violently if they knew developing nations would be helped to attain productive economies—that is if wealth was achieved in a thoughtful and altruistic manner respecting local cultural traditions and a level playing field. The fear of local peoples or Aboriginal societies is that the opposite is happening—that international corporations will not allow a reasoned development of wealth to occur. Corporations insist their development must be based on market conditions right from the start and if culture does not make money then out the window it goes. Compare this attitude to First Nations' land claims in Canada. In many circumstances present settlements include substantial allowances for cultural considerations. The recent news of the developments of the Mackenzie Valley pipeline includes guaranteed returns for the Inuit people. So it can be done. Not easily but with genuine concern, wealth can be created so cultures are not forced to compete with other cultures. Clearly the isolation and enthronement of culture in every wealthy society does not encourage less successful belief systems to join in the existing business atmosphere. Respect for the cultures of others while maintaining our own beliefs is not easy but it is the only way to develop wealth for all. It shows the true strength of what we hold dear. We have to find the common thread.

One successful amalgamation of cultures is modern Europe. Since the end of World War Two, Europe has steadily worked towards unification of many of the most prosperous nations. Now many less advanced nations are being welcomed into the Common Market of Europe. It is easy to forget that for centuries Europe was locked in endless wars and the championing of the "right" belief system. Even beliefs that had a common heritage caused horrendous wars that lasted for decades. Europe has finally put these turbulent times behind and moved on to embrace all the colors in their collective cultural rainbow. Their current economic struggles are probably only temporary; the effort put in place to resolve the issue is an example for us all and may be the best current example for the planet's future as well.

Generally though the rest of us are still locked into the first stage of our long development of survival in isolation from everyone else and we fail to see the great achievement of Europe as a future possibility in our own lives. In our paradigm of isolation cultural arrogance is still condoned and expected. It is everywhere. Still, we really do have an awful debt to our ancestors long dead, who believed themselves to be alone in the world and often at the cost of their own lives worked in dangerous mines or factories and then were forced into armies that left them isolated for days, weeks or even years from their families. Often they did not return, dying of their wounds or were abandoned by their Commanders as expendable. The French philosopher Jean Paul Sartre suggested, "The death of a soldier is seen as nothing more than the destruction of a tool."[259] Also the owners of industry, while creating freedom for millions by creating wealth remained locked to the helm of the ship that drove them-they forgot to free themselves! They had the money and the power, but were also its victims. Some eventually came to understand they had achieved everything isolation could offer them and then came upon the realization that something important was missing.

The fulfillment of a life's dream, filling in an existence of inadequacies, proving oneself to oneself, would normally be enough for any lifetime but once accomplished what to do? As I have written, every man (and now many women) have a list of "must do's so to speak that are essential commitments for their individual life. Some people may never develop them successfully to any sense of completion while others may conclude all of their goals and more at an early age. This is a crisis for both kinds of people. A lack of success can have never-ending consequences such as depression, drug abuse and violence, whereas the accomplished may languish in confusion or apathy sliding into middle age with the mind turned to past glories unable to find meaning in the perpetual present.

Many of the built-in social or cultural traditions as well as laws, all of the inventions of glorious machines and great ideas are really answers to other people's questions in their attempt to free themselves of their fate, and are not necessarily our questions. We are born into all these answers to other people's questions and we think this is reality, yet it is only solutions to their questions in their time and circumstance. Part of our fate is to learn which answers we have inherited that matter to us, and what are the questions for us to resolve. How do we choose which answers are valid to us, and which are not? What if several inherited answers are unacceptable yet are backed up in the outer culture by armed force? What if nudity to you was an answer yet to others a desecration? If life is truly about resolving our fates, as I believe it is, why are there so many impediments in the outer world attempting to prevent us from doing so? Are we a spiritual being living a physical existence or are we a physical being seeking a spiritual reality?[260] Why are so many people trying to stop us from living a free life?

We are restricted from fulfilling our fate by many of these pre-existing answers that have become habits for everyone else to live by and go unquestioned, having given up their quest to apathy or compromise. It could be said they did not completely resolve their own fates and so left a big mess for us newcomers to sort out. So not only do we have our own issues to resolve we also have the unresolved fates of millions of others weighing down the outcome. The pressure from so much baggage collapses many people into subordination and they add their unresolved questions to the weight already on the backs of the rest of us. Telling other people how to live is clearly the wrong way to go, because it simply does not work. As this is an unacceptable situation to live with for very long, we must see clearly what our individual fate is separate from the fate of others long dead, and move on by choice into present action with our answers intact and complete before we leave this life. We have an obligation to ask these questions so we do not add to the weight already piled high on the backs of coming future generations. Learning how to answer these questions ought to be the basis of our educational systems. If we fail to answer our own questions we end up with other peoples answers ruling our lives forever. My evidence for this is the fact that many of the most important revolutions[261] of the twentieth century were never agreed to publicly or voted on or even acknowledged as important to discuss. They are the Petro-chemical, Electronic, Nuclear, Television, Computer and Information Revolutions. We all just rolled over and played dead.

The most self-realized of the very wealthy individuals who recognized they had come to the end of what the acquisition of wealth could give them had been asking their own questions and some of them decided they should begin to give away all their great wealth. These are the philanthropists, the creators of non-profit societies, of charities and public works. Many men, tired of isolation and regardless of wealth or not, eventually realized that the whole purpose of an honorable manhood was to give back to his community in whatever manner and capacity he could; some get it sooner, some get it later, some never. They could have discovered this as young men before they had spent a lifetime struggling to create their personal empire, but with a script to work out, they had to learn it the hard way on their own. Either poor or wealthy, and when learned, a new way of life can begin that finishes the transformation of the man and brings out all of his natural goodness. He forgets his separateness and becomes a part of that greater creature; he lives life complete, through his own transcendence of his fate and all the inherited scripts he was taught.

Some will say this is just another script, and it could be, but you have to go through it first to know if it is or not. For some of us dropping dead on the ninth hole is Heaven, whereas for others it is on a mountaintop or working with children or in the garden. The transformation from self to no self or no-script has to occur regardless. Truly this is the spiritual purpose at the end of life, and one we prepare for all our lives.

Philanthropy, a spontaneous life choice, is the first step outside of the surplus management mentality. It includes many different kinds of giving such as money giving, giving of one's time, one's ideas, tools or property. A perfectly natural cycle starts to go full circle. Gifting is a very interesting subject and I believe this is part of the answer to the question of what happens to the mature male after he has raised his family, provided for a wife if married, and taken care of his elderly parents.

Of course we can see in Joseph Campbell's book "Creative Mythology" that even philanthropy is only a stage in a life—albeit an important one. The life cycle is something we do not pay much attention to at least not in the West; we think of retirement and the end of life. Joseph Campbell who so deeply explored the human reality, refers to Dante[262] on his ideal of the four stages of life as being far more complex and important:

- Adolescence to 25 years: Its virtues are four: obedience, sweetness, sensitiveness to shame, and grace of body. The aim of this period is increase; it is comparable to spring.

- Manhood—25 to 45 years: Its proper virtues are temperance, courage, love, courtesy, and loyalty; its aim is achievement, and its season, summer.
- Age 45 to 70 whose virtues are: prudence, justice, generosity and affability, that which enlightens, not only ourselves but also others. Usefulness and Bestowal.
- Decrepitude-70+: here the noble soul does two things:
- Returns to God as to that part whence (he) departed when (he) came to enter upon the sea of this life, and
- b) (He) blesses the voyage (he) has made.

There are many end-of-life theories from Aboriginal ones to modern novels. The important thing is not just retirement and death. We in the West have a lack of imagination here and few initiations to guide us. We have settled for an unfinished life instead of one seen, understood and blessed. Michael Meade,[263] the well-known drummer and storyteller, wrote in "Men and the Water of Life": "You could say that those feelings of chaos within life are actually calls from areas of unfinished initiation. Initiatory experiences inhabit the same deep psychic ground as birth and death. When the stages of life and radical occurrences in the life of an individual are not marked, old age becomes confusion and chaos. Dwelling with the little deaths in life changes the size and shape of the big death. Seen through the eye of initiation, death is not the opposite of life, death is the opposite of birth. Both are aspects of life." Our churches fill that need for some, but not for all. I hope my dad will finish his life in a manner similar to Dante's ideas.

Many men prior to this point are completely lost. Some never recover and die early; some do something extraordinary and that is care about others they have never met. They understand there is more to life than what you did while raising a family. I have seen it across the board: men from all walks of life joining clubs like Rotary, the Elks or men getting creative and starting their own organizations. I am sure many groups such as these exist throughout the world. I want to put to you that philanthropy is as natural a thing as sharing the "kill" and is as powerful an instinct as the protection of family from threat. Without it, children would not have access to many services now run by government, that originated as donations by wealthy or inspired individuals. Libraries, summer camps, churches and service agencies rely on philanthropy to survive and do their work. The hard working husband who could not afford to send his children to learn better skills looked to private bursaries and scholarships to pay for their education they needed.

At the same time though we must move on. The current paradigm of survival thinking which includes philanthropy is only the most dominant example of many existing kinds of masculinities. A new paradigm is beginning to appear not based on acquisition of power or the creation of wealth in traditional ways. I believe it is developing because enough wealth has already been created to free millions of people from ignorance and slavery. The Internet is one example of this fundamental shift. Information is everywhere and available to almost all strata of modern societies. Freedom and education to learn about freedom appear to be a growing trend. This is not philanthropy; it is a groundswell social transition.

Traditional male over-identification with provider and protector roles is now changing. What are the new models we can use? Many men seeking insight have joined men's support groups to explore these issues. They are easy to start. Many men are active in their communities because of them and because of the friendships they develop in those groups. Finding support to start one may not be that difficult. Hiring a counselor or psychologist for one or two nights to set it up would give you a necessary format for it to be successful. New models are beginning to show up and as minorities and women take on more of the wealth creation for a family, these traits will become even more noticeable as the list below suggests:

- Men tending their babies,
- Participating in men's groups,
- Becoming advocates for men's health,
- As teachers showing new ways for men to find friendship,
- Individual men going for a regular medical checkup,
- Everyday men encouraging male friends to open up about a personal problem,
- Men turning down the high-pressure job to spend more time with their children.

In the past many community-minded men would run for office, coach a soccer team, or become a member of a civic group encouraging voter reform or another civic issue of importance. What is new is men stepping out of the public eye to handle more domestic concerns and developing a new language to allow them to incorporate their emotions into their personalities. Other men could do well to become identified with this new masculinity and to foster it as it develops, for it is a step in a healthy direction. Non-profit societies are particularly well placed politically to encourage a new masculine identity that would not be seen as a threat to the hard-earned freedoms of minorities. Since our present culture has a strong equality stand for women, a strong inclusive stand for men would not be far off base and would be very timely. It is time for men to foster this new masculinity without the need to resort to hierarchy as the defining tool and power as the method. Unity in thought—unity in deed.

Many men seem to have missed this new and encouraging growth in masculinity. Along with cultural competition lies the disrespect shown to the elderly who can no longer generate wealth. Almost the entire culture, movies, comics, and fashions ridicule or at best ignore the senior members of our society. They are undervalued and uncared for; many left to die in nursing homes by selfish and unappreciative children. Just as their own fathers focused on creating wealth, so are they, casting out the weak and infirm, so they can get on with the job. I have said before this is the natural path to take in a survival driven culture; there are few choices and harsh realities to face. Some children are compassionate in making good decisions for their elderly and infirm parents. However in our wealthy industrial culture resurrecting the value of the elder could allow the natural cycle of a human life to feel more complete. I do see this happening much in the same way minorities have been freed by the generation of wealth and the philanthropy of mature individuals.

During the men's movement of the 80's, my own father came to several of the men's gatherings I helped to set up. He was given the opportunity to speak to the younger men about his experience as a man. I believe it was an important gesture of respect for him to be seen there. Men do not get a lot of this kind of praise. So by including our elders in family events, even if they say nothing, by asking them to speak at special times, by seeking their advice or having them praise the family in front of the grandchildren, we ensure the young never forget them. This is so important a role for the elders of a family—to get them involved. My father is now ninety-two and his exit from life is near, we celebrated his birthday and he is ready to go. I hope he can make peace with his worsening dementia.

Recent attempts at remaking masculinity have made many interesting and valuable contributions to our knowledge. However these attempts did not move us meaningfully forward although adherents in one of those attempts would say they experienced increased closeness with other men that they could not find anywhere else. This was the mythopoetic men's movement. This seventy's and eighty's movement produced a plethora of books on the wounded man. However, it generally reinforced the survivor paradigm rather than suggesting an evolution in masculine thought. However it did recognize the need for greater intimacy between men. Even though it has often been discredited as a reaction to feminist attacks on hierarchical social structures, men in many cultures began to reassess their identities.

Critics of the mythopoetic movement were alarmed by the focus on ancient role models (king, warrior, magician, lover) seemingly coming straight out of King Arthur's Court. This focus convinced some feminist observers that men were going backwards. The good of this revival was the deep bonding with other men that occurred and the rebirth of ritual in men's lives. It helped to bring back the ancient tribal closeness of the shaman and the supernatural. Many men were inspired in incalculable ways. The movement has died off and with the media's help has taken on an almost comic image of naked men dancing around a fire. Many cultural events are rooted in the time and place where they were created and addressed specific needs of that time and place.

The problem with the mythopoetic experience was the instrumental roles included in the teachings and experiences. Terms such as "King energy,"[264] and "Alpha Male" suggest a hint of class structure and hierarchy. These concepts are idealized and encouraged when they should instead be recognized as part of the survivor identity and be discarded for post-survivor role models using leveling mechanisms such as cooperative business models and democratic initiatory rituals like fairness. Leveling mechanisms are not "circles of emptiness" that some supporters of hierarchy might suggest. Granted, solutions may take longer but will satisfy greater numbers of people than self-appointed or even elected leaders could possibly achieve. In support of the mythopoetic movement, Robert Bly and others were sensing a lack in men at the time and were attempting to address this imbalance, as the many on going events showed.

By identifying ourselves with hierarchical terminology we continue to compartmentalize ourselves by pinpointing our place on the ladder of achievement and believe it is a fair conclusion to compare our personal success with others. We forget competition with ourselves is the only true measure of improvement.

I might go so far as to suggest that violent extremists living in the "Hero" archetype are in reality only frustrated individualists with no real vision, except their own "empire" to build. They talk a good line with no patience or ethics to speak of. Career heroes tend to like the spotlight and seek to keep it precisely by refusing to teach others. It is "on top" or nothing for those people. This is how most of us think, we want to keep what we believe is ours, ours.

Unfortunately for men who identify with the hero or warrior persona, there will be less and less tolerance for their outrageous behavior and they will be forced to seek opportunities further and further out on the edges of society, although there is still a definite need for them in these risky environments. For other men who seek fairness and democratic ideals, more and more opportunities will open to them. Men familiar with trust building exercises and attempt to create democracy on a daily basis are the new males of the modern era. They will find themselves within organizations; for example, they will be challenged by the very structure of meetings and will suggest alternatives to redefine the use of authority. There are new models to be found that are worth trying, if their groups are willing.

Within The Island Men Network here in Victoria, we attempted to resolve this issue by establishing a revolving wheel of job descriptions to produce our journal. We found it very valuable for dissipating and sharing power between diverse men and developing skills not normally tried or even considered by the traditional hierarchy in which we all live. Here is how it worked: if I had a strong desire to be the editor and do an issue from my view point, say for instance, power issues, I could first state this desire at a publication meeting, and this meeting would encourage statements from the other men too. If they could get excited about my topic, they would assist me to complete it. A danger here was that a strong character could dominate the process and have the group support only his topics. It was true that a mindful eye was needed to prevent this from occurring. This selection process for editor could be arranged as a "one time only" editor position to guarantee the process's effectiveness. Once around the wheel each person could suggest new topics to edit.

Having overcome this hurdle, the next step was to define the tasks required for that particular issue. Due to the fact that in the last issue my role of distributor taught me how to distribute the finished product, I had to teach the job to the person taking over from me. This task would include building and repairing the boxes we used for distribution on the street, delivering journals to the boxes, cleaning up messes at the boxes, such as vandalism, which did occur. As well I was to be instructed by the out going editor in order to enable me to function in my new role as the upcoming one. The end result was every man on the board had the opportunity and the pleasure of editing one or more journals that went to publication. It was very exciting and empowering to be apart of this non-hierarchical structure, to see something accomplished differently.

Years ago when I was completely self-employed, I used to hire many young people to help during busy times. I would train them, pay them well, listen to their stories and respect them as people. What happened? They went back to school, on to other kinds of work and left me to do it all over again. I was very frustrated. Then I meet Will. He had the same experience as an employer, and we began to brainstorm about how to get around this problem. We came up with the co-op model where we hired each other. He was an independent gardener and so was I. We kept our own business names and did our own income taxes, but called our new association "Harmony Landscapes Cooperative" which we placed on both our trucks. New members would have to be willing to change their truck ads to this joint one. Any work I could not do I gave to him and vice versa. I knew his skills and he mine. This has kept us busy during our down times. By that point we had expanded to five people, then three with the hopeful news that another would join soon. It went up and down but it worked. There was no hierarchy in this model, only equal members and their skills. We wanted it to be deliberately low key to reduce our workload and prevent it from becoming a "hiring hall." This way it is completely voluntary, with no dues and no obligations, other than to hire from the coop first and share the work. Eventually we wanted to get group insurance and dental plans etc since they are so much cheaper for groups than individuals, plus we had to watch how much time was involved in doing this too. The co-op eventually folded but the model is still representative of a possible solution to hierarchy for simple businesses.

When I first began my studies of power I experienced a period of intellectual paralysis. I could not function because every action I decided to take produced an opposite reaction in some other area. By way of example, I remember a conflict where I had acted out of fear. What stopped me in my tracks was the recognition that the person I was fearful of was possibly just as fearful of me in some other way. I did not understand enough of my inner workings at the time to be able to get past the fear. So if I was to function at all I had to find a way out of this conundrum. I decided to make as many conscious decisions as possible at every moment of my waking life. Since then I no longer feel that my very existence has terrible consequences for others or that I owe an apology to the ant I didn't see on the sidewalk. On the other hand I do take my existence here seriously, yet while living life in the moment I must remind myself to feel the fear of conflict and do it anyway. So joining a collective such as a men's group or publishing a local journal with no apparent boundaries was very disturbing at first. Fantasies of what could happen filled my mind with all kinds of dilemmas. It was the possible reactions from the public that disturbed me the most. Would they destroy the stands and trash the journals, or would they harass some of the writers? My fears also expressed themselves in the possibility that I would be made a fool of or feel overwhelmed by other powerful males. In some ways it was better than I thought. and at times worse; but what I gained was a sense of freedom I did not know before. And yes the public did some vandalism and showed up at some of our houses accusing us of outlandish behaviors. Regardless it was worth the problems and for the most part, they became comical and legend.

We used a leveling mechanism to share power within the Island Men organization. Leveling mechanisms can be used in many areas of life in order to improve communications at work, home or in a conflict situation. Our understanding of power and its positive uses are crucial to the use of democratic ideals. Indeed leveling mechanisms are the engines of democracy. They attempt to reshape the form power takes, as well as what structure controls it and what refinements and advances can occur. For the sexes these mechanisms provide challenges to the bio-cultural forces that now function as an impediment to modern civil society, such as historical sanctions against women entering politics. Our societies' great wealth acts as a dampening force to these ancient inherited blueprints of power by revealing them as constraining and restrictive and catering to the whims and dictates of elites. These democratic processes lead us to the creation of an even greater spectrum of wealth and a progressive educated freedom for vast numbers of citizens. As historical, biological and sexual definitions blur, our philosophical concerns drift toward the inevitable union of opposites. Power is no longer "power over" but "power with." Men and women can still be men and women but free to act on their own without hindrance by stereotypes. These examples of leveling mechanisms show that they are in fact a most important part of the evolution of any society and provide the best understanding of what is actually happening-the leveling of power structures.

Huge areas of additional reform can be obvious to the average eye and some may be below the vision of even trained observers. Other models to explore include new concepts of economic sustainability that are required to employ the continuing but slow decentralization of many Western societies, although conservatives may not see this decentralization occurring or worse see it as a danger. However the ongoing public outcry over the environment is probably an obvious example of this groundswell paradigm shift in thought. This process will encourage all of us to think and to make new although possibly miniscule decisions about our purchases, and our relationship to almost everything for that matter. When taken together they can have a powerful lobbying effect on decision-makers. The campaign against CFC's forced the appliance industry to find a new coolant for refrigeration products, and the development of hydrogen fuel cells builds on the public excitement of non-polluting transportation technology. Recycling efforts from curbside collections have been a huge success. There are so many citizen driven changes occurring we may fail to see them as they come to public attention. It is all very exciting and our future looks bright. Climate change and environmental degradation may in the long run turn out to be a hard adjustment period but just grist for the mill in our evolving human story.

An idea first brought to us by Einstein[265] is the beginning of a new science of unification theory. Current studies in physics are further developing this new definition of science by seeking the universal laws that hold everything together, instead of the traditional view that everything existed in isolation. "M" theory and beyond are beginning to show us the wisdom inherent in the interconnectedness of all things. The future holds interesting possibilities.

New ideas about power redistribution or democratization include unanimous decision making processes[266], worker rotation wheels, worker cooperatives, gender reconciliation processes, non-violent communication, mediation services, aboriginal circle sentencing, trust exercises, even parents asking their children's opinion on important social matters and many more. Not only are these fairness mechanisms operating in indigenous cultures, they are making major changes to Western ones as well. The process of Democracy is thousands of years old[267] and is one of the largest and most effective processes ever created. Also it was created in various places on the planet that were isolated from other centers of influence such as Europe and N. America and so shaped those cultures in varied and creative ways.

In a bold new experiment, South Africa has instituted a representative election system (1994)[268] where even parties that drew only 0.45 percent of the vote won two seats in their legislature. Here in British Columbia we just voted down a proposal for proportional representation for the second time.

However our collective struggle throughout history has inched forward hopeful of peaceful resolution of conflict. For example, models of fairness, one of our most important values, make it easier to step out of that hierarchical, competitive and survival oriented experience while still maintaining our business interests. I can focus on friendship, cooperation and mutual discussion to solve problems rather than relying on the loudest individual to supply the plan. Often the loudest or most forceful individual will have only a part of the solution which if carefully observed may closely resemble the traditional bio-cultural one.

We have moved from the Chieftain to the King and then to Democracy. Our level of maturity is still in question as we continue to resolve our problems with war making and denial of accountability for how the world's nations create hatred in other parts of the world.

I have noticed how easy it is to be confused over the right way to be in the world. Being a somewhat shy person as a child I have been climbing out of that misunderstanding all my life. It has been easy to believe it was best to mimic the external society for character examples to follow. It is too easy to believe that by deepening my voice and pushing out my chest in social situations that I will be safe from shyness or worse feelings. When nations see themselves as I did, of believing force could save me we are blind to our own troubles. Only when I allow the walls of protection to dissolve can I really exist in my true nature, and then let go of even the external crutches I used to help me attempt to expand. It is so easy to come to believe that daily experiences require a level of protection that we eventually forget we are even using since it becomes such a "natural" fit. Is the personal so different than the national? This attitude, it becomes part of us like we are wearing a shield we forgot to take off. Body armor, like real armor is in fact unhealthy to our well being without even knowing it is there. It can poison our relationships and delude us into a false sense of power and prestige that does not exist and becomes unnecessary as our real confidence grows.

One could say that a purpose of democracy is to produce in citizens the awareness of fair play and justice. Yet in the creation of democracy, freedom had to be repeatedly taken by force from the powerful few and given to the masses. Do not be fooled that it was given simply by a vote, although in rare instances a vote is what it took. Canada for example gained its independence from Britain in a gradual process eventually culminating in freedom and a new democracy. While as Emerson has said before, "All government in essence,[269] is tyranny." We still are not free. Since government seeks to control and dominate the individual, most Western governments would prefer not to inculcate in the individual or the greater culture a strong desire for greater freedoms. Examples of overly powerful companies that can place powerful lobbying efforts to protect their interests might include automobile, drug, aircraft or manufacturers of military equipment and computers.

Can it be that we just want to set up our own hierarchies the way we want? This may be true for some and at certain periods in time, but there must be a more compelling reason. After all, people keep attempting change. There must be something innate in us to want this. This innate desire for goodness is found throughout humankind, in all cultures and regions of earth. In males this quality is expressed in the most tragic of ways: the potential loss of his life through war. It is expected of males to sacrifice them-selves in this way and the duty has never been denied. Some might attribute it to religion or philosophy or even common sense but it is none of those. It is because it is innate in us to do so. We create philosophies and religions to reflect this inner reality and many of us live out our lives cultivating our own expression of this reality (police, military personnel, Coast Guard). There would be no hope for human life, as it currently exists if we could not evolve. As I have stated throughout this book, my belief is this kind of duty is slowly coming to an end and will be replaced by greater tolerance and broader individual freedoms, as we understand more compassionately our human nature. If this is not true we could not find a reason to live. Without hope for a better world we would wither and die on the spot. Yet some humans have endured horrendous situations such as torture or starvation and survived with help from such a positive outlook. Nelson Mandela is a great example. It's the positive outlook that is always with us, occasionally we choose to deny its existence yet its power runs through us every second of our life. Those who know this power have profound experiences in life and those who deny it live wondering what happened to theirs.

This goodness I wish to define is in every male, and female too. However the focus of this book is on men. I believe this is such a pivotal time for men that the male's innate goodness needs to be drawn out and celebrated. So much negative attention has been given to men over the centuries that some men and women feel there is no good at all in males, that they are a dying gender and that they should be extinct. Generally males are given a reprieve in our culture due to their fighting skills and reclaim a margin of value. Too bad for the rest of us guys though, now we have to do all that fighting and dying again, same old same old. Even Hollywood is at a dead end when it comes to men and the future, they have not got a clue what men will do after all the fighting and protecting and bacon delivery work is done. In truth, good men create love everywhere so there is no need to make them appear inaccessible, or for that matter ridiculous as in modern television representations of men and masculinity. Western culture seems to need to believe that men are inherently bad or stupid and that any goodness at all is scarce and unlikely to fall upon us, the oh, so deserving ones. So instead of facing the truth about how our fear runs us and that our expectations are more about our own inability to act independently without our "God Hero" to make it all safe, we, and they, go to work and buy stuff while thinking we are the "modern" people. The hatred and fear of men is everywhere, as well, the constant pressure on good men is unforgiving and unrelenting. An odd coincidence, yet I often marvel how good men survive at all when the pressure is so great to be shallow and insecure. On top of that just look at the weekly comics in any newspaper and frequently you will find a putdown of men-in a way it is a pandemic and invisible to everyone.

Have you ever felt guilty walking through a playground where there are only moms and kids? I have. Have you ever felt you had to prove you were a good man to skeptical and fearful women? All the time. This is a kind of judgment and fear men must live with, not so much that there really are that many evil men out there, but the media loves to portray this as true. It sells papers and movies celebrating this fear. The message is "Pedophiles are everywhere!" Do not forget because if you do, your little girl is a goner. Challenge yourself to discover the truth about this by finding the up to date statistics on crime.

In Canada go to this website[270] http://www.statcan.gc.ca/daily-quotidien/110721/dq110721b-eng.htm

For statistics on the USA go to this website[271] http://bjs.ojp.usdoj.gov/content/homicide/hmrt.cfm#longterm and you will see in proportion to population crime has come down over the last ten or so years, yet we still fear it so much.

The traditional goodness we have come to expect in a man is found in the methods and techniques that have been invented in order to provide for a family and protect them from harm. Even if it means the loss of their own lives, good men for centuries have given this gift to society. From this gift have arisen many of the institutions of philanthropy in its varied complexity of forms, and whether it is in striving for a cure to disease or being a good dad, it has been there since humans first existed. It may have began, as a curiosity to make things better and slowly became the gift of philanthropy where careers are built upon these high standards of service. The key ingredient here is a whole class of activities and processes I introduced earlier called leveling mechanisms.[273] In anthropology, leveling mechanisms refer to the distribution of wealth in a tribal environment. In this book I have broadened the concept to cover all human activities that produce a fair sharing of resources and power through human societies.

The best way to introduce these mechanisms is to describe how they have influenced human history. Actually they are everywhere:

One leveling mechanism, the development of the Magna Carta,[274] had a tremendous effect on early European societies. It is so obviously a great accomplishment yet so easy to forget. Here is a brief discussion of it:

Columbia Encyclopedia defines it as "the most famous document of British constitutional history, issued by King John at Runnymede under compulsion from the barons and the church in June, 1215." Now this is an extraordinary document, something that happened for a very good reason-fairness. This following quote is worth reading in its entirety because it is the beginning of our Parliamentary system of government and it helps us to see why this institution was created.

"Charters of liberties had previously been granted by Henry I, Stephen, and Henry II, in attempts to placate opposition to a broad use of the king's power as feudal lord. John had incurred general hostility. His expensive wars abroad were unsuccessful, and to finance them he had charged excessively for royal justice, sold church offices, levied heavy aids, and abused the feudal incidents of wardship, marriage, and escheat. He had also appointed advisers from outside the baronial ranks. Finally in 1215 the barons rose in rebellion. Faced by superior force, the king entered into parleys with the barons at Runnymede. On June 15, after some attempts at evasion, John set his seal to the preliminary draft of demands presented by the barons, and after several days of debate a compromise was reached (June 19). The resulting document was put forth in the form of a charter freely granted by the king—although in actuality its guarantees were extorted by the barons from John. There are four extant copies of the original charter."

"The charter definitely implies that there are laws protecting the rights of subjects and communities that the king is bound to observe or, if he fails to do so, will be compelled to observe. Historically most important were the vaguely worded statements against oppression of all subjects, which later generations interpreted as guarantees of trial by jury and of habeas corpus." "In later centuries it became a symbol of the supremacy of the constitution over the king, as opponents of arbitrary royal power extracted from it various "democratic" interpretations.

If you study history long enough, you will easily see the evil that men have done and you might be compelled to say that evil is all that men have done. However you cannot escape the fact that much of the remedy has also come from men. Of course this is now changing as women, thanks to feminism and their male supporters, have opened doors for other women to compete freely in the marketplace and government with men. Let us not forget the sacrifices our male ancestors made to create the freedoms and even more importantly the right to demand new freedoms we now enjoy.

The Magna Carta is a leveling mechanism that challenges hierarchical power and is a prime example of others that exist throughout the ancient and modern world. The study of anthropology lists many tribal cultures that have developed methods to control the wealth and power of individuals who are extremely successful. This is not to limit opportunity for these individuals but to guarantee that others are not excluded from sharing in this wealth, or injured in its acquisition. For the most part the process requires the wealthy individual to voluntarily give away all or most of his possessions at special events. This gift[275] elicits an obligation from the receiver in return for favors, often in the form of work or of giving prestige, thereby tying the community together. I will cover this area in more detail as the work proceeds.

Other examples of important leveling mechanisms in use today without us really being aware of their influence are:

- Endangered Species Legislation,
- Various Constitutions, Charter of Rights and Freedoms,
- Mandate of the United Nations
- Sustainable Economics / Appropriate Work Programs,
- Civil Society, non-profit societies, volunteering, fundraising events.
- Philanthropy, estate planning, donation of land or money to parks or universities, etc., and
- Aboriginal societies, the study of Aboriginal methods of justice, relationships, nature relationship.

All of the items in this list have one thing in common: a desire to make life fairer and ease the burdens on the poor and the vulnerable. Males have contributed those important qualities for those who rely on our help. Collectively those qualities are all leveling mechanisms and are a path-finding key to the unification of our dualistic way of thinking. As earlier sections suggested, the bio-cultural drives of males and females, as well as the institutions that were developed to maintain those drives required that our thinking be split into a universe of conflicting forces.

Hopefully as society continues to evolve and mature these problems will be addressed-the evidence of this occurring is there: By observing our wealth creation schemes in the past that has made a few powerful individuals wealthy, today many around the world are very well off. Theoretically this will lead us to a greater spiritual unification with ourselves by creating greater tolerance for differences or unusual attitudes or beliefs. How can we ignore the truth of this any longer?"

Along with tolerance comes the inherent responsibility for our own actions as well. We decide what is appropriate action, what we will do today or as the self-employed person might ask "can I take a day off or do I need to work?" We can give ourselves that choice, it makes us free and yet it makes us responsible too. How far can freedom or its truer form, responsible action, be taken in a democratic society? Wolff suggests, "For the autonomous man there is no such thing, strictly speaking, of a command."[276]

He states the situation clearly. If we are autonomous citizens we cannot in good conscience agree with some policies and laws made in our name without our agreement or consultation. He states, "On what grounds can it be claimed that I have an obligation to obey the laws which are made in my name by a man (a politician) who has no obligation to vote as I would, who indeed has no effective way of discovering what my preferences are on the measures before him?"[277]

So we are left with two choices,[278] either we become autonomous beings or we submit to a greater authority. It would seem that most of us have submitted to the authoritative model of culture in exchange for the right to participate in the survivor paradigm with all its individualistic wealth and privileges as a reward. So maybe we have to bend a bit until democracy evolves further. If it were true that humans are prepared and willing to move into a new paradigm then authority and the survivor paradigms would become non-existent. Individuals would cease to seek power in addition to their inherent skills and the value of each person would be honored as a gift. Fat chance is what the skeptics will say! It will be said that this is against human nature for this to occur, that it is naive to predict this, but again history suggests that in time, many small, unnoticed behaviors developing in sub-cultures can become mainstream cultural traits. Who would have thought that the hippy philosophy of environmental stewardship from the 1960's would eventually dominate many of the world's most important political debates of the twenty-first century?

Earlier yet is the significant contribution of the Levelers[279] of the 1640's "who came together during the English Civil War (1642-1648)[280] to demand constitutional reform and equal rights under the law. Levelers believed all men were born free and equal and possessed natural rights that resided in the individual, not the government. They believed that each man should have freedom limited only by regard for the freedom of others. They believed the law should equally protect the poor and the wealthy. The Levelers were the social libertarians of the day." I want to go into some detail here of their activities just to illuminate what it takes for social customs to be influenced enough to change society.

"The main leader (same source as above) of the Levelers was John Lilburne (known as Freeborn John). Lilburne was a Lieutenant Colonel in the Parliamentarian Army. Through his extensive writing and publishing of pamphlets, he was able to gain wide support for his ideas among army soldiers and the common people." He felt that "Those in government, before and after the (English) Civil War, felt alternative doctrines to be a threat. Tight controls were maintained over the means of communicating new ideas, by vesting the sole right to print and publish with agents of the state. Under Charles I all printing and publication were controlled by the Stationers Company, which held a legal monopoly."

Lilburne first became famous when, as a young man, he was arrested by officials of the Stationers Company while assisting in the illegal importation of texts from the Netherlands. Tried and convicted before the Star Chamber, he was flogged down the length of Fleet Street, pilloried, and then shackled in a prison cell. Lilburne was freed after two years, in time to enlist with the Parliamentary Army. After the war, Parliament was no more willing than the King had been to relinquish control of printing. The Stationers Company was not abolished, but reformed as the "Committee of Examinations." Lilburne soon fell afoul of the Examiners. Locked away at their behest in Newgate prison, he wrote England's Birth-Right Justified, an eloquent piece of writing in which he called for the dissolution of the "insufferable, unjust and tyrannical Monopoly of Printing."

In 1649, Lilburne published the "Agreement of the People,"[281] a manifesto for constitutional reform in Britain that gave birth to many of the ideas that are embodied in the U.S. Constitution and Bill of Rights. This particular version was smuggled out of the Tower of London, where Lilburne and others were being held captive.

Included in the Agreement of the People:

- Right to for all people to vote for their representatives,
- Right against self-incrimination,
- Freedom of religion and press,
- Equality of all persons before the law,
- No judgment touching life, liberty or property but by jury trial,
- Abolition of capital punishment except for murder,
- No military conscription of conscientious objectors,

- No monopolies, tithes, or excise taxes,
- Taxation proportionate to real or personal property.
- Grading of punishments to fit the crime, and
- Abolition of imprisonment for debt

In 1649 Charles I was executed. To his credit Lilburne did not approve of the sentence; instead he wished for a public trial by the common people so Charles could stand and face his greatest victims.

Leonard W. Levy wrote the following about Lilburne[282] in the Origins of the Fifth Amendment. "Lilburne was, or became, a radical in everything—in religion, in politics, in economics, in social reform, in criminal justice—and his ideas were far ahead of his time. From 1637 when he was but twenty-three years old until his death twenty years later, he managed to keep his government in a hectic state. In successive order he defied king, parliament, and protectorate, challenging each with libertarian principles. Standing trial for his life four times, he spent most of his adult years in prison and died (in exile in the Netherlands). Yet he could easily have had positions of high preferment if he had thrown in his lot with the Parliament of Cromwell. Instead, he sacrificed everything in order to be free to attack injustice from any source. He once accurately described himself as an honest true-bred, freeborn Englishman that never in his life loved a tyrant or feared an oppressor." Although the Leveler movement ended, and John Lilburne eventually died in prison, the ideas of the Levelers live on.

Lilburne was just like you and me except he refused to be ruled by dualistic thinking and the power driven individuals as well as the institutions they created-so we would think we were safe. That is what men are supposed to do, right? Make people feel safe? This is where the male role gets in the way of justice. It is not that we fail to progress, it is that we fail to notice existing and potential paradigm shifts and then to promote them. Yet of course this is how we change, by slowly absorbing these new ideas into our daily thoughts and behaviors. Many people found the Leveler ideas frightening until they gave them some consideration and incorporated the new ways into their own lives.

Yet as Wolff points out "If autonomy and authority are genuinely incompatible,[283] I state again, only two courses are open to us. Either we must embrace philosophical anarchism and treat all governments as non-legitimate bodies whose commands must be judged and evaluated in each instance before they are obeyed; or else, we must give up as quixotic the pursuit of autonomy in the political realm and submit ourselves (by an implicit promise) to whatever form of government appears most just and beneficent at the moment."

I wonder how many citizens have made this careful decision to submit or to face the consequences of going against a law they disagree with? So failing to decide, most of us go along with the survivor paradigm without thinking it through that it might not be the only show in town. Possibly it is the result of never being taught to make choices by insecure parents or to face decisions with real consequences and the desire to live with our choices. There is far too much fear and the fear of fear in our culture today.

I would like to suggest a kind of political process that would use leveling mechanisms to bring about stability and confidence in a given culture. Let's say that an issue needs to be decided, such as whether or not to build a new bridge to relieve traffic congestion. Currently we have boards of engineers and financial planners who sit on committees to decide these things for us who in turn are appointed by people we elect with the hope they will make good decisions for us. The results are often seen as lacking foresight, creativity and even honesty. The use of a leveling mechanism could be used to get a better decision: public debates could be used to inform the population about the issue then use local elections to pass or defeat it. This is not a new process but needs to be expanded to all areas of decision-making, eventually and effectively removing governments from power as well as separating knowledge from power, and replacing these current institutions with "public educators" who would be given the job of consulting with the public to make good voting decisions. They would be hired or fired by public referendum. Topics for voting would be accepted from the public on a first come first served basis, with all suggestions being given fair and equal treatment. The growing use of Internet voting might be a useful mechanism here. No longer would we be held hostage to political parties and individuals seeking power since a pre-requisite for this job would be political neutrality or at least a commitment to this ideal. A similar process is used today in local jurisdictions but not in all the ways it could be. In parliamentary democracies it is the job of the Speaker of the House of Commons to perform this role. It might be a small but useful step in furthering our democracy right now. The role of the Speaker could be enlarged dramatically to all areas of society. The Speaker would actually have no power, as his/her role would be brinkmanship. This is a simple example[284] of how leveling mechanisms could make our societies more fair and representative than they are now.

Emma Goldman, felt that the State (as it exists today) enslaves our spirit and dictates every phase of our conduct.[285] While I agree for the most part, I am glad that people are required to drive on certain sides of the road. Just imagine the chaos if drivers went everywhere they wanted to. On a daily basis you might find drivers fighting their way through your garden, destroying sensitive ecosystems of rare plants and birds or around your patio during a wedding. Who would care about anything unless some agreements are created? Here is the catch to having agreements—we the living, have laws decided by some committee that had the appointed responsibility to make them by somebody else-but we were not them. As Wolff said we have to go along with previously made laws unless we wish to challenge them, which today is a very difficult and time consuming effort. How many people challenge laws made in their name that they did not have any say in deciding? Here is the true beauty of democracy that many people gave their lives for—you and I could disagree or challenge laws that do not represent us. However it is like the laws are cast in concrete and must be jack hammered back into sift able conditions so their basic elements can be seen and examined.

In many situations laws are not challenged properly because the people these laws affect are either too poor or illiterate or overwhelmed to mount an adequate defense. One such example that has been adequately challenged (for the moment) is the SPP or the Security and Prosperity Partnership[286] discussions between Canada, the United States and Mexico. In short, it is an economic superhighway built expressly for commodities that would span all three countries with free labor zones that incorporate reduced labor standards, lower environmental regulations and lower wages. The real effect on the countries themselves would be a lessening of what makes each country unique. For example Canada cherishes strong environmental standards and the maintaining of its water rights. Canada's water would be on the table and unknown to many is already being shipped out in oil pipelines in order to move oil sands bitumen to the US market.[287] The individual countries would not be able to opt out of these agreements without severe financial penalties. The ultimate goal of SPP is the political, economic and military union of North America.

A recent film by Paul Manly, "You, Me and The SPP,"[288] has been crossing Canada. It highlights the fact many people are completely enraged that these high level discussions have been going on without public input or referendum. SPP has been called a shadow government that is anti-democratic and run without elected government involvement, but run instead by corporations. Like the Berlin Wall the West has its secret strangleholds that must be torn down so people are free too.

An even more disturbing occurrence is the ongoing escapades of The Bilderberg Society,[289] another secret "Club" whose membership includes many of the world's Presidents, Prime Ministers, leading corporate directors and wealthy businessmen. They meet regularly without public input or discussion and refuse to report agenda items or to allow press releases. With this kind of secrecy many understandable conspiracy theories have surfaced regarding their secret discussions. The most prevalent theory denounces Bilderberg as a power mongering crew of schemers who meet to plan and promote an eventual world government run by corporations rather than democratic processes. Imagine the money to be made and the injustices going unchallenged. Many science-fiction films predict these horrific future scenarios as true to life predictions, something we must not be complacent about any longer. Recent examples include: "Gattaca," "Moon," and especially for me at least, "Children of Men." If these Bilderberg conspiracy theories are true, disempowered societies could easily be created. How does this organization get away with its secrecy? It is up to you and me to hold these people accountable to the citizenry. The top down psychology of heads of state is the problem and not the solution.

Ian Buruma[290], a Professor at Baird College in New York wrote in the Globe and Mail in 2009, "[…] What's needed to revive liberal idealism is a set of new ideas on promoting global justice, equality and freedom. [In the 1980's] Mr. Reagan, Mrs. Thatcher and Mr. Gorbachev assisted in the end of an ideology that once offered hope and inspired real progress, but resulted in slavery and mass murder. We are still waiting for a new vision that can lead to progress-this time, we hope, without tyranny." Then 9/11 happened and paranoia became the new rule of the day. But it does not have to be so. We can address our mistakes and learn from them.

We have choices to make every day. However, as L. Susan Brown suggests of some people, "when faced with the ambiguity of their own existence, assert that if there is no God-given or absolute meaning in life then there is no meaning at all" they give up or become apathetic and self-serving. They seek the goodies a society may provide but have no willingness or ability to defend those rights for others. Again they believe they created it all themselves; so when they are defeated there is nothing left. Those who seek ultimate answers will be disappointed by life because situations change and so do the solutions. These individuals may attempt to evade the very responsibility of their own existence and become perfect fodder for hero types, or leaders that promise "every little thing" or religious conversion to the great hero in the sky or become willing victims of anti-democratic policies so their wonderful lives and the wealth they have accumulated will not be disrupted. Which of course, upon reflection this hoarding and lust for wealth can never be completely fulfilled; yet they want it regardless.

An important point is made by Simone de Beauvoir who wrote "[...] the human individual is [...] a being whose being is not to be [...] That is, they are never finished[291], they never achieve being." However, this lack of being is, in fact, a positive attribute as it gives to humanity the possibility of creating themselves, their world and their ethics freely or to restrict it. And "If humanity were like a god and could achieve being, there would be no question of an ethics, since meaning would be absolute." Ethics would be perfect and all chaos would be accounted for. So living with imperfection as our lot dictates, and if we decide to, we can work our way towards more and more inclusive solutions to our predicaments-and we do. This is our beauty. We have tried hierarchical systems and power-based systems for a solution but they just disenfranchise many people. Then we tried democratic principles. Now new kinds of leveling mechanisms are being implemented as valuable tools for responsible societies.

Some evidence of improvement can be seen in a report published by James Baxter in The Vancouver Sun (Oct 1, 1999) showing that consumers will be no longer fooled by irresponsible corporations. Nike[292] lost thirty percent of its sales in the two months after a fiasco of child-labor allegations were raised. A poll of 25,000 people worldwide taken in May 1999 by Environics International showed that one in five global respondents had punished a corporation at some point. Also a vast majority demanded that corporations be responsible for the health and safety of employees, eliminating child labor, ensuring the safety of the environment, and generally behaving ethically. We have the power in this life, and the Bilderbergs and others hold their meetings in secret because they know it-our failing is to let others lead us. We just cannot get away from the fact that leveling mechanisms are the only real protection from our own stupidity. Honestly, everyone has been greedy or abusive towards someone or something, like hitting the dog or blindly spanking a child, we need leveling mechanisms to teach us about ourselves and to remind us of ways to help find new and more appropriate solutions to problems and stresses. What else is there? Every time we really solve a problem leveling mechanisms are probably involved. This is self-evident.

The traditions of Aboriginal cultures are becoming widely accepted in some jurisdictions. Restorative justice or circle sentencing programs are being considered as an alternative to jail for some offenders. There is a lot of good change occurring and reason to hope. However a recent change in government in Canada may send prison reform back to the past.

However, National Post Journalist Christie Blatchford[293] (Jan 10, 2000) writing on restorative justice describes a situation where an Ontario police officer was shot at repeatedly with a clear intent to kill him. The event so traumatized the officer that when the offender was seeking parole, the officer refused to attend a restorative justice proceeding. He wanted nothing whatsoever to do with the man who nearly took his life. The lesson here is when there is doubt on either side that one or both are misrepresenting their stories, or the pain is too great, no healing can occur, at least not for a long time. Restorative justice can only work when both parties are attempting to be reconciliatory. This works for individuals as well as corporations and governments too. In this situation it is understandable a reconciliation process was unworkable, but there are many others where they can and do work.

Consider for a moment the sheer number of male inmates versus women. What is it about men? Many studies (see Statistics Canada website) have shown that poverty[294] and the hopelessness that goes with it are leading causes of criminal behavior in males. Our criminal justice system deals with this problem by removing an offender from his community and by placing him in a large building with hardened criminals. What is being accomplished here? A transformation? Yes, into a more experienced and better-informed criminal.

If however we took this same individual to another building or forest setting, brought together his extended family, his victims, friends, and community outreach workers and came to an agreement about his rehabilitation, do you think he would have a better chance than in the traditional prison system? Someone in the circle might give him a job as well as watch over him during work hours. When he was finished for the day he would be picked up by someone else, driven home and passed onto family members for the evening. What begins to happen is that the community slowly realizes the offender is more of a symptom of problems within the community rather than 'the' problem in the community. So other things can start to happen such as finding money to build a community center or skateboard park or a pool or bring in business to give youth better jobs. The problem gets dealt with and resolved by the average citizen rather than by a government agent who may or may not even live in the same city.

Blaming individuals will not create solutions. Yet our courts do blame individuals for their mistakes and often brutally. We think making potential criminals too afraid to do the bad thing will bring peace. We hope that they will somehow learn a lesson. We create fear instead of peace, and opposition to civil society becomes established in everyone's mind instead of loyalty to community. We create criminality because we fear it so much. The only way out is to accept people for who they are. Many of these antisocial men are seeking connection with wiser men than themselves because they know they are off base on some things. Often there is nowhere for them to turn other than girl friends who may not understand. Of course some do and so are loved deeply by these men. Sometimes these guys just need a little nudge to do the right thing. What stops them is the fear of their loyalty being abused. Of course that is nothing new to them, they have had that abused all their lives and they cannot take it in big doses. Without support they might do the wrong thing instead. Of course, say the skeptics, go easy on the criminals to your own destruction. Truly there are many who will take advantage of vulnerable people or exploit insecure situations to their benefit by committing a theft, a murder or genocide. These kinds of people require special handling so to speak. While we call them evil, it is really their actions that in the end are actually evil. We confuse the person for the deed. I am not talking about going easy on these wrong doers; what I am suggesting is to question our reaction to them. What result do we want from our handling of this situation? Do we want this wrong doer to suffer for his crimes, or do we instead want criminals to learn from their crime and to make restitution for it? Some might say there is no learning without suffering and our system of criminal justice is clearly focused on the suffering rather than the learning. We still want revenge; we want him to pay for what he did, yes something must be done to right the wrong, so what do we want, an inclusive society or a vengeful one?

I came across a copy of "Justice in Aboriginal Communities-Sentencing Alternatives" by Ross Gordon Green[295] and noted that even in the most advanced democracies a typical judicial proceeding looks something like this.

> "A foreboding court-room setting secures the seated Judge presiding on high, robed to emphasize his authority, armed with the power to control the process, and is rarely challenged. Lawyers stand in deference to his power. Council, with their prominent place in the room control the input of information, with their familiarity of the rules and of legal language exudes a confidence lay people are intimidated by and so remain quiet. This intimidation is intentional, and in order to increase the separation between Council and the public, the community is relegated to the back of the room often physically separated by a fence or bar and enforced by uniformed guards. This ritualistic performance is intended to keep ordinary citizens out of the process. This scene reinforces in the public mind of the Judge's pivotal wisdom and who supposedly has the resources to develop a just and viable conclusion."

Whereas a circle sentencing process laid out by Judge Stuart,[296] shows a very different scene.

"For Court, a circle to seat thirty people was arranged as tightly as numbers allowed. When all seats were occupied additional seating was provided in an outer circle for persons arriving late. Defense sits beside the accused and his family. The Prosecutor sat across the circle from the accused and to the right of the Judge. Officials and members of the community as well as Police officers and probation officers sat where they wanted. The process might begin with a prayer from an Elder of the community, and ritual smudging with sweet grass smoke. All religious beliefs are tolerated and welcomed. Everyone in the circle has the chance to talk or to remain silent. The Prosecutor will present the circumstances of the offence, the community perception of the seriousness of the crime, and make submissions as to sentence . . . the members of the circle are asked by the Judge to consider the problem and possible solutions. This allows the community to become specific when talking about the needs, strengths and resources available to the offender before them. The accused will be asked to address the circle and often speaks with much emotion and insight into the situation. If the victim is present, they are asked to speak to the circle. These processes are different in each community as they are designed to fit their particular circumstances and vision."

According to Canadian Chief Justice Bayda,[297]

> "A sentencing circle is much more than a fact-finding exercise with an aboriginal twist. While it may and does serve as a tool in assisting the judge to fashion a "fit" sentence and in that respect serves much the same purpose as a pre-sentence report, a sentencing circle transcends that purpose. It is a stocktaking and accountability exercise not only on the part of the offender but also on the part of the community that produced the offender. The exercise is conducted on a quintessentially human level with all interested parties in juxtaposition speaking face to face, informally, with little or no regard to legal status, as opposed to a clinical, formal level where only those parties with legal status participate and only at their respective traditional physical, cultural and ceremonial distances from each other."

The sentencing circle exercise permits not only a release of information, but also a purging of feeling, a paving of the way for new growth, and reconciliation between the offender and those he or she has hurt. The community to which the offender has accounted assumes an authority over and responsibility for the offender—an authority normally entrusted to professional public officials to whom the offender does not feel accountable.

At Pelican Narrows in Saskatchewan,[298] an actual assault circle is evidence of the evolving nature of circle sentencing. This circle involved ten offenders, both adults and youths, charged with a serious assault on a youth. The circle had twenty-five participants, including Judge Fafard, the offenders, members of their families, and other community members, two police officers and a defense council. The victim was not in attendance as Judge Fafard had recently sentenced him in another case. The circle opened with a prayer in Cree by a local elder. The judge outlined the range of sentences under the Criminal Code of Canada. All offenders were charged with aggravated assault, which carries a maximum penalty of fourteen years imprisonment. Corporal Bob MacMillan outlined the circumstance of the offence. The offenders had forced their way into the victim's home, where they had kicked and beaten him. The police believed beer bottles and logs had been used in the beating, which left the victim unconscious and bleeding.

Circle participants took turns speaking to the offenders and suggesting appropriate sentences. A consensus developed that one offender, the only one with a previous record, and apparently the instigator of the assault, should not receive the same sentence as the other nine because he had already appeared before the committee on a similar charge. They believed he needed a different kind of sentence, more focused on rehabilitation. Circle participants believed he should receive a short jail sentence, followed by probation with conditions similar to those imposed on the other nine offenders. These conditions included attending counseling sessions at the local alcohol rehabilitation center, undertaking 156 hours of community service work, abstaining from the possession or use of alcohol or firearms, taking a anger management course, and writing an apology to the victim. In addition, individuals and organizations from the community can step forward to assist in the rehabilitation of the offender. They might offer to make sure he attends the counseling session and the anger management course, while reporting back to the committee on compliance. Organizations might offer employment or volunteer opportunities that might lead to work and so on.

As can be seen from these examples there is a broad range of alternatives to traditional prison for offences. They just need to be tried, and they have been used throughout history. But in order to remember to use them we have to do the hard work of community building. Every community could implement alternative solutions in their own way and find what works best for them. Criminal justice issues are such an important area for men to engage in and to demand reforms. For too long we have this revenge filled need to torture people that commit offences. While the feelings are understandable, violent revenge by the state does not repair the damage to the offender or the victim, especially if we believe the offence was produced by a cause from within the reality of the community, such as high unemployment. Traditional justice methods are just barely substitutes for vigilantism by armed gangs or mobs. Only by intensifying the community involvement with the parties can the true issues involved such as poverty, drug addiction, immaturity, previously hidden physical or sexual abuse come to light and be assessed and treated within the same greater community. The trick here is to maintain the community involvement in the process.

So while these are good ideas, communities might just choose to not bother with these people and use the hierarchical system instead to deal with the offenders. The individual goes away but not the problem and the actual cause of the criminal act may still exist within the community. It keeps showing up in other young offenders and in other ways. Instead of assaults it becomes drugs or child porn rings. It is the cause of the criminal act that has to be addressed. Only then do we actually solve the problem.

The most powerful tool I have ever seen for intervening a conflict between two people or issues in a community is the "Talking Stick."[299] It is a First Nations invention and bestows the sole right of the holder to speak, completely free of any interruption and remains so until he or she is finished. This may take a while, but you get all the goods. What I mean is, you get the truth as this person sees it, at this time, free of complaints from others or safe from any attempts by others to influence the speaker. Any interruptions are immediately snuffed out by all present. Some times you may sit in silence for a long time before the person even speaks, and when they do something truthful and remarkable comes out. The talking stick is a very good example of the unification of opposites and non-dualistic thinking we have been discussing earlier in the book.

When the speaker is finished the stick is passed around a circle in order for another speaker to speak his or her truth. It is encouraged for the speakers to focus only on their own experiences and feelings, or similar experiences with other people and to allow any spontaneous emotion or memories to come to the surface. Frequently the speaker seems to be in another world because so often the difficulties encountered in life are really the result of injuries received many years ago at the hands of different people. The talking stick has given the speaker the opportunity to explore these past experiences and make connections and recognize patterns in their own behavior that has led to this current difficulty. It does require some experience to use a talking stick but not a lot, in fact it can be used effectively after only a few minutes instruction.

After several rounds with a stick the two parties can often let go of their anger toward each other upon seeing common experiences in life that have led to this conflict. Both are humbled by the recognition of the healing work they need to do on their own psyches. This process can take several hours with many turns at the stick. It can be used for formal community discussions as well.

So why do we not push for political reform like this so decisions can be made simply and fairly for all? Again we run up against the more traditional aspects of masculinity where fear of scarcity and control over resources (which includes ideas and people) keep danger to within tolerable limits. Too much change that is unregulated or having the appearance of anarchy sends the control freaks of business running together to get the world back into some kind of machine like system (think Bilderberg or Bacon's book). If it is not predictable it is dangerous in their kind of thinking. It is not that they are wicked people; it is that they allow fear to run their lives. They believe it is the smart way to go and by paying attention to their fears and the fears of others, they will profit in the end. Rather than valuing the qualities of fairness or the use of leveling mechanisms, they can only imagine power and hierarchical solutions. This is top-down thinking instead of a level playing field. Once you get into these kinds of power systems it can be like a drug, one that promises more and more rewards the longer you stick with it. This fear is the obstacle men must overcome to move on to a more appropriate masculine fit for today's world. So how would you convince your venture capitalist friends to consider leveling mechanisms instead of the bottom line or sales?

Let's take a look at a critically important sustainable business I know of in the logging industry. Merv Wilkinson, as a young forester started a logging company in Ladysmith B.C. in 1938.[300] He decided that clearcutting his land was not the best practice and after studying Scandinavian forestry practices he implemented a similar harvesting program here. So after sixty years of harvesting, the company now has more timber on its land than it did before the new practices were put in place.

By thinking sustainably we create jobs that will not disappear, maintain an ecological balance that has in fact been enhanced, maintained the hydrological cycle, enhanced the diversity of tree species and other wildlife values as well. The stumbling point for an investor is the slow turnaround of his money. However I believe it is clear that this business model is sustainable and does make a profit, if slowly at first. The point is that it would be an almost worry free investment and could be enlarged simply by buying up more land and begin to harvest using the same principals. Imagine if all the forests in British Columbia were under sustainable forest practices. There would no longer be unemployed loggers or mill workers because there would be a reliable and constant stream of wood. Businesses could plan on growth instead of closures and communities relying on forest companies for their base income could prosper and develop up to the carrying capacity of the growing forest. Now tell me who in their right mind would not invest in this? I believe there are many examples in other industries where this is also true; it is mainly a matter of looking.

Another critical solution needs to be found in order to resolve our issues with fear. To help understand why fear is such a problem and it seems to be everywhere in our world, I want to introduce an idea into our continuing discussion that fear is the key to many things conscious and unconscious. Niccolo Machiavelli, the famous writer who in 1532 shared a deep understanding of fear helps to illuminate part of the solution. In his remarkable book "The Prince" he delivers a significant crisis for us all: He suggests that if we recognize that to be feared in life rather than loved we may succeed in monumental strides forward but exist basically alone and driven by maintaining these fears in others and the worry of betrayal. If we prefer to be loved, we are vulnerable and can expect the full brunt of rejection, compassion, betrayal, criticism, and yes, love as well.[301] I call him "The Prince of Fear" because he describes the condition of our existence so well. He describes a choice that men and women make depending on their desire to be loved or feared for often-arbitrary advantages. Of course it may not be a choice we make but a deep built in character response to living. What a choice! Here is a quote from "The Prince", ". . . And men have less hesitation to offend one who makes himself loved[302] than one who makes himself feared; for love is held by a chain of obligation, which, because men are wicked (are human), is broken at every opportunity for their own utility, but fear is held by a dread of punishment that never forsakes you." We know this in our guts, and yet we do not have to be ruled by it, there is always our ability to not make a choice but to live in the middle ground, not being too vulnerable neither being too controlling either. Or we can choose to fall on our sword and knowingly live out our lives in cowardice and the terror that comes from ignorance.

How does one face such a dire reality? What he is suggesting is that in order to be successful or to become powerful we must decide to create fear in all those around us! We then create the boundaries, and falsities and then the hierarchies to protect us. We arm the police and convince the populace that criminals are everywhere. We surround ourselves with material goods to maintain our false image of ourselves as protected and upstanding citizens. No! We are not isolated, we say, we only want to live a good life. When in fact we have created a culture of fear and isolation. This is our own doing. Machiavelli warns us of our own folly—we only have to listen.

What is it going to be, fear or love?

It is obvious that a balance is required in order to function in life. If I seek to be only loved, individuals will surely abuse my trust, not deliberately but through forgetfulness. In other words sometimes people need reminders of boundaries between relationships. This is where fear (respect) comes into play. You state the boundary and if the fear of the loss of the relationship is great enough they will agree to a compromise in behavior. If not then you have not lost a friend because this person never was a friend. However some wounds are so deep that even numerous reminders are not going to be enough to stop boundary crashing behavior. Machiavelli suggests we choose our friends and especially our business partners with great care.

It is also possible to choose to ignore the Machiavellian dangers by remembering that we do not create opportunities by ourselves, we need others to open doors for us and we must not forget them, because they may turn against us and then we are doomed. We must in turn open doors for others as well as our benefactors or mentors. For example that plumber who did such a great job for you should be referred on to your friends; this is what opening doors for others means. He will say of you that you were a pleasure to work for, increasing your social prestige and reputation among your friends. Life works both ways, and if one does not do his duty Machiavellian principals come into force disrupting everything. It reminds me of ungrateful customers who complain about minor details of a job or the ones that squeeze the contractor for extra but unpaid little favors; other contractors will avoid them because word has a way of getting around about difficult clients. Likewise to the corner-cutting contractor who cheats his clients, word about him also has a way of getting around. Even if the satisfied customer or contractor does not spread the good word, the vacuum created will cause a decline in life's generativity. It is magical in a way the more we put into our lives the more we get out of it. If we comment on a good client to other contractors they will trust our opinion and possibly sub-contract work to us precisely because they sense we are a reasonable and positive person-one who can see good qualities in others. The client will also be considered a good referral. So what goes around comes around. At the same time though as a professional landscaper I have noticed I get most of my work from clients that actually like me-for reasons entirely of their own personality.

To sum up this idea for individual relationships, if one is unable to love, as depicted in the Machiavellian nightmare, we will never experience fear, thereby not gaining skills to deal with stresses in relationships or to respect the boundaries of others. If you will not allow yourself to feel fear, you may miss important clues about intimate relationships and thereby be seen as disaffected or uncaring and your friends and associates may abandon you.

As well, Machiavellian economics has a large following from the business community who may wish to develop the right kind of instincts for winning at the money game. Whether Machiavelli wished for us to create an attitude of fear in the culture of one's friends, clients and associates is not clear from reading his book. Instead what appears to be written is just the observation that he witnessed this behavior in other people during his lifetime. The fact that many men and business leaders are attracted to his words ought scare us enough to heed the warnings by keeping a close eye on corporate dealings.

No doubt many modern business people have seen that creating a climate of fear in the workplace can lead to success since few will challenge them and especially if their employees fear the consequences. A domineering, aggressively assertive and inconsistent employer comes to mind. A terse reminder of an overdue bill payment is another. Yet did Machiavelli propose these ideas as facts about human nature or as a warning to us that we can and might develop these capacities if we lose our way? A warning that was misinterpreted as "truth?" It's up to us in this matter it seems since co-operation has been shown to be a far more successful adaptation for survival than competition, but at the same time there is nothing like stiff competition to get the fear level up.

This is such a critical issue for our study because a major factor in individualistic thinking is the creation of fear in class politics. For example, employers will use fear as a motivation for greater production. Whereas the use of positive inducements including safe working conditions or profit sharing might have worked just as well or even better, but as was found by early capitalists if workers were paid very good wages they might not come back until they were in need again. Human nature is tricky to understand yet leveling mechanisms do work. Bully employers will use fear as a means to appear superior to their victims when actually the reverse is more likely the truth. The interesting thing about bullies though, is that they can have a special gift or unique perspective on humanity that is not yet defined and is much like a diamond in the rough. Remember the message from Alcibiades that the citizens gave up their own power to him and often paid for it in the end. So be careful whom you call "Hero." You could say Hitler was another bully who took over his people's unconscious aspirations in order to rule them-they paid for that with the total destruction of their nation. They believed power and fear are superior to compassion and empathy, yet at the end of our lives we all seek to be at the very least "considered or remembered" for something. Even the most fearful or hateful of us aspire to some good, even if it is as simple as feeding the dog every day, there is a part of us that feels some warmth in the simple act of caring.

The use of fear as a means of social control may well be something we all do in our personal lives too, the bringing up of an uncomfortable topic for discussion being an example. Yet we must clear the air and get on with life too. The individual that uses fear to dominate friends, family or employees is walking a tightrope. Read into this next quote from Machiavelli and find the twin threads of fear and love: "But when a prince[303] who founds on the people knows how to command and is a man full of heart, does not get frightened in adversity, does not fail to make other preparations, and with his spirit and his orders keeps the generality of people inspired, he will never find himself deceived by them and he will see he has laid his foundations well."

My take on this quote could resonate for all of us. We all at times must be in command of a given situation. Do we let children injure themselves without cause? Do we allow the local charity to fail if we can see a way through? I believe Machiavelli refers us to command well but never lose respect for our associates and dependents and especially for those who have opened doors for us. Of course the case could be made that here is a blueprint for a dictator who wants to hang around awhile too long. It depends on how you interpret Machiavelli. Every generation will interpret his writings according to their own filter.

His last warning about power though is quite clear:

"Whoever is the cause of someone's becoming powerful is ruined."[304] He based this on watching the ways people cultivate power and influence. So the point here is if you can give me power I will fear that you may also one day take it away. A person who operates on this kind of premise will never trust those below him because he fears the retribution he has earned from his own rise to power. He is caught in a perpetual struggle for dominance fearing the worst. The bully employer comes to mind as being careless and ungrateful. He suspects the very skills, opportunities, and influence other people provided to him will be used against him in order to bring him down. Machiavelli gives a warning to watch your back when playing with lions, but he also suggests you should be careful for whom you open doors.

Hopefully the wiser man would see the dangers of power questing and find another way to run his company, yet how could it be done? Leveling mechanisms are the right fit for this application too. Everyone looks out for everyone else, and power and influence are seen as tools to accomplish tasks the business has decided to pursue, not individualistic goals to elevate a single person. After all, and again, we have achieved our goals not entirely alone, for without the people who supported us or gave us inspiration or a referral we would be nothing and broke, actually we would be dead.

A way to conclude this section is to understand the thinking of Vladimir Lenin[305] one of the leaders of the Bolshevik Revolution in Russia: Lenin explained the need for the totalitarian state to exist (read fear and control) until the level of education and awareness of the people made the state unnecessary, unfortunately this growth never happened and that since both Marx and Lenin believed that when the classless society or "second or higher stage" of development occurred a new type of man would emerge. This did not occur either. Regardless of this assumption the human progression through democratic development is in fact creating a fairer, healthier, and more humane society than Lenin or Marx could have possibly created with force. Yet today with the global economic meltdown, Marxism seems to be having a reawakening of sorts, but our lesson here is that top/down economics only reinforce nature-based hierarchy.

A recent poll[306] in The Globe and Mail (June 13 2009) asks "Do you think the increased role of governments in running troubled banks and parts of the auto industry is a short term move to stabilize them or a return to a longer period of government ownership and control?" This leads us to conclude there were only two choices between conflicting ideologies to be made. If we live by ideologies we become limited by them and in truth produce no new improvement in democracy, which is what we have been doing for thousands of years, and our main goal. If we are not continuing with this game plan, then what are we doing? We go off spinning our tires, running rampant with no purpose or direction other than what we want for our self-indulgent little groups and ourselves. Democracy is an unfinished business. Forget ideology and embrace leveling mechanisms-learn about freedom instead. We do not need to worry about the banks if we are thinking about freedom, they will cease to be important and retake their positions as physical locations for savings accounts and checking accounts-period. The auto industry is really just a toolmaker that makes transportation tools-if the tool is no longer needed or is inadequate for the current demands then a new tool must be designed. It is very simple in fact to build a new tool. We know what is needed-hybrid electric or hydrogen fuel cell powered vehicles, the problem we have is who is going to build them, public or private? In matters of religious belief and instruction a private association is best suited to share their specific knowledge with the public, as are opinions or philosophies of any kind. Tools needed by society to advance on a physical plane are actually public endeavors best suited to a public accountability or through the use of by-elections or polls where changes are made by consensus rather than shareholders or market pressures. Market pressures do not necessarily reflect true needs, only desires. It is clear we need a paradigm shift in energy, as well as the tools that use it and the way we decide what gets built. We need to stick with leveling mechanisms. In this way we also avoid top-heavy state-run command economies while facing up to the real problems that exist. This is in fact the true role of any government: to govern, (read oversee) not rule-there is a difference. To repeat what I mentioned earlier a valid overseer or Speaker could act as a funnel and flow problems or issues needing further examination to a public process for a decision. This overseer would not make any decisions on its' own, the public would. This would be a true leveling mechanism at work in our affairs and would result in a fairer and more non-hierarchical society in which we might live and get things done. We just have to have faith that people would step forward to actually cast a vote.

As well, economic and political systems we have in place today do not adequately address societies need for honorable service (i.e. volunteering) or for the public process for determining the tools needed for today. For example most non-profits and charitable organizations still rely on a hierarchical structure for a sense of order. Admittedly the Society's Act[307] requires this structure to a certain extent, although if it is well understood then the legal requirements are very loose if the group decides it to be so. All that is really needed is an annual general meeting and a list of members. This AGM could meet over coffee for 10 minutes to decide on the required hierarchy for another year. My point is that these groups will often act in a hierarchical manner in order to live up to their title or position. I suppose it makes it easier for some members to function within a structure as opposed to a loosely organized group of individuals. Yet this need for structure must still rely on the ancient fear-based instrumental individualism I have written about so many times before. It would seem that the need for the structure becomes more important than the goal itself, and the vital transformative discussion is lost. We continue to forget that the process used sets the stage for the consequences we have earned. This is another kind of initiation.

Non-profit groups can talk themselves to death, so the group must assure the democratic ends of the organization. One can give and give but if the result is hierarchy and power, little democratic learning or real social healing will occur. So the message is this organization is not democratic but has a clear goal to pursue and as long as all the members agree to the goals there will be no-in fighting, but if a visionary is unsure of the next step then someone else is required to move the goal forward to fruition. This non-democratic aspect of service needs to be made clear at the outset so power struggles do not occur. This is critical to anyone engaged in an honorable service, especially for men. Without a doubt the work of the Board gets done easier with a hierarchy than without one yet a revolving hierarchy, a leveling mechanism, may be to everyone's interest so that even the least capable leader has a chance at being responsible and therefore of learning. What is the point of helping others unless we help ourselves as well? It seems to be the best way to guarantee renewed participation.

The Well Site Retreat Society, of which I am a founding member, has a retreat site for men in a rural area of Victoria. The site has been prone to vandalism and trespass so we put up signage telling people to not do certain things. The result was three events of vandalism and theft and one of theft and arson. Plus the sign got shot up too. What is the message here? Well it is difficult to be really sure, as this activity was a known problem before we came on the scene. However I cannot believe our signage had a neutral affect to these events. As was stated earlier our purpose to help men may have been corrupted by our actual message of private property and exclusion. So how are we helping the young men who are probably responsible for these violations? As well, who is to say that our signage is not seen as a violation of their sense of freedom or pleasure? So as a way to communicate when we were on the property and young men on motorcycles or ATV's came by we now introduce ourselves, welcome them to our property and describe what we are doing there. The effect was interesting, vandalism disappeared and rumors in the community had it that men normally antisocial were heard to say they would keep their eye on the place and woe to anyone caught messing with us. With our new introduction we had honored their presence on the land and they returned the favor.

One has to remember that this simple leveling mechanism worked and created good will for all around, including the potential vandals. Why is it so rare in other areas of our lives? Actually it is sad. We fear the other person so much and what they might do to us that we re-create just the right environment to piss these guys off, yet a little understanding goes a long way with the big burly guy who can be a wonderful man in the right environment. I am not suggesting these people are innocent either but I am presenting the idea that we create our own reality and earn its consequences.

Another earlier example shows again how we create our own reality and I learned a hard lesson in reality creation: On the retreat site again with a group of men and boys our job was to do some further installations on the new cabins we recently built. In the distance a group of dirt bikers on all-terrain vehicles rode up the trail. There was no time to discuss how we would meet them and an unfortunate encounter occurred. One of the men in our group stood in the way of the bikers with his big chest stuck out in an intimidating manner. His aggressive stance certainly stopped the bikers and they dismounted rather hastily. Our man approached them using commanding tones that they were trespassing (they were) and to leave immediately. I did not get to the scene fast enough to diffuse the hostility and the lead biker warned us that "you can talk tough now but when you are not here something might happen to those cabins." A month or two later all the windows were smashed and the doors broken. Admittedly this could have been the result of a coincidence, but not likely. A thought is that potential vandals have been hardened by years of competition without the hope that there is any relief for them as well as living with a serious lack of social integration and recognition. They are often loners who communicate poorly, in fact these are the kind of guys we want to become involved with our property, it furthers our outreach and builds relationships with alienated men. Again, this is the male inheritance of oppression we all live with, the distrust, the fear, and really, the lack of love that has been engineered partly by nature and partly by men themselves in order to create wealth and safety, and one of those creations is private property. As you can see, simple courtesy, the dispelling of any fears before the encounter occurred and an eye to the bigger goal could have saved the cabins. Now I welcome these aggressive men telling them they are free to come and relax and tell them what we are doing here for men and encourage them to look after the place as if it were their own. Sometimes though the best way to dissolve a problem will just not show itself, even with the best of intentions. For example, this morning I burned my porridge; my wife got up and suggested I use the timer in case I get distracted again. I responded that her tone was unkind and we were off into an argument. Half an hour later while driving downtown to write I realized that all I had to say was that she was trying to fix a problem that I could handle myself and just let me work it out on my own. Case solved but no, the right words were not there and so we fumble.

The Western leveling mechanisms I have discussed here are only one way to redistribute wealth and power. Leveling mechanisms have existed throughout history in the Aboriginal world and are often overlooked as primitive and unworthy of consideration. The First Nations people of the Pacific Northwest Coast of North America practiced the potlatch ceremony or the Tloo-qwah-nah, as they knew it. George Clutesi (cited earlier, p. 8) wrote a unique account of this ceremony and had published it with trepidation because the white authorities at the time might have harassed or arrested him as his kin were for having performed such a Tloo-qwah-nah. Potlatches were illegal until just recently, possibly because it was impossible for the white authorities to track all the gifts and obligations and what they meant. From the Nuyumbalees Cultural Centre on Quadra Island off the eastern coast of Vancouver Island, I spoke to a tribal elder about her interpretation of the potlatch. She informed me that a potlatch was always held after the death of someone in the tribe and for only that reason.[308] The honoring of a new chief or a marriage between tribes to establish a bond was based upon first having a funeral to establish the need to rekindle agreements and ties established by the departed. Even though one version of the Tloo-qwah-nah perpetuates and elevates the existing chief's influence as well as the tribe, the execution of the event exhausts the tribe's resources in both instances for some time to come. Much work by ordinary tribe members is required to replenish food stocks and staples such as meat, fish, firewood, clothing, drums and other gifted items that are used on a daily basis in tribal life. The benefits of the potlatch to the average member are small compared to the prestige earned by the chief. Yet the potlatch does add to the prestige of the tribe while temporarily impoverishing it. The acknowledgment earned from all the attending guests, many of whom came by canoe from great distances lasts for many years. The benefit translates into favors, marriages and trade agreements between the tribes, and this in time, had a much bigger impact on the average member of the tribe. It helped increase the wealth of the whole tribe rather than just the Chief.

The Highland Maya[309] of Central America have an economic system called a cargo-system that encourages the re-investment of wealth back into the community. This system is made up of a number of levels of prestige. Each level has a prescribed set of responsibilities and prestige tied to it. The purpose of such a system is to act as a leveling mechanism. William A. Haviland defines leveling mechanisms [310] as societal obligations preventing some individuals from accumulating more wealth than anyone else. This is a somewhat different version of the potlatch as described by Clutesi where the tribe itself is "leveled" rather than the chief. The prevention of the accumulation of wealth by an individual member of the society, and the subsequent distribution of the wealth of the culture to all of its members, should create an egalitarian society. However, in the case of the Highland Maya cargo system, this is not the end result because at the lowest level, young men are entering into the cargo system based on a hierarchy. Their term lasts for one year. At this level the young men are required to do menial tasks for older males in the system, running errands, and tending to higher members' beck and call. Each successive level requires a greater financial burden from the older males. However in exchange for undertaking this burden, greater prestige is granted to the man.

As the members of the cargo system progress, they host more elaborate festivals and feasts for the community. The level of celebration and financial debt these celebrations create, is commensurate with the level of prestige and honor that is generated. Therefore, even though financial wealth is not accumulated, prestige and social status is. The addition of prestige and social status give members of the cargo system a social advantage over non-members, and over lower level members of the system.

The cargo system is not really a leveling mechanism like the potlatch. The destructive structural effects of the hierarchy in the cargo system are somewhat minimized, but most importantly, the individuals are acknowledged and honored within the culture. Without this acknowledgement rampant abuse of power would occur, as we have seen throughout the developed world.

The above examples of the cargo trade, the potlatch and non-profits are good beginnings for us in the developed world to adapt and use in new and innovative ways to reduce our own structure. We in the West believe we are beyond reform; yet many areas need a good look. We have covered the critical areas which include reforms in inheritance laws, property laws, voter reform, justice reform and keeping an eye on corporations, to name a few. It is easy to become complacent; yet there are shadows close by.

"Man's true liberation, individual and collective, lies in his emancipation from authority and the belief in it" and that "True civilization is to be measured by the individual, the unit of all social life, by his individuality and the extent to which it is free to have it's being, to grow and expand unhindered by invasive and coercive authority." These quotes by Emma Goldman[311] describe her deep-seated belief that humans gain their humanity through the experience of freedom and through no other way. She believes freedom must be experienced directly in order to be felt. What I like about Ms. Goldman's quote is that many of the more restrictive social controls can be cast away, more than ever before, to allow greater freedoms and more choices for everyone. A good place to start is how we are governed or more accurately, how we are misgoverned, in areas I have discussed earlier such as voter reform. As well, if individuals were truly left alone other than in dire emergencies, much less resentment towards any remaining authority would follow. The early settlers experienced a similar kind of isolation. Their biggest fears were thieves, swindlers and cougars so a police presence is needed in even highly decentralized modern societies yet it is up to public perception as to whether this authority is oppressive or benevolent. Public awareness of police starts with the individual attitudes of the police themselves-they are public servants and can be hired and fired as any public servant is, in other words they are accountable to us. They may occasionally need to be reminded of this.

As we use leveling mechanisms more and more, and as the male role continues to adapt to the new reality so too does our education system come under the spotlight and is seen to be in need of improvement. Do we still need to train males to fit into a stereotypical industrial straight jacket? Clearly we do not train girls to be housewives any longer. So what does our education system need now? The evidence is mounting that males are changing; the statistics on young males that are enrolling in college[312] are down significantly from previous generations. Reactionary male organizations attribute this to feminist dominance on campus, and their fears of a feminist takeover. I do not believe this to be true. I believe it is directly a result of changing paradigms within the male role itself. Although I must admit I took some classes toward a social work degree and was shocked by the anti-male bias of a few professors. I was an enthusiastic class participant and was told several times to be quiet to allow less assertive women to speak. Funny, they never did speak even when I was quiet. I thought I was contributing to the class because it was so dull otherwise. While there may be some truth to the fears of a feminist takeover, in the global picture, I believe it is males that are changing and allowing these "takeovers" to occur. In fact these occurrences could not happen without male complicity or approval. This has been the male pattern throughout history, to open doors for others less fortunate, to create wealth for all, and over time dissolve the need for the very existence of that male role. As I have attempted to show through this entire book, the male role of protector and provider is not needed to the same degree as in the past. A new kind of male is needed now in egalitarian ways. For our fathers and grandfathers' sake, we owe them a great acknowledgment; yet our sons and daughters still need us. For the young men who find themselves adrift and aimless over the lack of a career, this is a time of reflection where creativity and imagination are the new tools we need for an altered future. Instead of law school, try art school; instead of getting an MBA, get a ticket to Manchuria; instead of enslaving yourself to an early mortgage and children, stick out your thumb and see the world. Nobody is telling you to be the mainstay any longer; it's all about sharing now. If they are yelling in your ear, ignore them and go do what you want to do. Explore. Be the first generation of men free of the wealth creation harness. With thanks, of course to all the men who came before.

If you do not feel confident enough to go on your own, there are many organizations seeking individuals to fill overseas aid positions. These are often voluntary without pay, but with food and accommodations provided an adventure awaits. If this is too far afield, the local soup kitchen can always use your help. Explore, invent, create, take some risks, and venture forth.

Local non-profit organizations are fine examples of causes being started by caring young people who see a need and feel an obligation to do something. For example here near Victoria, new industries starting in the forest sector include non-forest related start-ups that harvest stems, leaves or essences from plants and trees for floral and aromatherapy clientele. There is so much opportunity everywhere; so much need, just pick and do it. Or you could start your own business and do it the right way according to your values. You need to ask yourself one important question: Do you have anything else inside of you other than your needs and fears? If yes, you can probably succeed at self-employment. It is really not that hard; focus on an unmet need in your neighborhood; list off the things people have told you that you are good at; look back to school and list your subjects of interest, what you wanted to be available, or what was missing or a skill that came easy. Reach for the possible. From these areas you could find a possible direction. Get the training you might need, your licenses, then tell everyone you know, including the postman, the bus driver, your dentist and all your friends and relatives. Tell them what you are willing to do and for how much. Choose a reasonable rate of pay for your skill and work it. Good chances are you will succeed. However this will possibly be one of the most challenging and deeply rewarding things you will ever do.

A new vision about wealth could be created, possibly more cooperatively oriented than our current competitive economy with a more appropriate definition of the "Calling." Have a look at "The Money Myth Exploded"[313] found online at: michaeljournal.org that clearly explores how money works in our society. This new definition of a "Calling" could include an educational system that searches for the gifts in each individual. This could bring out the natural talents or callings in each of us. I wrote about my son who felt a career choice had to be hard work in order for it to be meaningful, but instead chose something that he enjoyed. My other son suggested he feels the same way and is following his desire to study Japanese. Making that career choice was very difficult for me too, but in the end I made a good choice in learning gardening instead of social work. Even though I would have been following my joy into Social Work I was not ready for that kind of work, as I had too many issues of my own. I do it now with the retreat center, but as a volunteer and not as a career. However I might be willing to try that now if the interest from the community is there. Occasionally clients of mine are filled with regret that they followed their fathers into a stressful career and did not follow their joy. They often wish they had become a gardener or a woodworker even if they were to make much less money. The pressure to stick with this outdated role model is regrettably still with us.

The problem of career or choice of work has haunted me many times in my life. Again, we developed the need for careers thousands of years ago when humans began to settle down in villages, towns and then cities. So much knowledge and structure were needed to run these complex societies. They chose a hierarchical way of doing things based upon the questions they asked of themselves and who they knew themselves to be at the time. Nowadays, we might try group knowledge instead of specializing and seeking knowledge to separate us and elevate us above others. We might seek knowledge of pleasure, which is actually very natural for us to do. All children know about this sensual reality from birth. They spend many hours exploring colors, tastes, textures and sounds. We slowly become alienated from our early love affairs with our senses and begin to relate only to our minds—as a computer might. We leave the aesthetics, emotions and the natural world behind and set off for an isolated pinnacle of knowledge where community is dead. Our education system teaches us how to think independently rather than as part of a community. Again we assume we are the creators of our world and all our wealth is ours to do with as we please and created by ourselves alone. We go to school to learn firstly the questions our ancestors asked, then to memorize the answers they discovered. Then at some point we might discover those answers cannot answer questions about our current lives. We have to ask our own. Failing this we become victims of our history. Now this education system I am referring to, one that informs and prepares the public on such topics as voting obligations, the law and its discernment, the philosophy of gender, good parenting is as important as traditional subjects such as reading, mathematics, science, the beauties of nature, art and music. Education must address the former list of topics that are the new needs of the day. The killer instinct is replaced with the ethical instinct. And yes we can still succeed and create wealth but in a more moral and responsible manner. Things or opponents do not need to be defeated or "killed" in order for us to have wealth. Collaboration might become a modern buzzword for new wealth creation styles.

I used to think that the way to create wealth for myself was to look to the market place for a need I could fill. This is a very good process for remaining within the traditional employer/employee system. If you have other skills that are not easily made into commercially oriented, skills such as compassion, artistic talent, spiritual or political insight, finding a specific need to fill may actually be quite difficult without a formal education. However, recognizing that if your skill is unusual, or if you desire something on the edge, and if you have the perseverance to create a need for your skill, the resulting occupation could be more rewarding. For example, my writing has been based on a long-term desire to understand myself and other men. It fits into few contemporary educational settings at the moment; yet I believe this will change. For now I have to create a need for my writing because there are few male positive men's studies departments anywhere that I am aware of. A pro-feminist men's studies program might open the door to limited understanding of masculinity but does not go as far as it could, although more and more courses focusing on male issues are appearing. What we need to hear is that males are approaching a redefinition of their bio-cultural role and that there are new ways for men to find meaning based on the traditional roles adapted to modern needs. A transcendence of traditional roles is already occurring. Women and men are shifting towards the middle. Self-actualization is the key to moving this shift along. A real danger is in believing that feminists are taking away men's traditional role of protector and provider. Men angry with this change lack imagination to see the silver lining in these new ways of relating. We males can now make a change that our developing world brothers will not have access to for maybe a hundred years or more, possibly never. Remember the wealthy men of the West who created enough wealth to enable disadvantaged groups including women to claim their rights as free individuals. This of course was all unconscious but we must remember that it was a scripted role in the male. It is now the time for us to move on as less burdened men by choosing the appropriate responsibilities and careers we have dreamed about since childhood. To me this describes the freedom to choose.

Yet do social studies courses in our public schools cover social issues such as the extreme views of skinhead philosophy or racist and fundamentalist beliefs? In literature what is the agenda for the choice of readings for students. Do they reflect survivalist agendas or are we led into romantic poetry that encourages the reader to dream of escape from a hard existence to an idyllic perfect world like the duped assassins of the Ismailis? In other words what is the agenda of education policy designers? Are they aware that their own unmet needs influence policy?

I remember in high school being a sensitive and idealistic student, and how boring the available literature was: war tales, Beowulf, Canterbury Tales and other rot. Clearly I was not ready for this material, I was too young. All I wanted to study was political writings and anti-war material and I wanted to talk about it in class. I was told to stick to less confronting material while at school. However I conspired to read all I wanted and yak away with friends at home. Funny how being denied something in public sends it underground and the issue becomes a rallying cry seeking revenge or redress.

In gym class I remember the barbaric method the instructors would use to choose players for opposing teams. Two captains would be chosen who then would pick the best possible players for his side. The unfortunate consequence was that poor or physically unfit players were chosen last. The social rub was tangible and humiliating. Who wrote that agenda? This is clearly a survivalist viewpoint.

How about science? The question is "Whose science?" Get an education, but be forewarned. What is it that you are really learning? Is getting a good job all that matters? What about ethical or moral considerations?

Over the years I have heard of many alternative styles of education. I don't know which are more successful than the others. I wish I had had the opportunity to try them as a child. My point is that state education is coming under greater challenges from a smorgasbord of education styles. Home schooling is catching on but are the kids getting enough opportunity to socialize? There are women's studies; surely it is time for men's studies. There are private business schools, private religious schools, psychologically oriented schools and even military schools. Are they all just various forms of the survival initiations we learned early on but in different guises? What would happen if a school opened that did not teach a survivalist curriculum? It would be an interesting experiment to try.

These alternative school models have been tried before and have developed into many different styles but basically they follow some simple guidelines. As John Taylor Gatto suggested in "Dumbing Us Down," these schools would have to be based on the desires of the student[314] and what they wanted to learn. Only total freedom of direction for the student would promise a true non-survivalist education. Looking a little deeper a student might wake up one day and realize they were curious about philosophy. Gatto felt genius was exceedingly common.[315] Of course there are so many directions one could go in; a new comer might be overwhelmed by too many choices. A guide could be appointed by the school board to assist the student in choosing meaningful directions of study. Choosing a school with a major in philosophy would be one choice. Another would be to spend a year traveling to different countries—that is an education in itself, if you keep your mind open. Another direction might be to spend time with a monk or a priest to discover their insights. Another might be to live alone in a mountain top cabin to see what thoughts might percolate up into consciousness. Aboriginal cultures might refer to these experiences as vision quests. Another would work and live with a boat-builder for a year. In most choices the three "R's" would have to be learned as well. The student could give an oral and written presentation at the end of this period and receive recognition for that learning. The study of philosophy may not lead to a career; in fact more questions will no doubt surface during this period. The student may end up building cedar canoes for a living; the journey is what is important. The end result will produce a better fit for both student and society, but especially a happier and more grateful citizen. If a society wants loyalty and citizens to take an interest in their community here is a way to get it.

In traditional education social convention, culture, gender roles, history, religion, ethics and morals are all imposed on us without our permission or agreement. So how do we know what is right? How do we resist what is unethical? If we ask someone else to tell us and if there are enough people saying the same thing, does that make it right? How about if enough are saying the opposite, does it make them bad? This is the value of the study of history, not of dates or people, but of successes and things that work. Making people's lives easier or more rewarding could surely be worth studying. We can learn from what does not work to create things and ideas that do work. Does this assume that our intentions are good? What is ethical behavior? How would we know it if we tripped over it? I do not mean that crap about doing the right thing. Where did you learn to do the right thing? What experiences did you have in order to learn something important? You might have acted in a certain way and seen the consequences. You might say you learned it from people you admired. You also may say you were surrounded by many people you admired, or maybe there was just one person out of the whole of humanity that you admired.

You know I have met many, many people who have told me they have never met anyone that they admired. Their experience of people is of deception and abandonment. That is an education too. So anything good in them comes from . . . where? While it is possible they were playing up their abandonment story, they seemed to believe it. They were feeling some kind of betrayal. So for these people something happens and we have an insight, totally new, completely original. This is learning too, different than just witnessing the actions of someone you admire. You let it in and it makes you silent, and you learn about pain. You have to do your own learning, and being open to considering other ideas can help.

Gatto writes about an interesting system of education provided to Europe's wealthiest children for centuries that operated on the belief that self-knowledge is the only basis for true knowledge.[316] They created situations where the child can be alone in an unguided setting with a problem to solve. Sometimes the problem is fraught with great risks. Now can you imagine anyone who had mastered such a challenge ever lacking confidence in his or her ability? We should trust children from a very early age with independent study where each child has a chance to develop private uniqueness and self-reliance. This is the purpose of "play." In our family home, my partner and I would often engage our two sons in "family meetings" where we would discuss important issues that affected us all. An example would be computer usage. Our sons were highly attracted to computer games and we were worried about their social development. We wanted them to spend more time actually playing outside in the dirt like I did when I was their age. Well, you can have these conversations and say what you are feeling but we were surprised by their response. They felt they were playing with their friends, just not the way we wanted them to play. We had to think about that for a while. Eventually we agreed they were having some kind of an interaction and that it was fun for them. We could not imagine spending that much time behind any monitor as fun but they did. We also realized that no matter what we did or said, they would get their computer time regardless of any restrictions we placed on them; that they would find a way. Previously we tried groundings, taking away laptops or game-boys only to see the same habit reset itself upon ending the punishment. In other words it had no impact. Dejected and feeling like failures as parents, we decided that after all it was their life to ruin if they wanted. We believed in their inherent ability to look after themselves; we had to trust it would be a passing phase.

Well many years later, our sons are as committed to gaming as ever, but have developed many real life friendships, just the kind we wanted them to have. Recently our oldest flew to Los Angeles to visit a girl friend, and our youngest who is now twenty was actually seeing a real flesh and blood girl for the first time. It is kind wonderful to watch his joy and bewilderment all at the same time. So who is to say, did we do the right thing or not? Apparently we did. As hard as it was, we did one thing right for them. We respected their choices, and they are still our friends. The most important thing we hope they have learned is the value of the "family meeting." We shall see. So leaving them "alone" in the wilderness can be interpreted in many different ways.

Shamanic ritual events or a First Nation vision quest has similar teaching power, where an individual is left alone in the wilderness for several days in order to gain insight into life. As part of my men's community, certain events we held required the young men to be separated from the older men and given a problem to solve. The problem was often simple but required the boys to work together to solve it. On one occasion they were sequestered on a small island in a lake nearby to the men's camp. They were instructed to find a way off the island for all the boys together, leaving no one behind. They were given one tool, an axe and some food for three days. By the end of day two they had build a raft by weaving branches and logs together and they all got off the island safely. This was a deep bonding experience that will hopefully stay with them for many years.

Another aspect of learning focuses on the consequences of doing what one wills versus doing what one wants. For example if I run up to a conductor in a train station and ask to have a train, the conductor might say track six, whereupon getting there I find it is not the train I need, I may be doing what I will, but not getting on the train that I want. Wolff suggests the basis for moral knowledge is: that I may know what I will for myself (such as candy), but it may not be what I want (health for example).[317]

In our Western individualistic society, our education naturally follows suit to reflect individual goals within the existing culture. However we then educate our children to see the future as an isolated experience of struggling to create a career or "calling." Most of us spend years to find the only familial support that might be had (wife, husband) then we buy an isolated, totally self-contained home complete with garage, freezer, lawn mower and tools. We have a family and teach our children to aspire to the same isolated existence. We call this learning? This is learning based on admiring our parent's isolation. What we fail to see is that we are the clear victims of market psychology gone mad. The net benefit of choosing an education based upon our interests and talents is the freedom to live a life unscripted by someone else's questions and answers.

As we continue in our journey into the future of Western masculinity, we see males still highly identified with provider and protector roles but experiencing increasing opportunities to adapt. There are many choices that you will have to face—mainly your loyalties. To restate the purpose of this section, we were to examine and reassess our masculine mythology, or that part of us we identify as male and move on to a potentially more complete and appropriate definition. What conditions are necessary for this transformation? We have explored the ten thousand blades of life that maintain the current hierarchical paradigm of masculinity. We have seen some of the new options for men based upon the use of leveling mechanisms and Aboriginal redistribution systems but as yet, we have not defined what conditions are essential to create this new and more contemporary model. Actually, it is more a matter of what conditions already exist and how we respond to them that will determine the future.

An interesting book has just been published on how even 1,000 years of time can create mutations in the general population. The constant in the equation could be a forced living situation, such as racial oppression, or a distinct dietary shift, such as milk products from cows. Some people are still lactose intolerant, the rest of us having adapted genetically to be able to digest it since prehistory where we were not able to use it as food. The extension of this idea might be that males assisting in the creation of democracy by forcing the signing of the Magna Carta 1,000 years ago, might have set in motion a genetic mutation coming to maturity now.

For example why has democracy flourished around the world in the last century, and why are males in the West more willing to embrace women and minorities in a shared workforce? We now expect these rights to be acknowledged and fairness to be expressed throughout our culture. So it is thoroughly possible that the conditions essential to create a newer male model are already here and in play.

Here is a short list of conditions I believe need to be in place for a paradigm shift to occur, or put another way, conditions that will be different after a mutation based paradigm shift occurs. Is it possible that all the advances as well as the slips we make are all genetically based? Are they the result of conditions we placed on our societies centuries ago? Will events that happen now create mutations 1,000 years from now? According to Professor Harpending and his colleague Gregory Cochran, in their book "The Ten Thousand Year Explosion" this appears to be true.[318] Yet we may also create the seeds of destruction by the same method.

The list of conditions to evoke an evolutionary process can include:

- Males must decide that the traditional role for men can be expanded to include non-traditional outcomes and greater flexibility in emotion.
- The limits of democracy can be pushed by asking the question who is oppressed and then addressing the causes of oppression.
- With the creation of appropriate leveling mechanisms based on worker rotation wheels, power-sharing strategies, removal of all ethnic, racial and gender discrimination, fairness in the workplace should continue to come into being.
- By managing our surpluses based upon need rather than desires we prevent creating the breeding grounds of power dynamics and abuse.
- When the true test of our potential is to beat our own best standard and to place far less value on comparison with others, aggression will be directed into fighting poverty.
- Reward for incentive would be reflected in the value the community holds for you.
- The ability to live in a non-dualistic society where good and bad are not so much values as they are opportunities for growth.
- Property has a new definition, one based on fair return for labor.

- And possibly the most important of all is thanking a man for his contribution. This is probably the very best way to disarm a fear-based competitiveness. This is especially true for men unaccustomed to being appreciated, which could include males who surround themselves with body armor such as expensive suits, muscle cars, money or possessions. The trick for us is to see his contribution.

CONCLUSION TO THE
FIVE FOUNDATIONS

"Democratic movements overthrow monarchies; establish
constitutions; set up election systems; pass laws that limit
state power and guarantee people's rights; found labor
unions; seek to redistribute wealth by reforming land
ownership, by changing inheritance laws, by taxing the
rich, by setting up welfare systems . . . "[319]

from "Radical Democracy" by C. Douglas Lummis

Our evolving challenge at this time in history is to integrate minorities
and marginalized citizens as equals into the larger economy and by the
same method redefine the male paradigm. Many courageous men and
women will lead this impending redefinition.

So how brave are we, my fellow wealth warriors? What is the next step,
and have we any idea of what that might be? How do we make the changes
required? Have we clearly defined what a good man is?

Try this on for size: "The democratic citizen must precede the
democratic society."[320]

We have to do it all together or not at all, as seen in the world of today,
that is 2012, unilateralist belligerence by other nations point to the still deeply
instilled bio-cultural programming that drives us to protect the waterhole
for ourselves and our own instead of sharing it. We still assume there are
limited resources and that there is not enough for all to have some. Yet there
will be more free time continuing into the future, education and access
to information. The most critical component of all is an excess of money
above expenses so that there is time to digest information in order to make
healthier decisions, to network and organize protest movements, to write
and demand change. At the same time I would bet my bottom dollar that if
the wealth dried up so would everyone's freedom. We would be transported
back to barbaric hierarchical structures so fast it would make our collective
heads spin! The old warrior system would become valued again for our very
survival. Chilling but probably true. Just look at the struggle with terrorism.

Have you noticed any traditional structures suddenly coming into force? Any fear based activities playing out in government or society at large?

> Biology running rampant,
> the head cut from the body
> it careens like a chicken
> just beheaded.

At the same time we must again perform a bow of appreciation to the creators of all this wealth, after all they created the possibility of our freedom (freedom to think, etc.). If it were not for this accumulation of inherited wealth and knowledge, our lives would be much shorter and without a lot of hope. Unfortunately, many forgot to free themselves!

One of the most important methods for deciding what to do or what to believe is based upon the kind of values we adhere to and how we access them. Here is an opportunity to see how you choose your path.

Check out these random value laden cultures: India, Aboriginal Australia and North America, also Classical Europe. Many early cultures used story telling, ritual and pilgrimages to holy sites as teaching tools. There is a huge resource of information on values in many locations including the Internet, public libraries, and bookstores and in academia.

From "A Question of Values" by Hunter Lewis,[321] here are six ways that we choose values:

- Authority,
- Deductive Logic,
- Sense Experience,
- Emotion,
- Intuition, and
- Science.

The six ways are defined as follows:

Authority:
Belief in what has been provided for me.

Deductive logic:
- Socratic questioning: asking of many questions without developing an opinion.

- The dialectic: debate between two opposing viewpoints.
- Syllogism: a conclusion logically deduced from two premises or statements:

An example: as the Buddha might have said[322].
- Human life is full of suffering, (premise one)
- Suffering is caused by desire, (premise two)

(conclusion)
- Suffering can be eliminated by eliminating desire.

The cataloging of common fallacies: or all things, which make the premise wrong or incomplete.

Sense Experience:
The five senses: Taste, touch, and smell, sight and sound. For example, I see you protecting your child.

Emotion:
- A consistent or ongoing social group such as identification with a country.
- Suggests a particular way to organize society, such as a bureaucracy.
- Requires an emotional stimulus such as a cause or an enemy.

Intuition:
The use of the unconscious to resolve problems. Try a thorough study of a problem before bed, and then go to sleep with the expectation of clarity when you awake, and by morning a solution may be at hand.

Science:
- Gather all the available facts (sense experience).
- Immerse yourself in the facts until a solution flashes in your mind (intuition).
- Think through all the logical implications of the proposed solution.
- Devise an experiment to test the reliability of the premise or statement.

Try all of them as an experiment! Take an old issue that you have not completely resolved fill in the appropriate information and carefully uncover the insights.

To recap, a new mythology began centuries ago; simple leveling mechanisms have permeated the global consciousness with the integration of selflessness throughout human existence. Our culture, institutions, daily thoughts and actions reflect this. We know that throughout history humans have created mythologies to explain their place on this earth, and just as we bestow our worldly goods on our families we naturally extend our love to humanity and the world through this ancient myth. Anthropology is the study of this reality in our ancient cultures. At the same time we modern humans have created mythologies and the initiations that provide other initiations. In our future the mythologies of selflessness will predominate as maturity slowly creates a new reality for us to live in. We see how our actions have created fairness and democracy around the planet and a new world is emerging from our knowledge that evil is a valuable tool for learning and growth. It is an opportunity. We have transformed our wickedness into spirit in practical ways because we wanted to and it made sense, not because we had to but because we wanted to. We have understood that our shallowness is a deep fear of the unknown and have committed to the clarification of our emotions as a tool for certainty and right action. We give thanks to our opponents for the good they have created as they have taught us many things. We have finally discovered that in truth there is no enemy, only answers to other people's questions. Humanity has reached its zenith and a new journey begins—that of the transcendence of our personalities and cultural histories. We have unified our contradictions into one great theme—a spirit of living with our eyes open, as we step into life.

My life is like the end of a long train journey
I am alone as I step on to the station platform
No one else got off

To the left is my truck with its shiny new paint
In the box my rototiller and wheelbarrow, friends I have worked with all these years
I look away

To the right a pile of books sit on a desk
A reading lamp, cozy armchair and a pot of coffee beckon me to sit
I turn away

In front of me a door into the station
It has no sign on it, yet it invites
It is dark I want to go in

I step through . . . .
Sparks and terrors, what have I done?
Go back to left or right, a safer known world

Yet I am happy taking the step

A loudspeaker calls out
The next train leaves in three minutes
I missed the destination

I am the train

The Five Foundations for an Evolving Life

The five foundations require men to:

1) Come to an understanding about our constructed masculine sociology and not to limit our lives out of fear or habit. Allow ourselves to expand to new areas of endeavor.

2) Acknowledge that our species is still very young and that nature works fine on its own, but it no longer provides the behavioral blueprint for us to follow. We can make different choices, as we have done in special areas throughout history. An example is the development of democracy.

3) Allow emotion to have a place in our lives, and to use logic and objectivity in the right places. Emotion is real at the moment although it can be part of the illusory phenomena as well. Yet it cannot be judged only felt, then you decide what to do with it if anything. Sometimes doing nothing is best.

4) Develop a clear understanding of what dualistic thinking is and commit to a non-dual thinking process. That is, not of competition but cooperation, not of winning but learning, not of better but of having more appropriate solutions. Make a commitment to create unity in your life and to grow in your own understanding of "The Great Illusion" that illustrates the relationship between fear and love.

5) Become familiar with the definition and use of leveling mechanisms and create faith in democracy wherever you go.

RESOURCES AND RECOMMENDED READING

Men's Studies:
- Victoria Men's Center Web Site:
- http://victoria.tc.ca/Community/MensCentre/index.html
    - Lists extensive activities; current and past, archives, articles and suggests referrals to other Men's organizations.
- Micheal Meade and Limbus : P.O. Box 4331 Seattle Wash. 98104. 1988. (Books and Tapes).
- For an existing Men's Studies Syllabi see Men's Studies Syllabi: by Sam Femiano, Ph.D, Ed.D. Editor, 22 East St., Northhampton, Maine. 01060. 413-584-8903.

Men's Groups:

- How to Start a Men's Group by Gervase Bushe Ph.D. Vancouver M.E.N. Ph. 1-604-251-5120.
- Tending The Fire : The Ritual Men's Group, by Wayne Liebman. 1991. Pub. by Ally Press, St Paul, MN. 55107.

Imaginative Processes: Full of exercises for getting in touch:

- The Little Book of the Human Shadow ; Robert Bly ; 1988, Harper-Collins, NY.
- Explores the unconscious and how to befriend it.
- All Rites Reversed?! ; Ritual Technology for Self-Initiation, by Antero Alli., Pub. Falcon Press, Phoenix, Arizona. 1987.
- Theatre of The Oppressed, by Augusto Boal. Pub. Community Press, N.Y.
- Dramatherapy; Theory and Practice 2, edited by Sue Jennings. Pub. Routledge, London, England. 1992.
- Dramatherapy-A Practical Guide for Teaching Drama. by Larry Swartz, 1988. Pembroke Publishers, Markham, Ontario.

- Creative Visualizations, by Shakti Gawain. 1985. Bantam Books, N.Y.
- Setting The Seen-Creative Visualization For Healing, by Alan Cohen, M.A. Pub. Cohen Publications, P.O. Box 450, Kula, Hawaii 96790. 1982.

Personal Growth:

- Raise Your Self-Esteem, (Cassette) 1987, by Nathaniel Brandon. Pub. Bantam Audio Pub. N.Y. His books too are worth the read.
- The Art of Loving, by Erich Fromm. 1956 Harper and Row N.Y.
- Stories of the Spirit, Stories of the Heart, Christina Feldman and Jack Kornfield ed. Harper Collins, San Francisco, 1991
- Tao-The Watercourse Way, Pantheon Books, NY. 1975
- Way of the Peaceful Warrior, Dan Millman, H.J. Kramer Pub.
- Sacred Journey of the Peaceful Warrior, Dan Millman, H. J. Kramer, Pub. Tiburon Ca. 1991
- Be Here Now, Ram Das, Lama Foundation, 1971.

BIBLIOGRAPHY

"God". "The Book of Nature."

(Editor), Alan Charles Kors, ed. Encyclopedia of the Enlightenment. New York: Oxford University Press, 2003.

Adler, M. J. Haves Without Have-Nots. London: Macmillan, 1991.

Alperovitz, Gar and Lew Daly. Unjust Deserts: how the rich are taking our common inheritance. New York: New Press, 2008.

Asher, Jeffrey. Statistics Canada, 1996.

Association, British Columbia Liberties. Squatters Rights. 2004. 15 12 2011 <www.bccla.org/positions/discrim/04squatter.htm>.

Averett, Susan L. and Mark L. Burton. "College attendance and the college wage premium: Differences by gender." Economics of Education Review 15.1 (1996): 37-49.

Bakan, Joel. The Corporation. Toronto: Penguin, 2004.

Barnum, P. T. There's a sucker born every minute. <http://en.wikipedia.org/wiki/There%27s_a_sucker_born_every_minute>.

Batmanglij, Najmieh. A Taste of Persia, An Introduction to Persian Cooking. 2006. 05 09 2011 <http://www.mage.com/cooking/A-Taste-of-Persia.html>.

Baumeister, Roy F. Is There Anything Good About Men? 2007. <http://www.psy.fsu.edu/~baumeistertice/goodaboutmen.htm>.

Baxter, James. "Canada Values Corporate Responsibility." The Vancouver Sun. Vancouver, 01 October 1999.

BDEA / BuddhaNet. "Buddhist Studies." Buddhistism in the West from the East. <http://www.buddhanet.net/e-learning/buddhistworld/to-west.htm>.

Beauvior, Simone de. Brown, L.Susan. The Politics of Individualism. Montreal : Black Rose Books, 1993. 167.

Bell, David A. The First Total War: Napoleon's Europe and the birth of warfare as we know it. New York: Houghton Mifflin Harcourt, 2007.

Bikini, Everything. The History of The Bikini. 2005. Everything Bikini.com. 24 June 2011 <http://www.historyofwaterfilters.com/bikini.html>.

Blatchford, Christie. The National Post. Toronto, 10 January 2000.

Bly, Robert. A Little Book On The Human Shadow. Ed. William Booth. New York: Harper SanFrancisco, 1988.

—. Iron John, A Book About Men. Reading: Addison-Wesley, 1990.

Bookchin, Murray. The Ecology of Freedom. Montreal: Black Rose Books, 1991.

Brockman, John, Steven Pinker and Richard Dawkins. What Is Your Dangerous Idea? Ed. John Brockman. 1. New York: Harper Perennial, 2007.

Bronte, Charlotte. Jane Ayre. n.d.

Bronte, Emily. Wuthering Heights. n.d.

Brown, Elizabeth. Feudalism. 2011. 24 June 2011 <http://www.britannica.com/EBchecked/topic/205583/feudalism>.

Brown, L. Susan. The Politics of Individualism. Montreal: Black Rose Books, 1993.

Buckingham-Hatfield, S. micro-credit. 2000. 18 12 2011 <http://www.answers.com/topic/micro-credit>.

C.G.Jung. Memories, Dreams, Reflections. Ed. Aniela Jaffe. Trans. RIchard and Clara Winston. New York: Vintage Books, Div of Random House, Inc., 1989.

Campbell, Joseph. Creative Mythology-The Masks of God. New York: Penguin Books, 1968.

Carol Locaust, Ph.D. The Talking Stick. 1997. 11 July 2011 <http://www.acaciart.com/stories/archive6.html>.

Chan, Carrie. Domestic Violence in Gay and Lesbian Relationships. 2005. <http://www.pdfdownload.org/pdf2html/view_online.php?url=http%3A%2F%2Fwww.austdvclearinghouse.unsw.edu.au%2FPDF%2520files%2FGay_Lesbian.pdf>.

Clausewitz, Carl von. Carl von Clausewitz: Business is War. <http://www.clausewitz.org/>.

Clutesi, George. Potlatch. reprint. Sidney: Gray's Publishing Ltd. (1973), 1969.

Cochran, Gregory and Harpending, Henry. The Ten Thousand Year Explosion-How Civilization Accelerated Human Evolution. New York: Basic Books, 2009.

Connell, R.W. Masculinities. 2nd Edition. Cambridge: Polity Press, 2005.

Constitution. The Levellers. 11 July 2011 <www.constitution.org/eng/leveller.htm>.

Cour, Peter de la. Weber, Max. <u>The Protestant Ethic and the Capitalist Spirit</u>. n.d. 61.

Danielson, Krissi. <u>Distinguishing Cloud computing from Utility Computing</u>. 2008. 15 12 2011 <www.ebizq.net/blogs/saasweek/2008/03>.

Dante. "The Four Stages of Life." Campbell, Joseph. <u>Creative Mythology-The Masks of God</u>. New York: Penquin Books, 1968. 633.

Daraul, Arkon. <u>A History of Secret Societies</u>. New York: The Citadel Press, 1961.

Das, Ram. <u>Be Here Now</u>. San Cristobal: Lama Foundation, 1971. de Soto, Hernando. <u>The Mystery of Capital: why capitalism triumphs in the West and fails everywhere else</u>. New York: Basic Books, 2000.

Diamond, Jared. <u>Guns, Germs, and Steel</u>. New York: Norton & Company, Inc., 1997.

Diamond, Jared M. <u>Collapse-How Societies Choose to Fail or Socceed</u>. New York: Penquin USA, 2006.

Douglas, C H. <u>Social Credit</u>. Third Edition. London: Eyre & Spottiswoode, 1937.

Douglas, T.C. <u>The Making of a Socialist, The Recollections of T.C. Douglas</u>. Ed. Lewis H. Thomas. Edmonton: University of Alberta Press, 1982.

E. F. Schumacher. <u>Buddhist Economics</u>. 05 04 2009. The E.F. Schumacher Society. 0Axis of Logic5 09 2011 <http://axisoflogic.com/artman/publish/Article_55356.shtml>.

<u>Early Modern Humans</u>. 2005. McGraw-Hill Science & Technology Encyclopedia. 12 4 2011 <http://www.answers.com/topic/early-modern-humans>.

Ecoforestry Institure. <u>Wildwood Forest, Ladysmith, BC: History</u>. 11 July 2011 <http://ecoforestry.ca/wildwood/history>.

Emerson, R.W. "In Fewer Words." <u>The American Mercury</u> (1938): 76.

Empedocles. "Eath, water, air and fire." Tarnas, Richard. <u>The Passion of the Western Mind-Understanding the Ideas That Have Shaped Our World View</u>. First Ballantine Edition April 1993. New York: Ballantine Books, 1991. 21.

Estulin, Daniel. <u>The True Story of the Bilderberg Group</u>. 2. Trine Day, 2009.

Even, Louis. <u>The Money Myth Exploded</u>. 01 02 2012 <http://www.michaeljournal.org/myth.htm>.

Farrell, Warren. Myth of Male Power-Why Men are the Disposable Sex. New York: Simon and Schuster, 1993.

FBI, Uniform Crime Reports, 1950-2005. Bureau of Justice Statistics. 01 02 2012. 01 02 2012 <http://bjs.ojp.usdoj.gov/content/homicide/hmrt.cfm#longterm >.

—. Homicide Trends in the US. 2005. 30 September 2011 <http://bjs.ojp.usdoj.gov/content/homicide/overview.cfm>.

Federation, Co-operative Commonwealth. "The Canadian Encylcopedea." Historica Dominion Institute. <http://www.thecanadianencyclopedia.com/index.cfm?PgNm=TCE&Params=A1ARTA0001902>.

Freire, Paulo. Pedagogy of the Oppressed. Trans. myra bergman ramos. 30th Anniversary. Continuum International Publishing Group, 2000.

Gatto, John. Dumbing Us Down: the hidden curriculum of compulsory schooling. 2, annotated. Gabriola Island: New Society Publishers, 2002.

Gillette, Robert Moore and Douglas. Hero, Magician, Warrior and Lover-Rediscovering The Archetypes of the Mature Masculine. New York: HarperCollins, 1990.

Goldberg, Herb. The Hazards of Being Male-Surviving the Myth of Masculine Privilege. New York: Signet, 1976.

Government of Canada. Canada's Oil Sands—Opportunities and Challenges to 2015: An Update. 23 July 2010. 11 July 2011 <http://www.neb.gc.ca/clf-nsi/rnrgynfmtn/nrgyrprt/lsnd/pprtntsndchllngs20152006/qapprtntsndchllngs20152006-eng.html>.

Green, Ross Gordon. Justice in Aboriginal Communities: Sentencing Alternatives. Illustrated. Saskatoon: Purisch Publishing, 1998.

Haviland, William A. Cultural Anthropology. Ed. Ted Buchholz. Seventh Edition. Orlando: Harcourt Brace & Company, 1993.

Hearne, Kevin. 1998. The Demonization of Pan. 08 02 2012 <http://www.mesacc.edu/~thoqh49081/StudentPapers/pan.html>.

"some may disagree with American way of life." Times Colonist. Ed. Denise Helm. Victoria: Victoria Times Colonist, 10 09 2002.

Highway, Thompson. Saul, John Raulston. A Fair Country-Telling Truths About Canada. Toronto: Penquin Group, 2008. 281.

History, The Book of Nature in Early Modern and Modern. Studies in Cultural Change. Ed. K van Berkel and A. Venderjagt. Groningen: PEETERS Publishing, 2006.

Hobbes, Thomas. Leviathan. London: Penquin Group, 1985.

—. Leviathan. Ed. J.C.A. Gaskin. Oxford: Oxford University Press, 1996.

Hobbes, Thomas. "Leviathan." Handbook, THe Philosopher's. Ed. Stanley Rosen. New York: Random House, 2000. 85-89.

Hughes-Hallett, Lucy. Hereos-Saviors, Trators and Supermen—A History of Hero Worship. New York: Alfred A. Knopf, Division of Random House, 2004.

Human Development Reports. "Human Development Reports." 2007-08. U.N.D.P. 09 02 2012 <http://hdr.undp.org/en/statistics/data/climatechange/planets/>.

Johnson, Katsuo Nishiyama and Jeffrey V. Karoshi Death. 4 Feb 1997. 11 4 2011 <www.workhealth.org/whatsnew/lpkarosh.html>.

Jung, Carl G. The Basic Writings of C.G. Jung. Ed. Violet de Laszlo. Trans. R.F.C. Hull. 21 vols. Princeton: Princeton University Press, 1990.

Kant, Immanuel. "Critique of Judgement 1790." The Philosopher's Handbook. Ed. Harry Rosen. New York: Random House, 2000. 194.

Kates, Gary. The French Revolution: recent debates and new controversies. Taylor & Francis, 2006.

Kierkegaard, Soren. "Fear and Trembling, Problema 1, Is There a Telelogical Suspension of the Ethical?" The Philosopher's Handbook. Ed. Stanley Rosen. New York: Random House, 2000. 170,171.

Kimbrell, Andrew. The Masculine Mystique. Ney York: Ballantine, 1995.

Kitch, M J. Capitalism and the Reformation. Ed. H. F. Kearney. London: Longmans Green and Co., 1967.

Krishnamurti, J. An Overview of Krishnamurti's Life and Work. 2011. Krishnamurti Foundation. <http://www.jkrishnamurti.org/about-krishnamurti/biography.php>.

Krishnamurti, J. The First and Last Freedom. Forward by Aldous Huxley. Wheaton: The Theosophical Publishing House-A Quest Book, 1954.

Kumarappa, J. C. Axis of Logic. 05 04 2009. The E.F. Schumacher Society. 05 09 2011 <http://axisoflogic.com/artman/publish/Article_55356.shtml>.

Kuttner, Robert. The End of Laissez-Faire: National purpose and the global economy after the Cold War. Philadelphia: University of Pennsylvania Press, 1991.

Lagasse, Paul and Columbia University, The Columbia Encyclopedia. 6, illustrated. Columbia University Press, 2000.

Lahey, Minam. "Leisure in The Global Village?" 12-15 05 1999. Canadian Association for Liesure Studies. Ed. Paul Heintzman. 09 02 2012 <http://www.pdfdownload.org/pdf2html/view_online.php?url=http%3A%2F%2Flin.ca%2FUploads%2Fcclr9%2FCCLR9_25.pdf>.

Landes, David S. The Wealth and Poverty of Nations-Why Some Are So Rich and Some Are So Poor. Ed. N.Y. New York: W.W. Norton, 1998.

Lee, Valerie L., William A. Haviland and Richard T. Searles. The Telecourse Faces. Harcourt, 1996.

Levy, Leonard W. Origins of the Fifth Amendment. New York: Oxford University Press, 1968.

Lewis, Hunter. A Question of Values. New York: Harper Collins, 1991.

Lummis, C. Douglas. Radical Democracy. New York: Cornel University Press, 1996.

Machiavelli, Niccolo. The Prince. Trans. Harvey C. Mansfield. 2nd. Chicago: University of Chicago Press, 1998.

Mawson, A R. Transient Criminality: A Model of Stress-Induced Crime. 1987. US Department of Justice. <https://www.ncjrs.gov/App/Publications/abstract.aspx?ID=109068 >.

Maybury-Lewis, David. Millenium. New York: Penguin, 1992.

McDowell, Maxson. http://www.jungny.com/carl.jung.46.html (Index of Terms). <http://www.jungny.com/>.

Mclaren, Angus. The Trials of Masculinity: Studies in the Policing of Sexual Boundaries. Chicago: University of Chicago Press, 1997.

McLaren, P and P Leonard. Paulo Freire: a critical encounter. reprint. Routledge, 1993.

McMartin, Pete. "The Life and Death of the King of Cassiar." The Vancouver Sun. Vancouver, 20 march 2010. A4.

Meade, Michael. Men and The Water of Life-Initiation and Tempering of Men. New York: HarperCollins, 1993.

Messerschmitt, James W. Capitalism, Patriarchy and Crime, Toward a Socialist, Feminist Criminology. Lanham: Rowan and Littlefeild, 1986.

micro-credit, Jeffrey Gangemi:. <u>University of Exeter-Business School</u>. 2005. Bloomberg LP. 11 July 2011 <http://www.businessweek.com/magazine/content/05_52/b3965024.htm>.

Mill, John Stewart. "on property." Gar Alperovitz, Lew Daly,. <u>Unjust Deserts</u>. New York: The New Press, 2008. 99.

Montagu, Ashley. <u>Man, His First Two Million Years</u>. New York: Columbia University Press, 1969.

Moore, Robert and Douglas Gillette. <u>King Warrior Magician Lover</u>. 1. New York: Harper Collins Publishers, 1990. <u>neighbourhood characteristics of crime</u>. 2008. Canadian Centre for Justice Statistics. 01 10 2011 <http://www.statcan.gc.ca/stcsr/query.html?qt=neighbourhood%20characteristics%20of%20crime&charset=iso-8859-1&qm=1>.

Nicholas, Elliott. "The Levelers: Libertarian Revolutionaries." <u>The Freeman Journal</u> 39.5 (1989).

Nuyumbalees Cultual Center, Quadra Island First Nations Elder. <u>History of the Potlatch</u> Rod Keays. 15 August 2010.

O'Brien, Barbara. <u>Buddhism/Right Livelihood: The Ethics of Earning a Living</u>. <http://buddhism.about.com/od/theeightfoldpath/a/right livelihood.htm>.

Perkins, William. Kitch, M.J. <u>Capitalism and the Reformation</u>. Ed. H. F. Kearney. London: Longmans, 1967. p. 106, 144.

Plato. "The Republic." Hughes-Hallett, Lucy. <u>Heroes-Saviors, Traitors and Supermen-A History of Hero Worship</u>. New York: Random House, 2000. 34.

<u>Post-Traumatic Stress Disorder (PTSD)</u>. 08 02 2012 <http://www.nimh.nih.gov/health/publications/post-traumatic-stress-disorder-ptsd/what-is-post-traumatic-stress-disorder-or-ptsd.shtml >.

Proudhon, P. <u>What Is Property?</u> Ed. Donald R. Kelley and Bonnie G. Smith. New York: Cambridge University Press, 1994.

Ptolemy. Shapin, Steven. <u>The Scientific Revolution</u>. Paperback Edition. Chicago: The University of Chicago Press, 1998. 22.

Ridley, Matt. <u>The Red Queen-Sex and the Evolution of Human Nature</u>. New York: Penquin, 1993.

Rilke, Rainer Maria. "Sometimes a Man Stands Up During Supper." Bly, Robert. <u>The Rag and Bone Shop of The Heart—A Poetry Anthology</u>. Ed. James Hillman, Michael Meade Robert Bly. Trans. Robert Bly. New York: HarperCollins, 1992. 60.

Rosen, Stanley, ed. <u>The Philosopher's Handbook: Essential Readings From Plato to Kant</u>. New York: Random House, 2000.

Rousseau, Jean Jacques. "The First and Second Discourses." <u>The Philosopher's Handbook, Essential Readings From Plato to Kant</u>. Ed. Stanley Rosen. New York: Random House, 2000. 98,101.

S.Brown, Laura. "Essential Lies:A Dystopian Vision of the Mythopoetic Men's Movement." <u>Women Respond To The Men's Movement—A Feminist Collection</u>. Ed. Kay Leigh Hagan. San Francisco: Pandora-HarperSanfrancisco, 1992. 96,99.

Sage Reference. <u>Encyclopedia of crime and punishment</u>. Ed. David Levinson. SAGE, 2002.

Saul, John Ralston. <u>A Fair Country, Telling Truths About Canada</u>. Toronto: Viking, 2008.

Saying, Traditional. <u>Caveat emptor, Latin for "Let the buyer beware"</u>. <http://en.wikipedia.org/wiki/Caveat_emptor>.

Searles, Valerie L. Lee and Richard T. <u>Study Guide for the Telecourse Faces of Culture</u>. Eighth Edition. Belmont: Wadsworth/Thomson Learning, 2002.

Sen, Ashoke. "String theory and Einstein's dream." <u>Current Science</u> 89.12 (2005): 2045-2053.

Shakespeare, William. <u>Romeo and Juliet</u>. n.d.

Shapin, Steven. <u>The Scientific Revolution</u>. Chicago: The University of Chicago Press, 1998.

Simon, Herbert. Daly, Gar Alperovitz and Lew. <u>Unjust Desserts-How the Rich Are Taking Our Common Inheritance and Why We Should Take It Back</u>. New York: The New Press, n.d. 101,136.

Smith, Adam. <u>"the hidden hand of the market would regulate the economy"</u>. 1759. <http://en.wikipedia.org/wiki/The_Theory_of_Moral_Sentiments>.

Smolin, Lee. "Seeing Darwin in the Light of Einstein;Seeing Einstein in the Light of Darwin." <u>What Is Your Dangerous Idea</u>. Ed. John Brockman. New York: Harper-Collns, n.d. 112-116.

Solzhenitsyn, Aleksandr. Barber, Benjamin R. <u>Jihad vs McWorld, How Globalism and Tribalism Are Reshaping The World</u>. New York: Ballantine Books, 1996. 236.

—. "To Tame Savage Capitalism." <u>The New York Times</u>. 28 November 1993. p.13.

Statistics Canada. <u>Canadian Crime Statistics</u>. Government of Canada. Ottawa: Minister of Industry, 2004, 2003.

—. <u>Deaths and mortality rate, by selected grouped causes, sex and geography—Canada</u>. 17 11 2010. <http://www.statcan.gc.ca/pub/84f0209x/2007000/t001-eng.htm>.

—. <u>Slight Increase in Spousal Homicides</u>. 2009. <http://www.statcan.gc.ca/pub/85-002-x/2010003/article/11352-eng.htm#a11>.

Steiner, Rudolf. <u>Compiled Lectures By Rudolf Steiner</u>. revised. Health Research Books, 2007.

Steve Muhlberger, Associate Professor of History, Nipissing University. <u>A History of the Vote in Canada: A Review Article</u>. 2 1 1999. <http://www.nipissingu.ca/department/history/muhlberger/histdem/canvote.>.

Stincelli, Rebecca. <u>Suicide By Cop-Victims From Both Sides of the Badge</u>. Stincelli & Associates. 11 July 2011 <http://www.suicidebycop.com/>.

Svendsen, Ann. "Stakeholder Engagement: A Canadian Perspective-Accountability Quarterly." 03 2000. <u>The Center for Innovation and Management</u>. 26 12 2011 <http://www.cim.sfu.ca/pages/resources_stakeholder.htm>.

Tarnas, Richard. <u>The Passion of the Western Mind</u>. New York : Ballantine Books, 1991.

Tawney, R.H. <u>Religion and the Rise of Capitalism</u>. London: Penquin, 1990.

The Columbia Encyclopedia. "Magna Carta." Sixth. New York: Columbia University Press, 2002.

The Well Foundation. <http://www.wellfoundation.org/main.cfm?cid=773>.

Tolle, Eckhart. <u>The Relationship of Our Material Existence to Spirituality</u>. 11 04 2011. 05 09 2011 <http://www.namastepublishing.com/blog/compassionate-eye/relationship-our-material-existence-spirituality>.

Valpy, Michael. ""It was the first time in my life that I cried while making my prayers"." <u>The Globe and Mail</u>. Toronto, 18 December 2004. T3.

Vanderkippe, Nathan. "What the forestry industry is teaching the oil sands." 25 02 2010. <u>The Globe and Mail</u>. 16 09 2010 <http://www.theglobeandmail.com/report-on-business/industry-news/

energy-and-resources/the-art-of-defusing-the-green-protests/article 1481763/>.

Venkatesh, Sudhir. Gang Leader For A Day. New York: Penquin, 2008.

Victoria Men's Center. Victoria Men's Centre. <web.me.com/vmen/VMC/ Resources.html>.

Wagner College, New York, N.Y. Men's Studies. 03 03 2011 <www. wagner.edu/news/node/1582>.

Wallach, Janet. Dessert Queen : The Extraordinary Life of Gertrude Bell. New York: Anchor Books, 2005.

Wasserman, Ira M. "The Effects of War and Alcohol Consumption Patterns on Suicide: United States, 1910-1933." Social Forces 68.2 (1989): 513-530.

Weber, Max. The Protestant Ethic and the Spirit of Capitalism. Trans. Talcott Parsons. New York: Scribner, 1976.

—. The Protestent Ethic and the Spirit of Capitalism. Trans. Talcott Parsons. New York: Routledge, 2008.

Weldon, John C, Allen H. Fenichel and Sidney H. Ingerman. On the political economy of social democracy: selected papers of J.C. Weldon. Montreal: McGill-Queen's Press, 1991.

White, Helen C. "The Religious Attitude Towards Usury in 16th Century England." Kitch, M.J. Capitalism and the Reformation. London: Longmans, 1967. 144.

Whitmire, Richard. Why Boys Fail: Saving Our Sons from an Educational System That's Leaving Them Behind. 2010. 04 01 2012 <http://www.amazon.com/Why-Boys-Fail-Educational-Leaving/ dp/0814415342#reader_0814415342 >.

Whitney Kisling, Lynn Thomasson. Profit Margins at 18-Year High Signal Bigger Dividends Coming for S&P 500. Ed. Nick Baker. 14 03 2011. 04 01 2012 <http://www.bloomberg.com/news/2011-03-14/profit-margins-at-18-year-high-signal-bigger-s-p-500-dividends.html >.

Wildwood Forest, Ladysmith, BC. 28 June 2011 <http://ecoforestry.ca/ wildwood>.

Wilson, Ellen J and Reill, Petter H. Encyclopedia of the Enlightenment. Infobase Publishing, 2004.

Wilson, Thomas. "The Secular Approach to Usury, Capitalism and The Reformation." M.J.Kitch. Capitalism and The Reformation. Ed. H.F. Kearney. London: Longmans, 1967.

Wolff, Robert Paul. <u>In Defence of Anarchism</u>. Berkely: University of California Press, 1998.

Wong, Bennet and Jock McKeen. <u>A Manual for Life</u>. Toronto: Hignell Printing Ltd., 1992.

Woodcock, George. <u>Proudhon</u>. Montreal: Black Rose Books, 1987.

Wright, R. <u>Nonzero: The Logic of Human Destiny</u>. Pantheon Books, 2000.

<u>You, Me, and the SPP</u>. Dir. Paul Manly. Prod. Paul Manly. 2009.

NOTES

1   p. xv, "shining with the light of the sun", Jung, Carl, Creative Mythology-The Masks of God, Campbell, Joseph, Penquin, 1968, p. 488.

2   p. xv, the Anima, Jungian therapy/analysis. Senior Jungian therapist, McDowell, Maxson, http://www.jungny.com/

3   p. xv, "one's secret intention for oneself...", Schopenhauer, Creative Mythology-The Masks of God, Campbell, Joseph, Penquin, 1968, p. 489.

4   p. xvi, Was I in Love or what? Anima issues, "The Basic Writings of C.G. Jung", Jung, Carl G, ed. Laszlo, Violet de, 1990, p. 162.

5   p. xvi, Too many answers, "A Question of Values", Lewis, Hunter, 1991, p. 60.

6   p. xxi, The Well Foundation, www.wellfoundation.org

7   p. xxii, Wagner College, New York, N.Y. Men's Studies. www.wagner.edu/news/node/1582 03/03/2011.

8   p. xxii, Bly, Robert, comments of feminist writer Laura S. Brown, Women Respond To The Men's Movement, Ed. Kay Leigh Hagan. San Francisco, p. 99, 1992.

9   p. xxii, on rape, "Essential Lies: A Dystopian Vision For The Mythopoetic Men's Movement", S. Brown, Laura, "Women Respond To The Men's Movement", Hagan, Kay Leigh, 1992, p. 99.

10 P. xxii, Hitler, Adolf, "Essential Lies: A Dystopian Vision For The Mythopoetic Men's Movement", S. Brown, Laura, "Women Respond To The Men's Movement", Hagan, Kay Leigh, 1992, p. 96.

11 p. xviii, Bly, Robert, (the key), "Iron John, A Book About Men", p. 1-27, 1990.

12 p. xviii, a work ethic template or initiation, "The Protestant Ethic and the Spirit of Capitalism", Weber, Max, 1930, p. 23-25.

13 p. xxix, the value of maintaining the role of the elder in our culture, p15, "The Ecology of Freedom", Bookchin, Murray, 1991, p. 82.

14 p. xxx, poem, "Sometimes a Man Stands Up During Supper", Rilke, Rainer Maria, "The Rag and Bone Shop of The Heart- A Poetry Anthology", translator Bly, Robert, 1992, p. 60.

15 p. xxxi, Business Is War, "Carl von Clausewitz: Business is War", Clausewitz, Carl von, http://www.clausewitz.org/

16 p. xxxv, Politics as usual is men's politics, "Masculinities", Connell, R.W., 2005, p. 204.

17 p. xxxv, gendered corporations, "Masculinities", Connell, R.W., 2005, p. 165,199.

18 p. xxxv, a world gender order, "Masculinities", Connell, R.W., 2005, p. 165, 199.

19 p. xxxv, A History of the Vote in Canada: A Review Article, "World History of Democracy", http://www.nipissingu.ca/department/history/muhlberger/histdem/canvote 1999.

20 p. xxxvi, the view that men are biologically or intrinsically competitive, "The Masculine Mystique", Kimbrell, Andrew, 1995, p. 31.

21 p. xxxvi, no biological urge in males, "Masculinities", Connell, R.W., 2005, p. 46.

22 p. xxxvi, on a misinterpretation of violence, "Guns, Germs and Steel- The Fates of Human Societies", Diamond, Jared, 1997, p. 277.

23 p. xxxvi, we had the raw materials in the right combinations, "Guns, Germs and Steel- The Fates of Human Societies", Diamond, Jared, 1997, p. 358.

24 p. xxxvii, Europeans are no different than other races, "Guns, Germs and Steel- The Fates of Human Societies", Diamond, Jared, 1997, p. 23.

25 p. xxxvii, The Calling, "The Protestant Ethic and the Spirit of Capitalism", Weber, Max, 2001, p. 39-55; 108.

26 p. xxxviii, fear produced by the expulsion from Eden, "A Fair Country, Telling Truths About Canada", Saul, John Ralston, 2008, p. 281.

27 p. xxxviii, not cast from Eden, quoting Highway, Thompson, "A Fair Country-Telling Truths About Canada", Saul, John Raulston, 2008, p. 281.

28 p. xxxviii, Aboriginal populations decimated, "Millenium-Tribal Wisdom and the Modern World", Maybury-Lewis, D., 1992, p. 14,

29 p. xxxviii, deforestation of Easter Island, Collapse-How Societies Choose to Fail or Succeed, Diamond, Jared, 2005, 79-119.

30 p. xxxviii, settling down allows a surplus, "Cultural Anthropology", Haviland, Willam A, 1993, p. 165.

31 p. xl, Karoshi Death, "The Job Stress Network", www.workhealth.org/whatsnew/lpkarosh.html, Johnson, Jeffrey V. and, Katsuo Nishiyama, 1997.

32 p. xl, Karoshi Death, 1400% increase in sudden death, "Myth of Male Power-Why Men are the Disposable Sex", Farrell, Warren, 1993, p. 203.

33 p. xl, stats on crime in Canada, See Canadian Centre for Justice Statistics, Pub. Ministry of Industry, 2004.

34 p. xl, Slight Increase in Spousal Homicides, See "Statistics Canada", Canadian Centre for Justice Statistics, Homicide Survey. http://www.statcan.gc.ca/pub/85-002-x/2010003/article/11352-eng.htm#a11

35 p. xl, stress contributes to suicide and criminality, Transient Criminality: A Model of Stress-Induced Crime, A R Mawson, 1987, https://www.ncjrs.gov/App/Publications/abstract.aspx?ID=109068

36 p. xl, The Victoria Men's Center, http://web.me.com/vmen/VMC/Home_page.html

37 p. xl, "Why Boys Fail: Saving Our Sons from an Educational System That's Leaving Them Behind" Whitmire, Richard, American Management Association, 2010. http://www.amazon.com/Why-Boys-Fail-Educational-Leaving/dp/0814415342#reader_0814415342

38 p. xli, the isolated male, "Gang Leader For A Day", Venkatesh, Sudhir, 2008.

39 p. xlii, immortality through sacrifice, "Heroes-Saviors, Traitors and Supermen-A History of Hero Worship", Hugher-Hallett, Lucy, 2004, p. 28.

40 p. xlii, the noble lie, quote "The Republic", Plato, "Heroes-Saviors, Traitors and Supermen-A History of Hero Worship", Hughes-Hallett, Lucy, 2000, p. 34.

41 p. xliii, hero, magician, warrior and lover, "King Warrior Magician Lover-Rediscovering The Archetypes of the Mature Masculine", Moore, Robert; Gillette, Douglas, 1990.

42 p. xliii, Alcibiades, and his self-destruction, "Heroes-Saviors, Traitors and Supermen-A History of Hero Worship", Hugher-Hallett, Lucy, 2004, p. 33-75.

43 p. xliii, 89, Achilles, "Heroes-Saviors, Traitors and Supermen-A History of Hero Worship", Hugher-Hallett, Lucy, 2004, p. 15-32.

44 p. xliv, on his refusal to lead, "An Overview of Krishnamurti's Life and Work", Krishnamurti Foundation, http://www.jkrishnamurti.org/about-krishnamurti/biography.php, 2011.

45 p. xliv, on creating an illusion, "A History of Secret Societies", Daraul, Arkon, 1961, p. 20-27.

46 p. xlvii, honoring the shadow, Bly, Robert, "A Little Book On The Human Shadow", 1988, p. 47-81.

47 P. xlix, 139 circle process (p. 67), quoting Bayda), "Justice in Aboriginal Communities: Sentencing Alternatives", Green, Ross Gordon, 1998, p.70

48   p. xlix, National Youth Action Strategy, "Participaction", http://participaction.com/en-us/Home.aspx

49   p. 2, the first Shamans and the beginning of hierarchy, "The Ecology of Freedom", Bookchin, Murray, 1991, p. 83.

50   p. 3, "a gradual change in the climate", "Man, his First Two Million Years", Montagu, Ashley, 1969, p. 53.

51   p. 3, food foraging, male and female, Haviland, Willam A, 1993, "Cultural Anthropology", Haviland, William A, 1993, p. 68, 157.

52   p. 3, early males were twice the size of females, "Cultural Anthropology", Haviland, William A, 1993, p. 68, 71.

53   p. 3, females chose to raise their young rather than hunt for meat, "Cultural Anthropology", Haviland, William A, 1993, p. 71.

54   p. 3, first spears or knives were created later by Homo Erectus, "Cultural Anthropology", Haviland, William A, 1993, p. 73.

55   p. 3, meat was often scavenged or stolen from other predators, "Cultural Anthropology", Haviland, William A, 1993, p. 69, 70.

56   p. 4, Early Modern Humans, Encyclopedia, McGraw-Hill Science & Technology, Answers.com, http://www.answers.com/topic/early-modern-humans, 2005.

57   p. 4, Domestication of plants and animals, "Cultural Anthropology", Haviland, Willam A, 1993, "Cultural Anthropology", Haviland, William A, 1993, p. 145.

58   p. 4, Goddess religions, "The Ecology of Freedom", Bookchin, Murray, 1991, p. 39.

59   p. 4, Domination itself did not exist, "The Ecology of Freedom", Bookchin, Murray, 1991, p. 79.

60   p. 4, elites were forming, "The Ecology of Freedom", Bookchin, Murray, 1991, p. 62-88.

61   p. 4, "thus, given the leisure time to think and administer…", "The Ecology of Freedom", Bookchin, Murray, 1991, p. 64

62   p. 4, Warrior Clans, "The Ecology of Freedom", Bookchin, Murray, 1991, p. 62-88.

63   p. 4, Surplus management during domestication of plants and animals, "The Ecology of Freedom", Bookchin, Murray, 1991, p. 74.

64   p. 5, Discussion on patriarchy, "The Ecology of Freedom", Bookchin, Murray, 1991, p. 120.

65   p. 5, "Is There Anything Good About Men?", Baumeister, Roy F., Oxford University Press, New York, N.Y. 2010. P 137.

66 p. 5, patriarchy as an ideology that arose out of the exchange of women, "Capitalism, Patriarchy and Crime, Toward a Socialist, Feminist Criminology", Messerschmitt, James W., 1986, p. x.

67 p. 6, male behavior is learned, "Capitalism, Patriarchy and Crime, Toward a Socialist, Feminist Criminology", Messerschmitt, James W., 1986, p. x.

68 p. 6, Violence in Lesbian Relationships, "Domestic Violence in Gay and Lesbian Relationships", Chan, Carrie, Australian Domestic and Family Violence Clearinghouse, http://www.pdfdownload.org/pdf2html/view online.php?url=http%3A%2F%2Fwww.austdvclearinghouse.unsw.edu.au%2FPDF%2520files%2FGay_Lesbian.pdf, 2005.

69 p. 6, "Infanticide: 23 were killed by a parent: 10 by a mother, 9 by a father, the rest by step parents", 1998-2011, Canadian Children's Rights Council, http://www.canadiancrc.com/Infanticide-Women_Who_Kill_Their_Babies.aspx

70 p. 6, "male elites based on agricultural surpluses", "The Ecology of Freedom", Bookchin, Murray, 1991, p. 62-88.

71 p. 7, the emergence of hierarchy, "The Ecology of Freedom", Bookchin, Murray, 1991, p. 62-88.

72 p. 7, history and purpose of the Potlatch, "Potlatch", Clutesi, George, 1969.

73 p.7, The Gift re Potlatch, see "A Poor Man Shames Us all", "Millennium-Tribal Wisdom and the Modern World", Maybury-Lewis, D., 1992, p. 63-89.

74 p. 9, Participation in the Cargo Trades of the S. Pacific, "Millennium-Tribal Wisdom and the Modern World", Maybury-Lewis, D., 1992, p. 63.

75 p. 9, The emergence of hierarchy, "The Ecology of Freedom", Bookchin, Murray, 1991, p. 62-88.

76 p. 10, "Guns, Germs and Steel- The Fates of Human Societies", Diamond, Jared, p. 74, 76, 77, 1997.

77 p. 10, A war against all, "Leviathan", Hobbes, Thomas, ed. Gaskin, J.C.A., 1996, p. xviii.

78 p. 10, Three principals of quarrel, "Leviathan", Hobbes, Thomas, 1985, p. 85.

79 p. 10, no common power to fear or to keep them quiet such as a god or laws, "Leviathan", Hobbes, Thomas, Handbook, The Philosopher's, ed. Rosen, Stanley, 2000, p. 85-89.

80 p. 10, every man must endeavor peace, but, "Leviathan", Hobbes, Thomas, Handbook, THe Philosopher's, ed. Rosen, Stanley, 2000, p. 85-89.

[81] p. 11, Buddhism in the West from the East, See "Buddhism in the West" at: http://www.buddhanet.net/e-learning/buddhistworld/to-west.htm

[82] p. 11, China's economic collapse, "The Wealth and Poverty of Nations-Why Some Are So Rich and Some Are So Poor", Landes, David S., 1998, p. 93.

[83] p. 12, the emergence of hierarchy, "The Ecology of Freedom", Bookchin, Murray, 1991, p. 62-88.

[84] p. 12, "men must compete in this culture", May, Rollo, "The Masculine Mystique", Kimbrell, Andrew, 1995, p. 74.

[85] p. 12, the Anima, Jungian therapy/analysis. Senior Jungian therapist, McDowell, Maxson, http://www.jungny.com/

[86] p. 13, males fall for the Romantic fantasy, "Myth of Male Power-Why Men are the Disposable Sex", Farrell, Warren, 1993, p. 82.

[87] p. 13, on feudalism, "Feudalism", Encyclopedia Britannica Online, http://www.britannica.com/EBchecked/topic/205583/feudalism, 2011.

[88] p. 13, People were supposed to know their place, Feudalism, "Tribal-Tribal Wisdom and the Modern World", Maybury-Lewis, D., 1992, p. 74.

[89] p. 14, Individualism was increasingly tolerated, "Tribal-Tribal Wisdom and the Modern World", Maybury-Lewis, D., 1992, p. 80, 89.

[90] p. 14, Individuation of the personality, "Memories, Dreams, Reflections", Jung, C.G., ed. Jaffe, Aniela, 1989, p.389.

[91] p. 14, The Troubadours songs of Romantic love, "Tribal-Tribal Wisdom and the Modern World", Maybury-Lewis, D., 1992, p. 96.

[92] p. 14, History of the Catholic Church (400 ad) had prohibited love marriages, "Cultural Anthropology", Haviland, William A, 1993, p. 236.

[93] p. 14, marriage as a socio-political arrangement, "The Passion of the Western Mind", Tarnas, Richard, 1991, p. 173.

[94] p. 14, Medieval Europeans believed in arranged marriages, "Tribal-Tribal Wisdom and the Modern World", Maybury-Lewis, D., 1992, p. 94-97.

[95] P.15, The emergence of hierarchy, "The Ecology of Freedom", Bookchin, Murray, 1991, p. 62-88.

[96] p. 15, Industrial revolution forced families apart, "Cultural Anthropology", Haviland, William A, 1993, p. 439-444.

[97] p. 15, males separated from family by work, "Tribal-Tribal Wisdom and the Modern World", Maybury-Lewis, D., 1992, p. 114.

[98] p. 15, Toll on the men shown in the record books, "Tribal-Tribal Wisdom and the Modern World", Maybury-Lewis, D., 1992, p. 136.

[99] p. 16, on the development of spirit of capitalism, "Capitalism and the Reformation", Kitch, M. J., ed. Kearney, H. F., 1967, p. 144.

100 p. 16, People were questioning authority of the Catholic Church, "Tribal-Tribal Wisdom and the Modern World", Maybury-Lewis, D., 1992, p. 74.

101 p. 16, "Traditionalism, to earn as much as is necessary and then go home", "The Protestant Ethic and the Spirit of Capitalism", Weber, Max, 1930, p. 60.

102 p. 16, Pre-capitalist labor, "The Protestant Ethic and the Spirit of Capitalism", Weber, Max, 2001, p. 60, 102-107.

103 p. 16, 96, High versus low wages, "The Protestant Ethic and the Spirit of Capitalism", Weber, Max, 2001, p. 23-25.

104 p. 16, people work so long as they are poor, "The Protestant Ethic and the Spirit of Capitalism", quote by Cour, Peter de la, Weber, Max, p. 61.

105 p. 17, Protestant Ministers and Capitalists started working together, "The Protestant Ethic and the Spirit of Capitalism", Weber, Max, 2001, p. 103-11.

106 p. 17, The Calling, "The Protestant Ethic and the Spirit of Capitalism", Weber, Max, 2001, p. 39-55; 108.

107 p. 17, the development of the "Calling", "The Protestant Ethic and the Spirit of Capitalism", Weber, Max, 2008, p. 56-79.

108 p. 17, establishment of the Protestant religions, "Millenium-Tribal Wisdom and the Modern World", Maybury-Lewis, D., 1992, p. 74.

109 p. 17, the new era of the individual, "Millenium-Tribal Wisdom and the Modern World", Maybury-Lewis, D., 1992, p. 73-74.

110 p. 18, "Millenium-Tribal Wisdom and the Modern World", Maybury-Lewis, D., 1992, p. 74.

111 p. 18, the glorification of God, "The Protestant Ethic and the Spirit of Capitalism", Routledge Pub., Weber, Max, 2008, p. 64.

112 p. 18, on Luther and Calvin, "Religion and the Rise of Capitalism", Tawney, R.H., 1990, p. 103, 114.

113 p. 18, brotherly love, may only be practiced for the Glory of God, "The Protestant Ethic and the Spirit of Capitalism", Weber, Max, 2001, p. 64.

114 p. 19, the certainty of Grace, "The Protestant Ethic and the Spirit of Capitalism", Routledge Pub., Weber, Max, 2008, p. 69.

115 p. 20, Never ending relaxation was seen as a danger to Godly men, "The Protestant Ethic and the Spirit of Capitalism", Weber, Max, 2001, p. 119, 157.

116 p. 20, "only through activity was the Glory of God increased", "The Protestant Ethic and the Spirit of Capitalism", Weber, Max, 2001, p. 68.

[117] p. 21, Character of Sport, "The Protestant Ethic and the Spirit of Capitalism", Weber, Max, 1930, p. 182.

[118] p. 21, right work, Buddhist understanding. See "Buddhist Economics" at: http://axisoflogic.com/artman/publish/Article_55356.shtml

[119] p. 21, Buddhist Economics, Kumarappa, J. C., The E.F. Schumacher Society, 2009, http://axisoflogic.com/artman/publish/Article_55356.shtml

[120] p. 22, obligation to find a calling, "The Protestant Ethic and the Spirit of Capitalism", Weber, Max, 2001, p. 19, 25.

[121] p. 22, "rational organization of our social environment", "The Protestant Ethic and the Spirit of Capitalism", Routledge Pub., Weber, Max, 2008, p. 64.

[122] p. 22, lack of religious direction, "The Protestant Ethic and the Spirit of Capitalism", Routledge Pub., Weber, Max, 2008, p. 54.

[123] p. 22, "The Book of Nature", See Bibliography, Bible: nature read as if it were a book.

[124] p. 23, on intense worldly activity, "The Protestant Ethic and the Spirit of Capitalism", Routledge Pub., Weber, Max, 2008, p. 67.

[125] p. 23, On usury Calvin felt it compared to paying rent on land, "Religion and the Rise of Capitalism", Tawney, R.H., 1990, 116.

[126] p. 23, we live in a constant state of war, by Hobbes, Thomas, "The Philosopher's Handbook", ed. Rosen, Harry, 2000, p. 83-89.

[127] p. 23, The separation of men...from the family, "The Masculine Mystique", Kimbrell, Andrew, 1995, p. 39.

[128] p. 23, tribal cultures stifled the individual, Durkheim, Emile, "Millenium-Tribal Wisdom and the Modern World", Maybury-Lewis, D., 1992, p. 88.

[129] p. 25, religious dissenters in The Netherlands, "Tribal-Tribal Wisdom and the Modern World", Maybury-Lewis, D., 1992, p. 75.

[130] p. 25, The Bank, an institution required by a capitalist economy, "Tribal-Tribal Wisdom and the Modern World", Maybury-Lewis, D., 1992, p. 75.

[131] p. 25, Italy had banks before The Netherlands but were controlled by The Church, "Tribal-Tribal Wisdom and the Modern World", Maybury-Lewis, D., 1992, p. 78.

[132] p. 25, Usury, "Tribal-Tribal Wisdom and the Modern World", Maybury-Lewis, D., 1992, p. 80.

[133] p. 25, "English Preachers saw..." "The Religious Attitude Towards Usury in 16th Century England", White, Helen C., "Capitalism and the Reformation", Kitch, M.J. 1967, p. 144.

134   p. 26, Church Ministers frowned on capitalists taking usury on loans, "Capitalism and the Reformation", Kitch, M. J., ed. Kearney, H. F., 1967, p. 144.

135   p. 26, William Perkins quote in, "Capitalism and the Reformation", Kitch, M.J., 1967, p. 106, 144.

136   p. 26, Banks loaned to unknowns, "Tribal Wisdom and the Modern World", Maybury-Lewis, D., 1992, p. 80.

137   p. 26, Calvinist Ministers banned capitalists from Communion, "Tribal Wisdom and the Modern World", Maybury-Lewis, D., 1992, p. 80.

138   p. 26, Bankers were refused communion over usury, "The Protestant Ethic and the Spirit of Capitalism", Weber, Max, 1930, p. 201.

139   p. 26, usury as lazy money, "The Secular Approach to Usury, Capitalism and The Reformation", by Wilson, Thomas, "Capitalism and The Reformation", M.J.Kitch, ed. Kearney, H.F., 1967.

140   p. 27, the start of Canadian Socialism, "Federation, Co-operative Commonwealth", Historica Dominion Institute, http://www.thecanadian encyclopedia.com/index.cfm?PgNm=TCE&Params=A1ARTA0001902,

141   p. 27, regarding Mohammed Yunis and Micro-credit, Buckingham-Hatfield, S., http://www.answers.com/topic/micro-credit, 2000.

142   p. 27, on the loss of Canadian business, "A Fair Country-Telling Truths About Canada", Saul, John Raulston, 2008, p. 213.

143   p. 29, British effect on Arab blood feuds, "Dessert Queen : The Extraordinary Life of Gertrude Bell", Wallach, Janet, 2005.

144   p. 31, the increasing use of mirrors, "Tribal-Tribal Wisdom and the Modern World", Maybury-Lewis, D., 1992, p. 81.

145   p. 31, "Caveat emptor", Latin for "Let the buyer beware", http://en.wikipedia. org/wiki/Caveat_emptor

146   p. 31, "there is a sucker born every minute", others: Joseph ("Paper Collar Joe") Bessimer, Barnum, P. T., "There's a sucker born every minute"., http:// en.wikipedia.org/wiki/There%27s_a_sucker_born_every_minute

147   p. 31, "the hidden hand of the market would regulate the economy", Smith, Adam, http://en.wikipedia.org/wiki/The_Theory_of_Moral_Sentiments,_1759.

148   p. 32, suicide and alcoholism low during war and high post-war, "The Effects of War and Alcohol Consumption Patterns on Suicide: United States, 1910-1933", Wasserman, Ira M., Social Forces, Dec/1989, p. 513-530.

149   p. 32, where are the elderly men?, Asher, Jeffrey, http://www.canlaw.com/ rights/whokills.htm_1996, and also see Statistics Canada: http://www. fathersforlife.org/health/cod_Canada_1992.htm1996.

150 p. 32, forty-seven years ago, "Cultural Anthropology", Haviland, William A, 1993, p. 240.

151 p. 35, males not living up to masculine standards, "The Trials of Masculinity: Studies in the Policing of Sexual Boundaries", 1870-1930 Chicago: University of Chicago Press, 1997.

152 p. 36, Officer Assisted Suicide, "Suicide By Cop-Victims From Both Sides of the Badge", http://www.suicidebycop.com/, Stincelli & Associates, 2008.

153 P. 37, Americans idealize passion, believe in the individual, "Tribal-Tribal Wisdom and the Modern World", Maybury-Lewis, D., 1992, p. 117.

154 P. 37, Mahatma Gandhi was asked how many planets will India require for development- "two planets", "Human Development Reports", 2007-08, http://hdr.undp.org/en/statistics/data/climatechange/planets/

155 p. 38, can competition work for the benefit of everyone?, "The Red Queen-Sex and the Evolution of Human Nature", Ridley, Matt, 1993, p. 93.

156 p. 42, geographical determinants "Guns, Germs and Steel- The Fates of Human Societies", Diamond, Jared, p. 408, 1997

157 p. 44, geographical determinants, and Chatham Islands, "Guns, Germs and Steel- The Fates of Human Societies", Diamond, Jared, p. 408, 1997.

158 p. 46, A Taste of Persia, "An Introduction to Persian Cooking", Sweet and Sour tastes/ Ancient Persia, http://www.mage.com/cooking/A-Taste-of-Persia.html 2006.

159 p. 47, dualistic analysis of nature—Greek rising and falling columns of air and falling rock, "The Philosopher's Handbook: Essential Reading From Plato to Kant", Rosen, S., 2000.

160 p. 47, Scientists and philosophers sought initially to reinforce the notions of hierarchy, "The Scientific Revolution", Shapin, Steven, 1998, p. 119-166.

161 p. 47, "the Natural Mechanical view was...", "The Scientific Revolution", Shapin, Steven, 1998, p. 153.

162 p. 48, "described research as a kind of worship", Boyle, Robert, "The Scientific Revolution", Shapin, Steven, 1998, p. 153.

163 p. 48, feelings are unhelpful in men, "The Hazards of Being Male-Surviving the Myth of Masculine Privilege", Goldberg, Herb, 1976, p. 43-44.

164 p. 48, humanity can only know so much knowledge, "The Protestant Ethic and the Spirit of Capitalism", Routledge Pub., Weber, Max, 2008, p. 60.

165 p. 49, regarding "A Manual of Life", Wong, Bennet; McKeen, Jock, 1992, p. 35.

166 p. 50, the democratization of our desires, "Leisure in The Global Village?", Lahey, Minam, City University of New York, 1999, http://www.

pdfdownload.org/pdf2html/view_online.php?url=http%3A%2F%2Flin.
ca%2FUploads%2Fcclr9%2FCCLR9_25.pdf

[167] p. 51, rising and falling of matter referring to their proper place in the cosmos, quote Ptolemy, "The Scientific Revolution", Shapin, Steven, 1998, p. 22.

[168] p. 51, "Nonzero: The Logic of Human Destiny", Wright, R., 2000.

[169] p. 52, What is fear? "The First and Last Freedom", Krishnamurti, J., Theosophical Society, Wheaton Ill., 1954, 186.

[170] p. 53, a philosophy based on unity, "Encyclopedia of the Enlightenment", (Editor), Alan Charles Kors, 2003.

[171] p. 53, equality is tied to freedom, "The Ecology of Freedom", Bookchin, Murray, 1991, p. 144.

[172] p 53, Einstein, Albert on a network of relations; Darwin, Charles on natural selection leading to a genuine novelty, "Seeing Darwin in the Light of Einstein; Seeing Einstein in the Light of Darwin", by Smolin, Lee, "What Is Your Dangerous Idea?", Brockman, John; Pinker, Steven; Dawkins, Richard, ed. Brockman, John, 2007, p. 113-119.

[173] p. 53, Darwin, Charles on natural selection leading to a genuine novelty, "Seeing Darwin in the Light of Einstein; Seeing Einstein in the Light of Darwin", by Smolin, Lee, "What Is Your Dangerous Idea?", Brockman, John; Pinker, Steven; Dawkins, Richard, ed. Brockman, John, 2007, p. 113-119.

[174] p. 54, Aristotle suggested the perfection and unchanging nature of the suns and stars, "The Scientific Revolution", Shapin, Steven, 1998, p.71.

[175] p. 54, Galileo did not see sunspots, "The Scientific Revolution", Shapin, Steven, 1998, p.71.

[176] p. 55, "The Great Instauration", of Sir Francis Bacon p.68, "The Scientific Revolution", Shapin, Steven, 1998, p. 20.

[177] p. 56, Rene Descartes quote on machines built by artisans, "The Scientific Revolution", Shapin, Steven, 1998, p. 32.

[178] p. 56, Johannes Kepler principles of geometry, "The Scientific Revolution", Shapin, Steven, 1998, p. 59.

[179] p. 57, Newton's Mathematical Principles of Natural Philosophy, Isaac Newton, "The Scientific Revolution", Shapin, Steven, 1998, p. 61.

[180] p. 57, "English "moderns" contrasted themselves with "ancients", "The Scientific Revolution", Shapin, Steven, 1998, p. 66.

[181] p.57, the Horned God of wine and pleasure named "Pan", "**The Demonization of Pan.**", Kevin Hearne (c) 1998. http://www.mesacc.edu/~thoqh49081/StudentPapers/pan.html

182   p. 57, on natural philosophy, the Book of Nature, enculturalization of masculinity(via a hierarchy or order such as the clock), natural mechanical theory of Newton, Robert Hooke's natural philosophy, "The Scientific Revolution", Shapin, Steven, 1998, p. 78, 90, 110, 125.

183   p. 57, "The Book of Nature", was a source of God's revelation while viewing nature, "The Book of Nature in Early Modern and Modern History, Studies in Cultural Change", ed. K van Berkel and A. Venderjagt. Groningen: PEETERS Publishing, 2006.

184   p. 58, "modern empiricism", "The Scientific Revolution", Shapin, Steven, 1998, p. 69.

185   p. 58, "when systems of institutional control are working . . . ", "The Scientific Revolution", Shapin, Steven, 1998, p. 124.

186   p. 58, Bly, Robert, "A Little Book On The Human Shadow", 1988, p. 52.

187   p. 58, "learning as an arm of state power", "The Scientific Revolution", Shapin, Steven, 1998, p. 127.

188   p. 59, "learning as an arm of state power", "The Scientific Revolution", Shapin, Steven, 1998, p. 127.

189   p. 59, Bacon's "New Atlantis", "The Scientific Revolution", Shapin, Steven, 1998, p. 130.

190   p. 59, "the codes regulating civil conversation...", "The Scientific Revolution", Shapin, Steven, 1998, p. 134.

191   p. 59, "science as religions' handmaid", "The Scientific Revolution", Shapin, Steven, 1998, p. 135.

192   p. 59, "we lost technological control over nature", "The Scientific Revolution", Shapin, Steven, 1998, p. 139.

193   p. 59, "Christ would come for a millennium", "The Scientific Revolution", Shapin, Steven, 1998, p. 140.

194   p. 60, Rene Descartes "we cannot share in God's plans", "The Scientific Revolution", Shapin, Steven, 1998, p. 148.

195   p. 60, Dualistic philosophy, "The Relationship of Our Material Existence to Spirituality", Tolle, Eckhart, http://www.namastepublishing.com/blog/compassionate-eye/relationship-our-material-existence-spirituality, 04/11/2011.

196   p. 60, "If Science fails to report objectively...", "The Scientific Revolution", Shapin, Steven, 1998, p. 162.

197   p. 61, Darwin, Charles writings used to bolster, "those who won in the race of life were superior", "The Masculine Mystique", Kimbrell, Andrew, 1995, p. 79.

[198] p. 61, evolutionary scientists, "he who co-operates will often survive far better", "The Masculine Mystique", Kimbrell, Andrew, 1995, p. 82.

[199] p. 61, "It might therefore be said that science . . . ", "The Scientific Revolution", Shapin, Steven, 1998, p. 163.

[200] p. 61, "the more a (or any) body of knowledge...", "The Scientific Revolution", Shapin, Steven, 1998, p. 164.

[201] p. 61, Paradox: the more a body of knowledge appears . . . , "The Scientific Revolution", Shapin, Steven, 1998, p. 164.

[202] p. 61, "science remains also the most respected . . . ", "The Scientific Revolution", Shapin, Steven, 1998, p. 165.

[203] p. 64, James O'Toole quote, Adler, M. J., "Haves Without Have-Nots", 1991, p. 55, 89.

[204] p. 64, Betty Friedan quote, "The Politics of Individualism", Brown, L. Susan, 1993, p. 6.

[205] p. 66, PTSD is an anxiety disorder that some people get after seeing or living through a dangerous event, http://www.nimh.nih.gov/health/publications/post-traumatic-stress-disorder-ptsd/what-is-post-traumatic-stress-disorder-or-ptsd.shtml

[206] p. 67, "freedom is a function of ownership", quoting Wm. Gary Kline, "The Politics of Individualism", Brown, L. Susan, 1993, p. 117.

[207] p. 67, "property in the person", "The Politics of Individualism", Brown, L. Susan, 1993, p. 3.

[208] p. 67, Rousseau's first and second discourses, "In Defense of Anarchism", Wolff, Robert Paul, 1998, p. 42-57.

[209] p. 67, evils of property, "The First and Second Discourses", Rousseau, Jean Jacques, "The Philosopher's Handbook: Essential Reading From Plato to Kant", Rosen, S., 2000, p. 101.

[210] p. 68, equality disappeared and property was introduced, "The First and Second Discourses", Rousseau, Jean Jacques, "The Philosopher's Handbook: Essential Reading From Plato to Kant", Rosen, S., 2000, p. 98.

[211] p. 68, to annul his singularity in order to become the universal. Quote:"Fear and Trembling, Problema 1, Is There a Telelogical Suspension of the Ethical?", from Kierkegaard, Soren, "The Philosopher's Handbook", ed. Rosen, Stanley, 2000, p. 170,171.

[212] p. 69, savage capitalism, Solzhenitsyn, Aleksandr, "Jihad vs McWorld, How Globalism and Tribalism Are Reshaping The World", Barber, Benjamin R., 1996, p. 236.

213 p. 69, "laissez-faire doctrines are fatal", "Jihad vs McWorld, How Globalism and Tribalism Are Reshaping The World", Barber, Benjamin R., 1996, p. 240.

214 p. 69, on global intelligentsia, "The End of Laissez-Faire: National purpose and the global economy after the Cold War", Kuttner, Robert, 1991, p. 24.

215 p. 71, the two poles of identity, "The Politics of Individualism", Brown, L. Susan, 1993, p. ix.

216 p. 72, Schiller, Friedrich quote "it is only through beauty that mean makes his way to freedom", "The Philosopher's Handbook: Essential Reading From Plato to Kant", Rosen, S., 2000, p. 193, 236.

217 p. 73, Clayoquot Sound, Nathan Vanderkippe, What the forestry industry is teaching the oil sands, http://www.theglobeandmail.com/report-on-business/industry-news/energy-and-resources/the-art-of-defusing-the-green-protests/article1481763/ 2010.

218 P. 73, Clayoquot Sound, "Stakeholder Engagement: A Canadian Perspective", Ann Svendsen, Center for Innovation In Management, Accountability Quarterly, http://www.cim.sfu.ca/pages/resources_stakeholder.htm March 2000.

219 p. 73, "power vs authority, Def.", "In Defense of Anarchism", Wolff, Robert Paul, 1998, p. 4.

220 p. 75, a definition of anarchy is self-responsibility, "In Defense of Anarchism", Wolff, Robert Paul, 1998, p. 71.

221 p. 75, some may disagree with American way of life, Times Colonist Newspaper, Sept 10, 2002. http://www.timescolonist.com/

222 p. 76, "obligation to obey laws", "In Defense of Anarchism", Wolff, Robert Paul, 1998, p. 29.

223 p. 76, on autonomy, "In Defense of Anarchism", Wolff, Robert Paul, 1998, p. xix, 15, 29, 71.

224 p. 79, unfinished beings, "Pedagogy of the Oppressed", Freire, Paulo, 2000, p.84.

225 p. 83, understanding the "Great Illusion", The Four Noble Truths, Ajahn Sumedho, http://www.buddhanet.net/4noble.htm

226 p. 83, "In the dualistic society that we live in, a crime committed is punishable by law, whereas in a non-dualistic world-view, all actions are the soul's way of learning about the Self. Even when a being breaks the law of non-violence, it means that that being is still in a deluded state and is in the process of learning about truth.", by Miruh on September 9, 2010, http://spiritualhealingjourney.com/living-in-a-non-dualistic-world/

227   p. 86, server computers for the future, "Distinguishing Cloud computing from Utility Computing", Danielson, Krissi, www.ebizq.net/blogs/saasweek/2008/03.

228   p. 87, Profit Margins at 18-Year High Signal Bigger Dividends Coming for S&P 500, Bloomberg TV., Whitney Kisling, Lynn Thomasson, ed. Nick Baker, nbaker7@bloomberg.net, March 14, 2011, http://www.bloomberg.com/news/2011-03-14/profit-margins-at-18-year-high-signal-bigger-s-p-500-dividends.html

229   p. 89, all human beings are worthy of respect, quote :"Critique of Judgement 1790", Kant, Immanuel, from "The Philosopher's Handbook", ed. Rosen, Harry, 2000, p. 194.

230   p. 90, labor plus nature =moral basis for property, quote Mill, John Stewart, "Unjust Deserts", Gar Alperovitz, Lew Daly, 2008, p.99.

231   p. 90, If I clear land I should enjoy the benefits, "What Is Property?", Proudhon, P, ed. Kelley, Donald R.; Smith, Bonnieg, 1994, p. 67-86.

232   p. 91, clearing land, labor and environmental standards, land shares, the old regime (nobility and the clergy), "What Is Property?", Proudhon, P, ed. Kelley, Donald R.; Smith, Bonnieg, 1994, p. 95, 96.

233   p. 92, King Louis XIV "The State! I am the State", "In Defense of Anarchism", Wolff, Robert Paul, 1998, p. 4.

234   p. 92, the exploitation of man by man, "What Is Property?", Proudhon, P, ed. Kelley, Donald R.; Smith, Bonnieg, 1994, p. 92.

235   p. 92, Winstanley, Gerrard, leader of the Diggers, 1640, "Radical Democracy", Lummis, C. Douglas, 1996, p. 92.

236   p. 95, Since the employer cannot promise to employ the worker forever, "What Is Property?", Proudhon, P, ed. Kelley, Donald R.; Smith, Bonnieg, 1994, p. 92.

237   p. 96, quote "but land is much scarcer . . . ", "What Is Property?", Proudhon, P, ed. Kelley, Donald R.; Smith, Bonnieg, 1994, p.73.

238   p. 98, progress of a kind, "What Is Property?", Proudhon, P, ed. Kelley, Donald R.; Smith, Bonnieg, 1994.

239   p. 98, increases in property values owed to the state, Ricardo, David, "Unjust Desserts-How the Rich Are Taking Our Common Inheritance and Why We Should Take It Back", Daly, Gar Alperovitz and Lew, p. 100.

240   p. 99, on Herbert Simon quote 15 times the income is made today in comparison to 1870, Alperovitz, Gar; and Daly, Lew, "Unjust Deserts: how the rich are taking our common inheritance", 2008.

241 p. 99, "an enormously productive social system", Herbert, Simon, "Unjust Desserts-How the Rich Are Taking Our Common Inheritance and Why We Should Take It Back", Daly, Gar Alperovitz and Lew, p. 136.

242 p. 99, Quote "equality is tied inextricably . . . ", Bookchin, Murray, "The Politics of Individualism", Brown, L. Susan, 1993, p. 91.

243 p. 100, Goldman, Emma, quote "Property" means dominion over things . . . , "The Politics of Individualism", Brown, L. Susan, 1993, p. 126.

244 p. 100, Goldman, Emma, 1. man must sell his labor, 2.subordinate to the will of a master, 3. right to buy and sell your labor is an unfair exchange, (p. 127), "The Politics of Individualism", Brown, L. Susan, 1993, p. 126.

245 p. 100, C. B. MacPherson quote "political society is a human contrivance for . . . ", "The Politics of Individualism", Brown, L. Susan, 1993, p. 54.

246 p. 100, domination and subordination hierarchies, "The Politics of Individualism", Brown, L. Susan, 1993, p. 3.

247 p. 102, property ownership, "The Mystery of Capital: why capitalism triumphs in the West and fails everywhere else", de Soto, Hernando, p. 16, 2000.

248 p. 102, ownership in the developed economies followed by the inherent difficulties creating wealth in the developing world, "The Mystery of Capital: why capitalism triumphs in the West and fails everywhere else", de Soto, Hernando, 2000, p. 39-68.

249 p. 104, "surpluses belonged to the state", Alperovitz, Gar; and Daly, Lew, "Unjust Deserts: how the rich are taking our common inheritance", 2008, p. 108.

250 p. 104, a plan for a percentage of national worth distributed to the population, "Social Credit", Douglas, C H, 1937, p. 205.

251 p. 105, eighty-five percent of our income is inherited, Alperovitz, Gar; and Daly, Lew, "Unjust Deserts: how the rich are taking our common inheritance", 2008.

252 p. 106, copyright law in Canada, Business Development Center, "Register a Trademark in Canada",

253 p. 108, need for strong public oversight of corporations, Bakan, Joel, "The Corporation", 2004, p. 163.

254 p. 108, marketing of the Bikini, "The History of The Bikini", Everything Bikini.com. 2005, http://www.historyofwaterfilters.com/bikini.html

255 p. 110, cheerful motorist greeter, "The Life and Death of the King of Cassiar", McMartin, Pete, The Vancouver Sun, 3/20/2010, p. A4.

256 p. 110, Squatter's Rights in Canada, "Rights-of-way, Easements, Squatters' Rights and Restrictive Covenants", Michael G. Cochrane, 2007, http://www.mycanadianrealestatelaw.com/rightsofway.html

257 p. 113, St. Kevin Monastery in Ireland, "It was the first time in my life that I cried while making my prayers", Valpy, Michael, The Globe and Mail, 12/18/2004, T3.

258 p. 115, "money making on the Church steps", Tawney R.H., Religion and the Rise of Capitalism-A Historical Study, Penquin, London UK, 1990, p. 159.

259 p. 119, quote by Jean Paul Sartre, "The Masculine Mystique", Kimbrell, Andrew, 1995.

260 p. 120, Are we a spiritual being living a physical existence . . . , "Compiled Lectures By Rudolf Steiner", Health Research Books, 2007, p. 119.

261 p. 120, Revolutions not debated, "The Masculine Mystique", Kimbrell, Andrew, 1995, p. 122.

262 p. 121, Dante's end of the life cycle, "Creative Mythology-The Masks of God", Campbell, Joseph, 1968, p.633.

263 p. 122, initiation, "Men and The Water of Life-Initiation and Tempering of Men", Meade, Michael, 1993, p. 12.

264 p. 125, the source of the term King Energy, "King Warrior Magician Lover-Rediscovering The Archetypes of the Mature Masculine", Moore, Robert; Gillette, Douglas, 1990, p. 49-74.

265 p. 129, Einstein's science of unification, "String theory and Einstein's dream", Sen, Ashoke, 12/05/2005, p. 2045-2053.

266 p. 129, "Participation in Unanimous Decision-Making: The New England Monthly Meetings of Friends", Ethan Mitchell, 2012, http://philica.com/display_article.php?article_id=14

267 p. 130, Proudhon wrote that humanity has been going through a process of leveling for the last four thousand years, "Proudhon", Woodcock, George, 1987, p. 58.

268 p. 130, proportional Rep in S Africa, "In Defense of Anarchism", Wolff, Robert Paul, 1998, p. xvii.

269 p. 131 "all government in essence, is tyranny", "In Fewer Words", Emerson, R.W., The University of California, 1938, p. 76.

270 p. 133, The national crime rate has been falling steadily for the past 20 years and is now at its lowest level since 1973, Statistics Canada, 2010. http://www.statcan.gc.ca/daily-quotidien/110721/dq110721b-eng.htm

271 p. 133, decrease in US homicide rates over time, "FBI, Uniform Crime Reports, 1950-2005", Feb 2, 2012, http://bjs.ojp.usdoj.gov/content/homicide/hmrt.cfm#longterm

273 p. 133, Leveling mechanisms, "Cultural Anthropology", Haviland, William A, 1993, p. 186-87.

274 p. 133, important leveling mechanism. See, "The Magna Carta", "The Columbia Encyclopedia", 2002.

275 p. 135, "Essay on the Gift", Mauss, Marcel, "Millenium-Tribal Wisdom and the Modern World", Maybury-Lewis, D., 1992, p. 66

276 p. 136, Strictly speaking . . . , "In Defense of Anarchism", Wolff, Robert Paul, 1998, p. 15.

277 p. 136, who has no obligation to vote as I would, "In Defense of Anarchism", Wolff, Robert Paul, 1998, p. 29.

278 p. 136, autonomous beings, "In Defense of Anarchism", Wolff, Robert Paul, 1998, p. 71.

279 p. 136, "The Levelers", www.constitution.org/eng/leveller.htm

280 p. 136, "The Levelers: Libertarian Revolutionaries", Nicholas, Elliott, The Freeman Journal, May, 1989.

281 p. 137, on Lilburne, "Origins of the Fifth Amendment", Levy, Leonard W., 1968, p. 272.

282 p. 138, Leonard Levy on John Lilburne, "Origins of the Fifth Amendment", Levy, Leonard W. 1968, p. 272.

283 p. 138, If autonomy and authority are genuinely incompatible, "In Defense of Anarchism", Wolff, Robert Paul, 1998, p. 71.

284 p. 140, first use of leveling mechanism as applied to fairness, "The Ecology of Freedom", Bookchin, Murray, 1991, p. 85.

285 p. 140, felt the state enslaves our spirit, Goldman, Emma, "The Politics of Individualism", Brown, L. Susan, 1993, p. 113-142.

286 p. 140, Paul Manly film, "You, Me, and the SPP", Manly, Paul, 2009.

287 p. 140, water exports with oil sands bitumen to US, Canada's Oil Sands - Opportunities and Challenges to 2015: An Update, http://www.neb.gc.ca/clf-nsi/rnrgynfmtn/nrgyrprt/lsnd/pprtntsndchllngs20152006/qapprtntsndchllngs20152006-eng.html 23 July 2010.

288 p. 141, a film on the Security Prosperity Partnership, Manly, Paul, 2009, http://www.youmespp.com/about-youmespp/

289 p. 141, Bilderberg society, "The True Story of the Bilderberg Group", Estulin, Daniel, 2009.

290 p. 141, "promoting global justice", Buruma, Ian, Globe and Mail, November 9, 2009.

291 p. 142, unfinished beings., quoting Beauvior, Simone de, "The Politics of Individualism", Brown, L. Susan, 1993, p. 167

292 p. 142, Nike lost 30% on sales for bad child- labor laws., Baxter, James, "Canada Values Corporate Responsibility", also 25000 people world wide polled that 20% of them had punished a corporation at some point, Environics International, The Vancouver Sun, May, 1999.

293 p. 143, officer refuses to attend restorative justice meeting. Blatchford, Christie, The National Post, January 10, 2000.

294 p. 143, studies on poverty and hopelessness = crime, See Sage Reference, "Encyclopedia of Crime and Punishment", 2002 p.1213.

295 p. 145, judicial proceeding, "Justice in Aboriginal Communities: Sentencing Alternatives", Green, Ross Gordon, 1998, p. 67

296 p. 145, sentencing circle described by Judge Stuart, "Justice in Aboriginal Communities: Sentencing Alternatives", Green, Ross Gordon, 1998, p. 67

297 p. 146, circle process (p. 67), quoting Bayda), "Justice in Aboriginal Communities: Sentencing Alternatives", Green, Ross Gordon, 1998, p.70

298 p. 146, Pelican Narrows, "Justice in Aboriginal Communities: Sentencing Alternatives", Green, Ross Gordon, 1998, p. 114.

299 p. 148, on the use of a talking stick, "The Talking Stick", Carol Locaust, Ph.D, http://www.acaciart.com/stories/archive6.html, 1997.

300 p. 149, Merv Wilkinson, and "Wildwood", http://ecoforestry.ca/node/333

301 p. 150, to be feared or loved", Machiavelli, Niccolo, "The Prince", 1998, p. 66.

302 p. 150, Is it best to Love or fear?, "The Prince", Machiavelli, Niccolo, 1998, p. 65.

303 p. 153, "but when a prince", "The Prince", Machiavelli, Niccolo, 1998, p. 41.

304 p. 154, the creator of a powerful person is ruined, "The Prince", Machiavelli, Niccolo, 1998, p. 16.

305 p. 154, "second or higher stage of man", Lenin, Vladimir, "Haves Without Have-Nots: Essays for the 21st Century on Democracy and Socialism", Adler, Mortimer Jerome, 1991, p. 55.

306 p. 154, Is running troubled banks becoming government ownership?, "The Globe and Mail", June 13, 2009, Poll.

307 p. 156, non-profit rules, BC Society Act 2012, http://www.bclaws.ca/EPLibraries/bclaws_new/document/ID/freeside/00_96433_01

308 p. 159, history of the Potlatch, Quadra Island First Nations Elder, Nuyumbalees Cultual Center, Quadra Island, BC., 2010.

309 p. 159, Highland Maya, prevention of the accumulation of wealth, and protection to the lowest member of the system, Haviland, William A.; Searles, Richard T. Lee, Valerie L.; "The Telecourse Faces", 1996, p. 147, 158, 159.

310 p. 159, def. of leveling mechanisms, "Cultural Anthropology", Haviland, William A., ed. Buchholz, Ted, 1993, p. 186,187.

311 p. 160, "Man's true liberation…" Goldman, Emma, "The Politics of Individualism", Brown, L. Susan, 1993, p. 122.

312 p. 161 stats on lower male attendance at college, Averett, Susan L.; Burton, Mark L., College attendance and the college wage premium: Differences by gender, See "Economics of Education Review", 1996, p. 37-49.

313 p. 162, the power banks have over us, "The Money Myth Exploded", Even, Louis, "Michael" Journal, 1101 Principale St., Rougemont, QC, Canada J0L1M0), (514) 856-5714, http://www.michaeljournal.org/myth.htm

314 p. 166, following the desires of the student, "Dumbing Us Down: the hidden curriculum of compulsory schooling", Gatto, John, 2002, p. 20.

315 p. 166, genius was common, "Dumbing Us Down: the hidden curriculum of compulsory schooling", Gatto, John, 2002, p. xi.

316 p. 167, "self-knowledge", "Dumbing Us Down: the hidden curriculum of compulsory schooling", Gatto, John, 2002, p. 34.

317 p. 169, I may know what I will, not what I want, "In Defense of Anarchism", Wolff, Robert Paul, 1998, p. 53.

318 p. 170, will events today create mutations one thousand years from now?, "The Ten Thousand Year Explosion-How Civilization Accelerated Human Evolution", Cochran, Gregory and Harpending, Henry, 2009, p. 187, 227.

319 p. 173, Democracy is, "Radical Democracy", by C. Douglas Lummis, 1996, p, 160.

320 p. 173, "the democratic citizen must preceed the democratic society", "Jihad vs McWorld, How Globalism and Tribalism Are Reshaping The World", Barber, Benjamin R., 1996, p. 286.

321 p. 174, List of Values, "A Question of Values", Lewis, Hunter, 1991, p. 10.

322 p.175, The Four Noble Truths, http://www.rinpoche.com/fornob.html, Thrangu Rinpoche

Index

consumers must consistantly place
a high level of expectations on
them 70
if forced by consumer demand
corporations will produce what
shoppers want 70
influence over copywrite 107
Corporations
as persons 63, 70, 98, 109, 118
Credit Union
in contrast to banks 27
money is kept locally 27
critical thinking x
culture
geographical influences 37, 44, 46,
48, 79, 124, 131

elites
  in hierarchies. See power
Emerson
  all government in essence, is tyranny
    131
empirical evidence
  direct sense experience is the best
    teacher 58
English Revolution
  Oliver Cromwell 92
Enlightenment, The 53
environmental stewardship
  embraced by the 60's generation
    136
Europe
  ancient memories 10
  endless medieval conflict 11
  formation of the E.U. 11
  redistribution theories 98
  the success of xl, 9, 25, 118, 119, 130
evolution is ours for the asking xxiv.
    See Buddhism

F

fairness xxix, xxxiv, xlix, 42, 76, 91,
    94, 111, 112, 114, 126, 128,
    130, 133, 149, 170, 176.
    See thank him
  our most important value xxix, 82
fair voting
  South Africa 130
fate
  ours to discover 22, 34, 64, 119,
    120
father and son xviii
fear xi, xiii, xvii, xxii, xxiii, xxiv,
    xxxiii, xlvii, 1, 10, 17, 30, 39,
    49, 52, 53, 55, 57, 62, 67,
    74, 77, 79, 80, 81, 84, 85,
    92, 93, 96, 107, 109, 113,
    114, 117, 118, 128, 132, 139,
    144, 149, 150, 151, 152, 153,
    154, 156, 157, 158, 174, 176,
    178. See men; See heirarchy;
    See non-dualistic thinking
  of being overrun by emotion 57
  the deep hurts and rejections of the
    past 77
fear of the discovery xiii. See fear
Feelings in males
  counterproductive in provider/
    protector based society 48
Feminist. See Messerschmitt, James
    W.
Feudal system. See Feudalism
Feudal times
  most goods were produced and
    consumed in the home. 18
First Nations
  Potlatch 7, 148, 158
first principals
  chop wood; carry water 33
f--- off, and seeing that this magic
    phrase xiv. See Autobiography
freedom
  To go shopping? 38, 64, 66, 78
  who are apart from what we buy 66

G

Galileo
  discovered sunspots; church furious
    54
Gandhi, M.
  two or three planets would be
    needed for India to create
    western style wealth 37
gangs xxii, xxviii, xxxi, 35, 148.
    See initiation; See survival
Gatto, John Taylor 166, 167
  education based upon the desires of
    the student 166
  felt genius was exceedingly common
    166
generativity. See Circle Sentencing
Gifting
  the mature male role 121

N

Y

CPSIA information can be obtained at www.ICGtesting.com
Printed in the USA
LVOW080008301012

304952LV00003B/2/P